THE EBAY SURVIVAL GUIDE

THE EBAY® SURVIVAL GUIDE

How to Make Money and Avoid Losing Your Shirt

by Michael Banks

NO STARCH
PRESS

San Francisco

Publisher: William Pollock
Production Manager: Susan Berge
Cover Design: Octopod Studios
Developmental Editors: William Pollock, Patricia Witkin
Copyeditor: Marilyn Smith
Compositor: Riley Hoffman
Proofreader: Tina Barland/ICC
Indexer: Ted Laux

For information on book distributors or translations, please contact No Starch Press, Inc. directly:

No Starch Press, Inc.
555 De Haro Street, Suite 250, San Francisco, CA 94107
phone: 415.863.9900; fax: 415.863.9950; info@nostarch.com; www.nostarch.com

Library of Congress Cataloging-in-Publication Data

Banks, Michael A.
  The eBay survival guide : how to make money and avoid losing your shirt / Michael Banks.
    p. cm.
  Includes index.
  ISBN 1-59327-063-1
1. eBay (Firm) 2. Internet auctions. I. Title.
  HF5478.B36 2005
  381'.177--dc22

                                                    2005022840

For Dee and Mick

BRIEF CONTENTS

PART IV: HOW NOT TO GET RIPPED OFF AND WHAT TO DO IF YOU DO

CONTENTS IN DETAIL

PART I
HOW EBAY WORKS

1
WHAT YOU'LL FIND ON EBAY   9

2
HOW EBAY AUCTIONS WORK   27

3
FINDING STUFF ON EBAY: THE BASICS 35

4
FINDING STUFF ON EBAY: HIGH-POWER SEARCHES 47

5
WHAT IS IT WORTH? 61

PART II
EBAY FOR SELLERS

6
SELLER DO'S AND DON'TS   77

7
FIGURING OUT WHAT TO SELL   91

8
SOURCES OF ITEMS TO SELL   99

9
LISTING ITEMS: WHEN AND HOW   109

10
HOW TO CREATE LISTINGS THAT SELL   137

11
IT DIDN'T SELL!   157

PART III
EBAY FOR BUYERS

12
BUYER DO'S AND DON'TS   167

13
BID TO WIN!   185

14
HOW TO TURN A LOSS INTO A WIN   201

15
PAYING FOR AND GETTING YOUR ITEMS   207

PART IV
HOW NOT TO GET RIPPED OFF AND WHAT TO DO IF YOU DO

16
SHILLS, SLEAZES, AND SELLER SCAMS
223

17
BOGUS PRODUCTS AND MONEYMAKING SCAMS
239

18
HOW TO INVESTIGATE OTHER EBAY MEMBERS 247

APPENDIX
EBAY-SPEAK: ABBREVIATIONS AND ACRONYMS 253

INDEX 255

ACKNOWLEDGMENTS

Thanks are due Susan Berge, Riley Hoffman, Christina Samuell, Leigh Poehler, Marilyn Smith, and Patricia Witkin of No Starch Press, for the long hours they put into the editing and production of this book—and to publisher Bill Pollock, for suggesting it.

Special thanks to Debbie Morner for the eBay support.

INTRODUCTION

A familiar adage is that a thing is worth what someone is willing to pay for it. Collectors may rant and rave all day about how much a baseball card, old radio, or toy is worth, but in the end, a given item will sell for a price that represents its value to a buyer, as well as that buyer's ability to pay.

Obviously, it can be difficult to price an item you're selling or to know how much to offer for an item you want to buy. This is particularly true of rare or one-of-a-kind items. (Of course, price guides may give an idea of what a thing might be worth, but both buyer and seller should keep in mind the fact that price guides are what the name says: *guides*, not absolute indicators of an item's value.) Fortunately, there is a solution to this quandary: the auction.

At its most basic, an auction is a means of selling something for the highest possible price, or, if you're a buyer, a chance to buy something for a reasonably low price. With an auction, the seller doesn't need to worry about the buyer's resistance to his asking price, and neither party needs to haggle. The item sells for what it is truly worth to the buyer at that time.

In practice, an auction is a means for multiple buyers to tell the seller what an item is worth to them by *bidding*, or offering a specified amount for it, with the operating assumption that the seller will accept the highest bid offered. (Where multiples of the same item are offered by one or more sellers, this might be thought of pricing based on demand.) In the process, the seller usually realizes the highest possible price for whatever he is selling. If there are only a few interested bidders, the selling price may be low, unless the buyers are well heeled and determined to own the item in question. The greater the number of bidders, the higher the price is likely to go.

This book is about auctions in their most modern form and popular venue: online auctions on eBay. As an introduction, let's see how auctions have evolved from ancient times to their latest electronic form.

A Brief History of Auctions

The first auctions of record took place around 1,500 years ago in Babylonia, where they were used to sell brides to young men. This approach ensured that the "best" brides went to the wealthiest men. (A few brides drew negative bids; the "sellers" had to throw in some cash to get someone to take them.)

NOTE *The word* auction *is derived from the Latin* auctio, *which means "an increasing." Why we use a word derived from Latin rather than Babylonian is a subject best left for etymologists to ponder.*

This selling technique quickly evolved as a means of disposing of just about any property quickly, without complications or haggling (except the battles conducted among the bidders). Today, auctions provide the same streamlined—albeit suspenseful—approach to buying and selling.

The First Online Auctions

People have been buying, selling, and trading things online since the late 1970s, when early computer hobbyists set up the first computer *bulletin boards*. A typical computer bulletin board system (BBS) consisted of a personal computer connected to a telephone line.

The BBS had special software that allowed it to communicate with another computer. Once connected to a BBS, you could post private and public messages, and upload and download files, but very little else. At the same time, a few American universities were linking their large mainframe and minicomputers in a similar fashion, through a network dubbed USENET. Most of the dialogue on these message systems consisted of technical discussions. Before long, computer geeks started buying and selling computer hardware and software online.

Buying and selling stuff wasn't quite as popular as pirating software (which is why many computer bulletin boards existed), but it was something a lot of people did. Most of the items you could find for sale online in those early days were computer-related, which made sense. After all, the best place to find the highest concentration of techie types was any bulletin board or an online service such as CompuServe, The Source, or America Online. I recall selling a computer printer and buying some software through postings on CompuServe message boards in 1981.

BBSs and USENET became popular among the techie crowd, but not among the general population. In those days, you needed to know how computers worked before you could even think about linking with another computer.

The very first online auction took place sometime between 1979 and 1981, when someone decided he might be able to generate more interest in an item, and get more money for it, with an auction rather by using a "For Sale" notice. It was a good idea, since an auction carries with it quite a bit more urgency than a conventional sale, and there's always the competition factor, which often spurs people to spend more for something than they might have in other circumstances.

So, our hypothetical first online auctioneer posted a public notice that described the item he was selling (I say "he," since 90 percent of those online were male), stated a closing time, and solicited bids. Bids were either emailed to the bidder or posted as replies to the seller's original message. After the auction closed, the seller announced the high bidder, and the deal was consummated. (Unless, of course, the seller was a rip-off artist or the buyer wasn't serious.)

It was all fairly simple and direct. No live interaction or automation was involved. Photos were rarely used, largely because the ubiquitous digital camera was yet to be invented, and very few people had scanners.

By 1983, all of the major online services of the time had auctions, though those pre-Web online auctions weren't likely to draw large numbers of bidders. The bidder pool was restricted by the fact that you needed online access, and fewer than a million people were online in the mid-1980s. The number of potential bidders was further limited to those who happened to use the bulletin board or online service that hosted a given auction. The result was that most online auctions drew a few dozen bidders at most, and usually far fewer.

But the online world evolved, and more sophisticated tools became available. Then came the Web, and suddenly it was possible to make an online auction accessible to each and every one of the now tens of millions of modem-equipped computer users looking for something to do online.

Enter eBay

Although some may claim to have gotten there first, no one can say definitively when the first Web-based auction took place.

In any event, HTML wizards—the people who actually create web pages—were developing pages that presented auction items, collected bids and bidder information, kept track of auction winners, and perhaps automated other bidder/seller interactions. Once the 1990s rolled around, a few specialized online auction companies popped up, but none really attracted the public's attention—until eBay.

eBay began late in 1995 as AuctionWeb, a small operation run by Jeff Skoll and Peter Omidyar. The two put together a website that offered a primitive version of what eBay is today. Sellers could post items for auction, and bidders could bid on them for a specified period of time. When an auction was completed, the buyer and seller completed the deal via email.

NOTE *The official legend seems to be that when Omidyar created his auction site, he was moti-vated by a noble and altruistic desire to "level the playing field" and make online trading fair. But it is far more likely that he was thinking something along the lines of, "What can I come up with to make money with the Internet?" as was his partner.*

By the summer of 1996, AuctionWeb was charging a 25-cent fee for a list-ing, thus confirming many users' predictions that the service was not going to be a free ride forever. Even with the per-listing charge, the site's usage grew and grew. The operation changed its name to eBay, and venture capital was sought and found.

By 1998, eBay was well financed and growing faster than ever. Eventually, it became the most popular site on the Web, went public, went international, and did things like buy Sotheby's and PayPal. And it's still growing in popu-larity and sophistication.

Auctions and eBay Today

eBay has changed how we think of auctions. Before the late 1990s, the word *auction* was likely to conjure up images of hard-bitten farmers vying for live-stock or having their farms sold out from under them. Or perhaps it brings to mind a picture of paddles waving in the genteel parlors of Sotheby's or Christy's, where artistic masterpieces go for millions.

Say the word *auction* today, though, and the first thing most folks envision is an eBay page. Ironically, many of those same people would never dream of tramping around a stranger's house inspecting furniture, yelling a bid in a storefront auction gallery, or trying to master the wink-and-nod approach of covert bidding. But now they routinely participate in three, four, or even a dozen auctions every week. Why? Because of the way eBay brings auctions directly to millions of buyers and sellers: easily, conveniently, and on their terms.

When you're eBaying (now a household name, eBay is commonly used as verb, right up there with Googling), you don't need to worry about acci-dentally bidding $500 for an old picture frame or looking stupid because you lost track of the bidding and bid below the current price. eBay auctions are private, so you don't need to go anywhere, and you don't even need to get dressed—all the action takes place in your home. Better still, eBay gives buyers access to items they might never have found otherwise.

To sellers, eBay brings convenience. It has converted thousands of pack-rats into avid sellers. Rather than open a store, lug a carload of junk to a flea market, or bring in an auctioneer, anyone with something to sell can work from home. And there are all those millions of potential buyers.

About This Book

Whatever you intend to do on eBay, welcome to the book! *The eBay Survival Guide* is a nonconformist, irreverent, and realistic handbook for both buyers and sellers. You'll learn how eBay works; how to find things on eBay (including things others might want, but can't find elsewhere); how to bid effectively and win; the best times for buying and selling; how to draw bidders without spending a bunch on eBay auction features; how to spot shills, fraudulent sellers, and deadbeat buyers; and a lot more.

The information contained here is based on my eight years of experience with online auction sites, as well as the experience of dozens of other buyers and sellers. You'll find a lot of practical how-to information, and also some philosophical points to ponder and put into practice. These pages examine not only where, how, and when to do what on eBay, but also how to deal with people, government entities, and other elements that may become involved with your eBay activities. In addition, you'll find information about how to handle the offline aspects of online buying and selling, and some useful information about using the Internet in general.

Unlike most computer books, *The eBay Survival Guide* is not a dreary "point-and-click" how-to. Instead of forcing you through hundreds of pages of reference material, I focus on showing you what is there, and how to use it.

And mixed in with all that are some fascinating, stupid, and scandalous (and true) tales of eBay adventures.

Ready to begin?

PART I

HOW EBAY WORKS

1

WHAT YOU'LL FIND ON EBAY

eBay is different things to different people. To buyers, it is a source for all sorts of merchandise, collectibles, or just weird stuff. Depending on their degree of involvement, sellers view eBay as a way to get rid of good junk, a place to make extra money, or the source of their livelihood. Unfortunately—and through no fault of eBay—a few scammers regard the service as a vehicle for their rip-offs. To a few other folks, eBay serves as a source of entertainment. To still others, it's a valuable research tool (as you will learn, this is not as unlikely as it may seem).

In the upcoming chapters, you'll take a look at each of the various aspects of eBay. In this chapter, you'll get an overview of the organization and structure of eBay, along with what it offers and the basics of how it works.

What Is eBay?

eBay's stated mission is "to provide a global trading platform where practically anyone can trade practically anything."

eBay also devotes itself to a policy of trust, safety, and privacy. Trust is, as eBay maintains, the key to its success and the key to successful transactions between buyers and sellers. (Actually, the trust is more on the buyers' end, since buyers almost always pay before sellers fulfill their commitment.) Safety is supported by eBay's registration policies, the Feedback system, and the rules under which buyers and sellers must operate. eBay further commits itself to protecting users' privacy.

But eBay is much more than just a website devoted to giving people who have something to sell a place to display their wares to potential buyers. In a broader sense, eBay is an enormous database (and it truly is enormous; on any given day, it lists millions of items for sale). Users access this database via the Internet to browse or search listings, sell items, bid on or buy items directly from sellers, arrange for payment and shipping, communicate with one another and, not incidentally, pay eBay for the services it provides.

Although it began as a free service, eBay does charge sellers various fees, including those for posting items for auction or direct sale and for adding enhancements to auction listings. Sellers are also charged a small percentage of an item's final sale price. These are simply overhead costs for anyone who does business on eBay. Buyers are never charged a fee by eBay.

Getting Around eBay

Getting around on eBay is similar to navigating any other website. Almost all navigation involves clicking links, which may be highlighted text, icons, or button-shaped graphics.

To get started, let's take a tour of eBay's home page. Figure 1-1 shows the top portion of this page.

Home Page Promotions and Features

Most of the center of the home page is taken up by promotional offers and featured items that change daily, like specials on a restaurant menu. Promotions on the home page include the In Demand box. The links in the In Demand box lead to lists of auctions for specific kinds of goods—digital TVs, camera phones, and so forth. The theme items to the right of the In Demand box—in this example, College Superstore and Hot Gifts for Her—lead to lists of auctions of related merchandise.

Below the In Demand box, you see the Featured Items links. Sellers pay extra to have their items featured on the eBay home page. If you're a buyer looking for bargains, you might not be too excited about the offers you see here. Sellers may be charging a bit more for their wares to make up for the cost of the promotional link. If you see a featured item that interests you, it's a good idea to do an independent search to see whether you can get a better deal. (See Chapters 3 and 4 for more information about searching eBay auctions.)

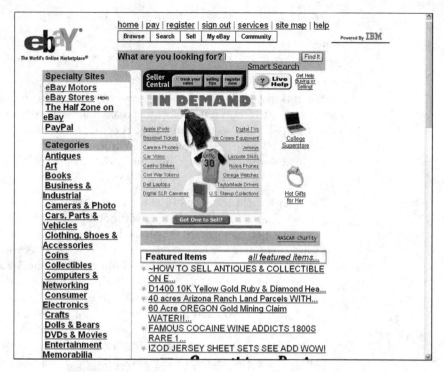

Figure 1-1: eBay's home page (top portion)

On the other hand, if you're a seller, you may want to cough up the cash and have your item featured on eBay's home page. It will be in a position to capture the attention of anyone who arrives at www.ebay.com.

While promotions and featured items change daily, the rest of the home page remains pretty much the same.

eBay's Main Menu

At the top of the home page, the eBay main menu, shown in Figure 1-2, offers a variety of links.

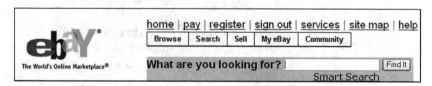

Figure 1-2: eBay's main menu

Briefly, the selections on the main menu are as follows:

Home

This takes you to eBay's home page after you stray from it.

Pay

This link goes to a page that offers several services. In addition to allowing you to pay for merchandise, you can also sign up for an online payment service (which allows you to pay or receive payments for items immediately) or pay your eBay seller fees. You can also register as an eBay member here—something you must do before you can buy or sell items.

Register

This may appear in place of the sign out or sign in link. If you're not yet registered as a buyer or seller, or you need to set up a new account, start here. The process is fairly simple and involves filling out some online forms. If you want to register as a bidder, eBay will ask you to provide some basic contact information, including your name, mailing address, phone number, and email address. You'll also need to create a user ID, which is the name you'll be known by on eBay, and supply a password (use something you can remember but is not easy to guess). To register as a seller (which you can do when you sign up as a buyer, or later with the same user ID or a new one), you'll need to provide the same information. eBay will also want a credit card or checking account number to which your eBay seller fees can be charged.

NOTE *If you use a so-called "anonymous" email address, such as one at hotmail.com or yahoo.com, you will need to provide a credit card number to verify your identity. This is the only circumstance under which you must provide a credit card number if you are registering as a buyer only.*

Sign out/sign in

This link logs you off eBay, or, if you're not logged in, takes you to eBay's Sign In page.

Services

This link takes you to a mixed bag of selections grouped under General Services, Bidding and Buying Services, and Selling Services.

Site map

The site map is a text outline of what you can find on the eBay website. It offers clusters of menus and links under these headers: Browse, Sell, Search, Help, Services, and Community.

Help

This link is a gateway to eBay's online Help system, as well as related services such as eBay's Customer Support and Security Center. We'll explore eBay's Help system later in this chapter.

Browse

Click the Browse link to see a page with an alphabetical list of eBay's main categories (some with partial lists of subcategories). Clicking a category name displays a list of subcategories. Click any of the subcategory links, and you'll see the first page of items listed in the selected subcategory.

Search

This selection leads to what, for most, is the heart of eBay: a collection of search tools.

Sell

Click here to begin the process of listing your item for sale on eBay.

My eBay

My eBay is your own personal set of pages on eBay, accessible only when you sign in with your unique username and password. With it, you can keep track of any bids you make, create a reminder list of auctions to keep an eye on (called a *watch list*), manage your sales, and more. We'll explore My eBay later in this chapter.

Community

The eBay Community page is a collection of services for communicating with other eBay members in chat rooms and via bulletin boards. It's also where you can keep track of eBay events (online and off), access news from eBay (general news and system announcements), join eBay groups for buyers and sellers, contact eBay, and so on.

Specialty Sites

Moving to the top-left area of the home page, you'll see a menu labeled Specialty Sites. This is a collection of sites that are significantly different from the rest of eBay, as well as external sites that eBay owns or operates (also known as *affiliates*).

The Specialty Sites selections change frequently, as eBay experiments with name changes and new ideas. To give you an idea of what these sites are about, here are brief descriptions of the sites listed as I'm writing this chapter:

eBay Motors

eBay Motors, shown in Figure 1-3, is a website devoted to the sale of new and used automobiles, boats, motorcycles, as well as parts and literature for these vehicles. At this site, you'll also find ATVs, mopeds, buses, aircraft, RVs, campers, and just about any other kind of motor-driven vehicle. Although the eBay Motors site looks a little different from "regular" eBay, it works pretty much the same.

Figure 1-3: eBay Motors site

eBay Stores

The eBay Stores site, shown in Figure 1-4, provides eBay sellers with the means for selling items at a set price, rather than through an auction. In some cases, this can be more cost-effective than auctions, and it also offers several more advantages.

Half.com by eBay

Shown in Figure 1-5, Half.com is an arm of eBay that specializes in books, movies, music, and video games. It features an "express sell" system that helps sellers create new listings by automatically providing information such as a book's ISBN, cover image, and publisher after the seller types in a title or selects a product from a menu. For buyers, Half.com offers a quick way to zero in on specific media, thanks to the prefilled product information in listings. This is in contrast to eBay's conventional searches, which rely on the sometimes incomplete or inaccurate information provided by sellers.

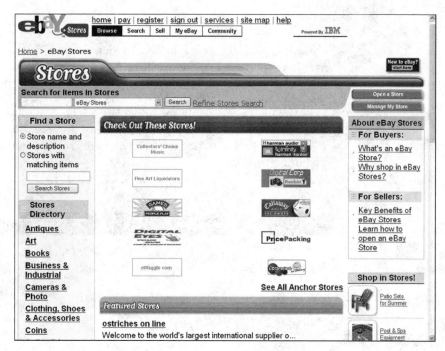

Figure 1-4: eBay Stores site

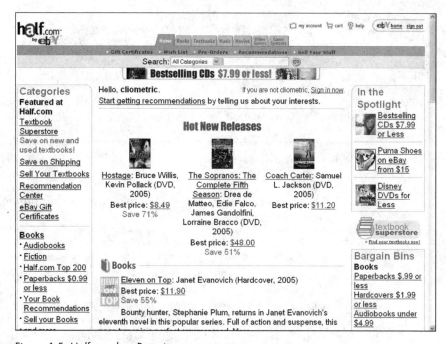

Figure 1-5: Half.com by eBay site

PayPal

PayPal is one of several online services you can use to pay for items purchased on eBay (or, from the seller's viewpoint, to collect your money), as shown in Figure 1-6. The service is free to buyers. Sellers are charged a fee and a small percentage of each transaction. In addition to offering just about the best rates for both buyers and sellers, PayPal is owned by eBay and interfaces seamlessly with eBay. This has a number of advantages, as PayPal "knows" when you win and auction, and eBay "knows" when you've used PayPal to pay for it. PayPal offers additional benefits, including financing.

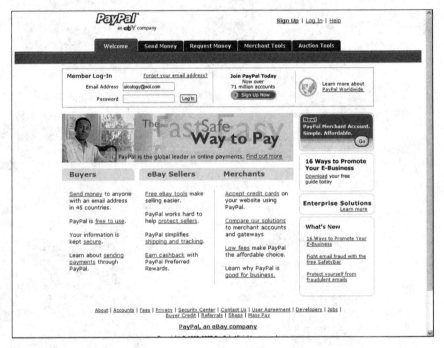

Figure 1-6: PayPal home page

Rent.com

Rent.com is an eBay-owned service you can use to find an apartment or other rental property.

Want It Now

Want It Now is a specialized bulletin board on which you can post a request for an item or items you cannot find on eBay or Half.com. As shown in Figure 1-7, Want It Now offers dozens of categories in which you can post requests for free, and these posts can be searched by sellers. This makes it a potentially useful selling tool, particularly for unusual items. A Want It Now listing consists of a subject header (up to 55 characters in length) and a description of the wanted item (which can be up to 500 characters long). Want It Now listings remain active for 60 days, after which they are automatically deleted. If a seller finds a request for an item he has, he can contact the potential buyer and direct her to an auction or Buy It Now listing he has posted. The system does not allow direct messaging, however, so Want It Now cannot be used to make deals outside eBay.

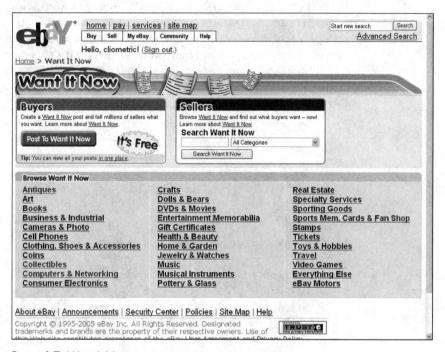

Figure 1-7: Want It Now page

eBay Categories

eBay is organized according to a system of merchandise categories. Each category has several levels of subcategories beneath it. For example, the Antiques category offers 16 subcategories, among them Asian Antiques, Decorative Arts, Maritime, and so on. Each of these subcategories has multiple subcategories. It's not uncommon for a category to have up to five levels beneath it. For example, the Collectibles category's Radio, Phonograph, TV, Phone subcategory has two additional subcategories under it, like this:

Collectibles ▸ Radio, Phonograph, TV, Phone ▸ Radios ▸ Other Radio Items

These categories cover just about anything you might imagine.

NOTE *eBay users might like to see additional categories or subcategories. Why not, for instance, a category for food items? And how about a Scam category for multilevel marketing (also known as pyramid schemes) and those "free" offers that really aren't?*

Global Sites

Still farther down the left side of the page, as shown in Figure 1-8, is a box labeled Global Sites. The Select One drop-down menu lists more than a dozen international eBay sites. Most menu selections and other items on these sites are in the same relative position as you would find them on eBay for the United States, so you should have few navigational problems, even though each site uses its home country's language. If you're fluent in the language in question, you're ahead of the game. If not, you may want to try an online translation service to help make sense of the foreign eBay. (One of the best is AltaVista's Babel Fish Translation, a free service located at http://babelfish.altavista.com.)

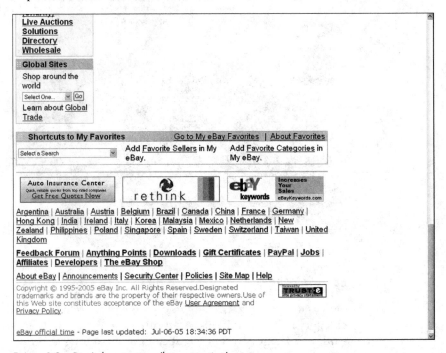

Figure 1-8: eBay's home page (lower portion)

A few foreign sites operate under a different name, like *Mercado Libre* (Free Market) in Argentina and Mexico. Some are eBay associates, meaning that eBay does not own them.

You can sign in at eBay sites in other countries and bid on items, but be sure to check the auction listing to see whether the seller will ship to your country. If it's not explicitly stated, email the seller and ask.

You'll also want to check whether the seller accepts the currency of another country. Some accept PayPal or another online payment system that allows you to pay in the currency of other countries. (PayPal automatically calculates the exchange rate for you; it pays foreign sellers in their currency, while subtracting the equivalent in dollars from your account.) However, there is sometimes a delay in posting or acceptance of PayPal payments in foreign currencies, which can result in an item costing a bit more or less (in your home currency) than you had planned on. A few sellers will accept cash.

The Bottom of the Home Page

Various company logos are lined up beneath the promotions and featured items on the home page. Clicking one of those links will take you to another site or to an eBay page related to the item in question.

Here are some other notable links you'll find if you scroll all the way down the home page:

The eBay Shop
At this site, you can buy shirts, coffee cups, and other items that carry the eBay logo.

NOTE *eBay sellers who like to plan ahead may want to consider stocking up on the latest eBay-imprinted pens, mugs, hats, and so on. With a little luck, you can cash in by reselling these items five or six years from now, after they're out of production!*

Security Center
The Security Center is loaded with tips, frequently asked questions (FAQs), articles about safe buying and selling, and links to eBay's rules and policies. This page also provides a link to where you can report problems.

NOTE *eBay rarely steps in to resolve problems between users. It provides suggestions and automated resources for users to resolve conflicts themselves, but almost never settles disputes directly.*

Feedback Forum
eBay Feedback is a rating system that buyers and sellers use to rate their trading partners. This page provides fast access to any user's Feedback, and it also offers links for leaving Feedback, responding to Feedback, viewing others' Feedback, and getting help with Feedback. (You will find more about eBay's Feedback system at the end of this chapter.)

About eBay
This leads to a page of links that present information about just about every aspect of eBay as a company—its history, stock, and so forth.

Affiliate Program
The eBay Affiliate Program rewards those who link to eBay with commissions on registrations, bids, and sales.

Developers
This links to a page with information and a registration form for those who wish to develop an eBay-related software/Internet application.

eBay Downloads
eBay downloads are software tools that enhance and support the buying or selling process on eBay. Some of these downloads are free.

Using eBay's Help System

As with most commercial websites, eBay offers a specialized Help system. The Help page is shown in Figure 1-9.

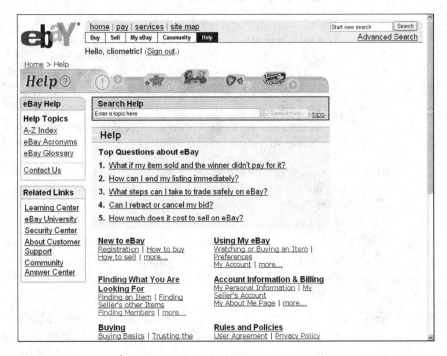

Figure 1-9: eBay's Help page

If you're new to eBay—or have been a buyer and are just getting into selling—visit the Learning Center, where you can access tutorials, a tour, bulletin boards, and other very useful information resources. For more in-depth learning, eBay University offers online (and on CD) courses on how to use eBay for buying and selling.

Also accessible from eBay's Help page (and of special interest) are eBay's Security Center and the Community Answer Center. The Community Answer Center (also known as the eBay Answer Center) provides bulletin boards where you can post questions and get answers from other eBay users (and perhaps eBay staff). The boards are organized by topic and are searchable.

eBay tries to anticipate customer needs by providing a wealth of information in its Help system and in user discussion forums. If you can't find an answer to your question on the company's website, you can contact eBay Customer Support via email, or click the **Live Help** icon to connect with an agent (just be prepared to wait awhile).

A FEW WORDS ABOUT EBAY BULLETIN BOARDS

You should be aware that, just as with the rest of the Internet, not all information found in eBay's bulletin boards is reliable. Information is posted by eBay staff on some boards, but not all, and not everything comes from eBay. Sometimes, eBay members post erroneous information (usually unintentionally). So be sure to double-check anything important you find on a board—especially if it is about another eBay member—before acting on it.

Also note that some of the "boards" are actually chat rooms, where (as might be expected) almost no one talks about eBay.

You may find it useful to create an eBay ID for use exclusively in posting on bulletin boards. Many members do this, because it allows them to keep their personal and seller/buyer personas separate, and say what they feel without fearing some sort of repercussions on their sales or bidding activities.

Communicating with eBay

Communicating with eBay is not unlike communicating with any other large company that has several million customers. You probably won't get an answer to a question within minutes (unless you're using eBay Live Help). However, eBay confirms receipt of an email question within a few minutes after it is sent, and promises a reply within 24 to 48 hours. The vast majority of questions receive replies within that time period.

You can get into eBay's contact system through the Help system. However, before you get to a link that will allow you to email eBay Customer Service, you'll see some exhortations that you find the answer to your problem yourself, along with links to a good deal of Help and FAQ material. eBay would prefer that anyone with a problem find the solution herself, using either the Help system or one of the bulletin boards. This is actually a good idea. It makes for less of a drain on eBay resources, and people who work out their own solutions tend to remember those solutions and learn more useful information along the way.

NOTE *eBay staffers are active on several of the bulletin boards in Seller Central (a collection of bulletin boards and information sources for eBay sellers). You'll also find eBay employees posting in eBay Workshops bulletin boards.*

The fastest way to get to an eBay message link is via the Contact eBay Customer Support link on the main Help page. This leads to eBay's Contact Us page, shown in Figure 1-10.

As you can see, the page is a special kind of form, on which you select the general sort of problem or question you want to report, then refine it with one or two additional selections. (The choices are determined by what precedes them.) The choices offered cover the most frequent types of questions and problems eBay members have.

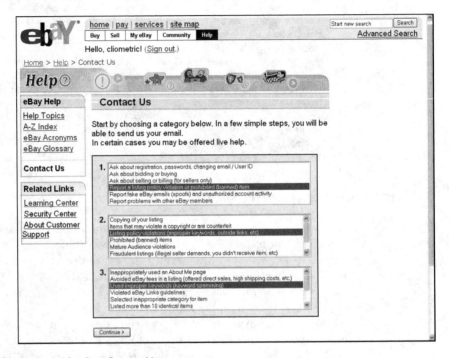

Figure 1-10: eBay Contact Us page

NOTE *Sometimes the simplest way to get an answer to a question is to ask another eBay member directly. You can post a question on one of the bulletin boards or send an email to a member. You can contact any eBay member by clicking his or her user ID and typing a message in the form that appears. The message will be forwarded to the member's email address, which will not be revealed to you, although yours will be shown to the member you're contacting, so she can reply to you.*

Touring My eBay

eBay provides a comprehensive set of online tools to help you manage all your eBay activities. These tools are made available through a page called My eBay, which is the first page you see when you sign on to eBay, as shown in Figure 1-11. To reach My eBay, click the My eBay link on eBay's main menu.

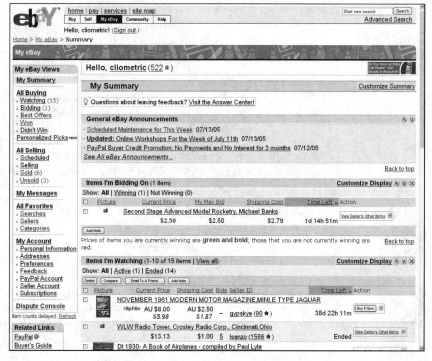

Figure 1-11: My eBay page (partial)

With My eBay, you can manage buying, selling, your favorites, and more. Here's a quick rundown:

Buying

Several lists keep track of what you're bidding on, what you've won, and items you are watching. In addition to listing the auctions and providing links to them, My eBay also displays your maximum bids, totals for your purchases, and more.

Selling

A listing of all your active auctions and flat-price sales is displayed, along with the number and amounts of bids for each item. Separate lists show auctions that have ended, one for unsold items and one showing items that have sold. Cumulative totals for bids and sales are provided, too.

Favorites lists

My eBay provides access to lists of your favorite searches, sellers, and categories.

Messages

Notification of announcements and messages from eBay and other eBay members are displayed on the My eBay page, with links to the messages and a My Messages page.

Your account

All elements of your account are available, from managing personal and financial information, to setting preferences, checking your Feedback profile, managing your seller account, and more.

Dispute Console

The Dispute Console, which is where you initiate and manage complaints against nonpaying bidders and sellers who don't deliver, is accessed from My eBay.

In addition, the My eBay page provides all eBay's menu links, plus links to related services such as PayPal, eBay Stores, searching, and more.

Introducing eBay's Feedback System

One of eBay's most important features is the *Feedback* system. The Feedback system is a means of gauging how good members are at fulfilling their obligations as buyers and sellers.

Each time a sale is completed, both parties rate their trading partner by leaving Feedback on the transaction. This is done via a link on an item's listing page, a link next to the completed item on your My eBay page, or from Feedback pages. You have a choice of rating the buyer or seller as Positive, Neutral, or Negative.

If the rating is Positive, the member receives one Feedback point. If a Neutral rating is given, the member receives no points. If the rating is negative, one Feedback point is subtracted from the member's total score. This score is displayed next to the member's ID online, along with what percentage of the member's Feedback is Positive (for example, you might see 95%, 100%, 84.9%, and so on). eBay buyers and sellers often refer to other members' Feedback scores to judge whether they want to trade with those members. A typical member's Feedback page is shown in Figure 1-12.

Most eBay members do their best to maintain a high Feedback rating. But realistically, on a day-to-day basis, few sellers remove bids or block bidders based on Feedback scores, and few buyers refuse to bid on an item when they see a Feedback score below 95%. People generally look at a member's Feedback score when they are having problems getting paid or getting their merchandise.

But it's better to have a good reputation than a bad one. And, in addition to giving you a good reputation, maintaining a high positive Feedback rating can qualify you for certain benefits.

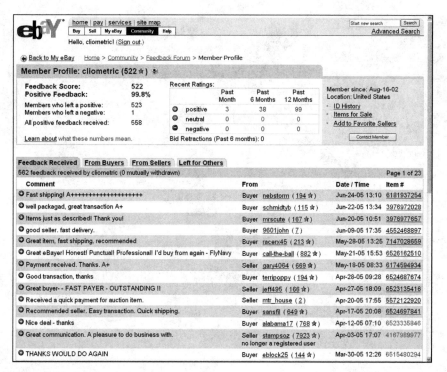

Figure 1-12: Feedback page

You have by now noticed that eBay has more than a few inconsistencies. While most aren't on the same level as referring to a bulletin board as a chat room, there is still quite a bit of potential for confusion. The service is apparently an ongoing project of not just one committee, but several committees that don't seem to communicate with one another. Most inconsistencies are easy to figure out (like a link labeled eBay Education that leads to a page called Learning Center). If you find something that doesn't make sense, remember that you can back out of it with your browser's Back button. You can't break anything on eBay, and there is no way you can rack up a charge or delete something without knowing what you're doing beforehand. You can always look to this book for clarification, of course.

Now that you've explored the basics of eBay, you're ready to take a look at how auctions work. The next chapter describes standard auctions, as well as the variations you'll find on eBay.

2

HOW EBAY AUCTIONS WORK

Although eBay offers several ways to buy and sell items, the most common technique is the standard auction. In an eBay auction, bidders who want to buy an item ostensibly enter the highest price they're willing to pay for it. I say "ostensibly" because bidders frequently revise their maximum offer upward and end up paying more than they had intended. This happens for a couple of reasons. First (and most often), a bidder who was willing to pay, say, $50 for an item decides that she can afford $55 when someone else bids $52. After all, it's only another $5 (or, as some might see it, another $3). A few days later, she may go to $100 when she is outbid at $95. And so it may go, up and up, until—win or lose—our bidder who wasn't going to pay more than $50 is bidding twice that or more, one small increment at a time. The moral of the story: It's easy to spend too much, if you do it a little at a time.

Excessive bidding also occurs when bidders get caught up in the psychology of competition and raise their bids just for the sake of beating someone else. In this case, the auction becomes less a matter of obtaining the item and more about winning. And so it goes, until one bidder with more money, guts, or competitive fire wins out over all the others. Fortunately, you *can* avoid such competitive escalation and still win, as you'll learn in Chapter 13, a primer on bidding strategies.

In this chapter, I'll cover the basics of participating in eBay auctions.

Anatomy of an Auction

eBay auction listings are usually fairly straightforward. Now and then, you get some silliness where people include photos of their cats or children, or 4,000 words of rules and threats they hope will keep insincere bidders away. Usually, however, when you view an auction, you'll see a title, an item description, some shipping information, a starting bid (and perhaps a Buy It Now price) and, more often than not, one or more photos. A typical eBay auction listing is shown in Figure 2-1.

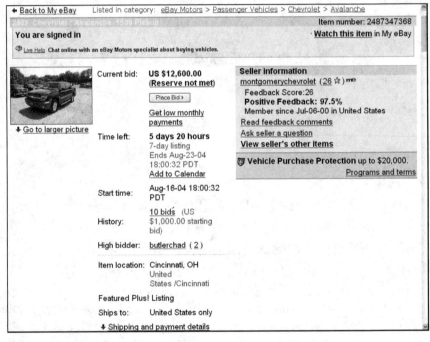

Figure 2-1: Typical eBay auction listing

Quite often, the most important elements of a listing (sellers take note!) are the starting bid and the item title. The first question anyone asks before buying something is "How much?"

Additional information in the listing (much of which is automatically added by eBay's software during the posting process) includes the amount of time left until the auction closes, the number of items available (usually one, except in the case of a Dutch auction, which I'll explain in the "Auction Variations" section later in this chapter), and the location of the item. You may also see icons and links for payment services.

NOTE *When a listing takes a long time to load—typically due to large image or sound files the seller has included with the listing—you can speed it up by clicking your browser's **Stop** button. In most instances, the eBay auction framework (item title, bid amounts, time left, and so on) will appear, along with the item description. If the photos haven't loaded, scroll down until you see a frame or blank area where you think the photos might be, right-click, and select **Show Picture** on the pop-up menu. This saves you from waiting for the entire page to load but enables you to view the areas you do want to see.*

Seller Information

The seller's ID is included with every auction listing, followed by a number and a star in parentheses. The number is the member's Feedback score, and the star changes color as a member's Feedback score increases. A gold star appears by the user's ID after he completes ten sales and/or purchases. The highest ranking is a red "shooting star," accorded those who have more than 100,000 Feedback points.

Beneath the user's Feedback information is a link labeled "Ask seller a question," which you can use to email the seller (anonymously, if you wish).

Bidding on an Auction

If you read an item's description and decide to bid on it, zip down the page to the "Your maximum bid" entry box, as shown in Figure 2-2.

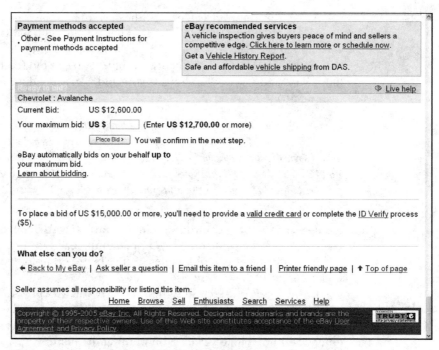

Figure 2-2: Ready to bid area of a listing

Displayed next to the box for your bid is the minimum bid you can make. If no one else has bid on the item, this will be the same as the opening bid amount set by the seller. If others have made bids, the minimum bid is the next increment over the highest bid. The increment amount is determined by eBay, and it increases as the bid price increases, as shown in Table 2-1.

Table 2-1: Bid Increments on eBay (in U.S. Dollars)

Current High Bids	Bid Increment
0.01 to 0.99	0.05
1.00 to 4.99	0.25
5.00 to 24.99	0.50
25.00 to 99.99	1.00
100.00 to 249.99	2.50
250.00 to 499.99	5.00
500.00 to 999.99	10.00
1,000.00 to 2,499.99	25.00
2,500.00 to 4,999.99	50.00
5,000.00 and over	100.00

As you can see from Table 2-1, if the current high bid on an item is $1,000, the minimum bid is $1,025. Similarly, if the current high bid is $4.25, the least you can bid is $4.50. And if an item has a bid of $510, you'll need to offer at least $520 before eBay will accept your bid. (You can bid fractional amounts, like $520.26 or $531.54, as long as your bid is greater than the required increment.)

NOTE   *Because eBay employs proxy bidding, if you bid $6.00 on an item when the current bid is $4.25, eBay will place a bid of only $4.50. The proxy system bids your maximum only if someone else comes within a certain percentage of it. If someone else takes the bid up to $5.50, eBay will place your maximum bid of $6.00 automatically. However, if another bidder bids only $5.00, eBay will increase your bid to just $5.50.*

You can bid more than the minimum bid, but for various reasons (as discussed in Chapter 13), you should not start off with the maximum amount you're willing to pay. If you bid your maximum early in the auction, you're inviting someone else to bid higher. You're better off holding back and seeing if you can outbid everyone else at a lower price.

If you're registered and signed in, eBay will accept your bid when you place it. The screen that follows will tell you where you stand in the bidding. If you've been outbid, you can enter another bid, vow to come back later and enter a winning bid, or give up on winning the item.

After You Bid

Whether or not you are the high bidder, the auction will remain open for additional bids until its preset ending time. When the auction ends, eBay will notify the winner and the seller.

PayPal and other auction-related sites may also send notifications, and the seller may send a manual notification to the winner, as well. Some buyers get upset if *all* these things happen—it's too much like being dunned by automated bill collectors. So, as a seller, you'll want to be aware of just how many systems are mailing your buyers, and keep the notifications to a minimum.

Another message you may see after you bid is "Reserve not met." This means that you haven't offered the reserve price the seller has set for this item, as explained next.

Reserve Price

A *reserve* is the minimum price a seller will accept. This is optional, however. You may wonder what the point of a reserve price is. Why doesn't the seller just set the minimum bid at the lowest price she will accept? Some sellers use the reserve in combination with a ridiculously low minimum bid (like $1 for a two-year-old automobile) as a device to lure potential bidders into having a look at the item. ("Hey, a car for a dollar! I'm in!") The reserve makes sure the seller doesn't get burned if only one or two people bid.

Most sellers who use reserves don't bother with ridiculously low minimum bids. They simply post the item with a reasonable minimum bid.

Sellers pay a couple of bucks extra to set a reserve, but most feel the additional cost is worth the safety net. Some buyers, on the other hand, get annoyed when they click an item that has an attractive price only to find the message "Reserve not met" glaring at them. Many consider really low minimum bids with reserves to be cheap tricks.

In case you are wondering, eBay's software doesn't divulge the amount of the reserve. It's up to the sellers whether they want to share this information.

NOTE *The letters NR in an auction item title mean No Reserve. The limited number of characters in auction headers has resulted in a number of shorthand references like this. See the appendix for a list of the most common abbreviations and acronyms.*

Auction Variations

Some variations on the typical auction bidding just described include the Buy It Now option, Dutch auction, and fixed-price auction.

Buy It Now

eBay offers an option called Buy It Now, which allows the seller to set a price for which a bidder can buy the item, ending the auction immediately.

The seller is charged a small fee for this. When the buyer clicks the Buy It Now button, it is the same as if the auction had run its course and the buyer was the highest bidder.

The Buy It Now option usually disappears from an auction when the first bid is placed. If an auction has a reserve *and* the Buy It Now option, however, Buy It Now remains in place until someone bids more than the reserve. Thus, someone can grab the item using Buy It Now, even though there are bids on it.

Dutch Auctions

A Dutch auction is an auction in which more than one of the same item is offered. The seller specifies how many items are available, and sets the minimum price (with or without a reserve). When a bidder bids on the auction, he also indicates how many items he wishes to buy. He must outbid other bidders to be able to take more than one of the item. The next highest bidder gets to choose how many of the items she wants, and so on, until all the items are taken. Otherwise, the auction is the same as a single-item auction.

Say there are five pearl necklaces in a Dutch auction, offered for $14.50, and user A bids for two of them at $14.50 each. Then, user B comes along and bids for two at $16.50. At this point, user A has the minimum successful bid; that is, the minimum winning bid. If you want just one necklace, you will need to outbid user A, though you don't necessarily need to outbid user B. If you want three or more, however, you will need to outbid user B.

NOTE *Some buyers are confused by Dutch auctions and end up bidding more than necessary. Remember that you do not need to outbid the highest bidder to win. As long as there are items left (all the items offered are not taken by those who have bid), you can win one or more items. So, before you bid on a Dutch auction, check how many items are left. If there are a lot, you're probably safe to bid the minimum.*

Fixed-Price Sales

A fixed-price auction is similar to the Buy It Now option, but no concurrent auction is in progress. Multiple items may be offered, and buyers may purchase more than one of them at the fixed price. The difference between this and a regular or Dutch auction is that, once you bid, you have won the item(s). You don't need to wait for the sale to end to close the deal.

eBay Stores

eBay Stores offer sellers with a large number of items a way to sell them for flat prices. Instead of putting dozens or hundreds of items up for auction (or as fixed-price listings), you post them to your own area of eBay, called an eBay Store. Figure 2-3 shows a typical page from an eBay store.

Figure 2-3: Typical eBay Store

Basically, an eBay store is a collection of listings that stay active longer and cost less to post than conventional eBay auctions. You, as the store proprietor, create the categories in which you'll list items, and then post the items for 30, 60, 90, or 120 days. You can also place selected items from your stock up for auction on eBay. (See http://stores.ebay.com for information about setting up a store.)

eBay's Search system will not pull results from eBay Stores, but there are ways for buyers to search all stores, one store, and individual categories within a store. (See Chapters 3 and 4 for information about how to search eBay Stores.)

When a buyer finds an item she wants, she buys it, and the sale is consummated, just as with any other eBay sale.

This covers the basics of buying on eBay. Of course, you have to find something before you can buy it, which is exactly what Chapters 3 and 4 show you how to do. You'll learn the basics of searching for items on eBay, along with quite a few tricks that can give you an edge on other buyers. eBay sellers will want to study these chapters, too, to learn how to make their merchandise easy to find.

3

FINDING STUFF ON EBAY: THE BASICS

eBay would be nearly worthless without a means of searching through the millions of items offered for sale on any given day. If you needed to hunt through all the descriptions manually, you would rarely find what you wanted.

eBay provides some excellent search tools within its Search and Browse systems. With these tools, you can search for items that meet specific criteria and browse lists of items by category. In addition, you can sort lists by multiple criteria, limit searches using search controls, and filter out items that don't fit your interests. You can also use eBay's search features to find information about other eBay members' buying and selling habits, discover the going prices of items, get historical data on auctions, and much more.

This chapter introduces you to the basics of searching on eBay. You'll learn how to tell eBay's Search system what you want to find and what you *don't* want to find. You can use the search techniques you learn here in any eBay venue, including auctions, fixed-price sales, and eBay stores.

Entering Search Text

Searching eBay involves *keywords*, also known as *search text*. On eBay, every word that a seller puts in an auction's title or description is a keyword. Figure 3-1 shows an example of a search text entry in the eBay Search box.

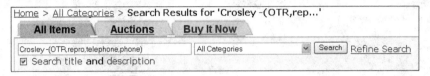

Figure 3-1: Search text entry

NOTE *Searches in eBay Motors and in eBay stores operate the same as those described for conventional eBay auctions.*

By following some basic rules, you can find just about anything on eBay:

Title and description searches

On most of eBay, you can search auction titles only or titles and descriptions simultaneously. Where a description search is also available, you'll see a check box for it beneath or next to the Search text box, as shown in Figure 3-1.

Wildcard searches

You can use the asterisk (*) as a "wildcard" in eBay searches. Type the first few letters of a word, followed by an asterisk (no spaces) to find all words that begin with those letters. For example, if you type **sti***, eBay will find words such as *still, stile, stir,* and *stilt.* In the same way, if you enter **196***, eBay will find all items that have 1960 through 1969 in their descriptions or titles, as well as *196a, 196b,* and so on. eBay does not permit wildcard searches containing fewer than two letters.

Phrase searches

To tell eBay to find only exact phrase matches, put quotation marks at the beginning and end. For example, **"little red wagon"** will find descriptions that contain the phrase *little red wagon* (that is, the words in that exact order), but it will not find descriptions that contain those three words in any other order or separated by other words.

NOTE *You may have used search tools elsewhere on the Internet that allow the words AND and OR as commands to find or omit certain word combinations. eBay does not use AND and OR as commands; they are treated just like any other keyword. As explained in the next chapter, certain symbols are used instead.*

Words that appear in an auction's Item Location field also qualify as keywords. Thus, if you enter the word *Milford* in a search, the results may include items located in Milford, Ohio, and Milford, Connecticut. In the same fashion, eBay user IDs turn up as keywords in searches, as does information in a listing's Ship to field. All text is entered by the seller.

Using Your Search Results

A list of auctions that match your search criteria will be displayed in a *search results list*, as shown in the example in Figure 3-2.

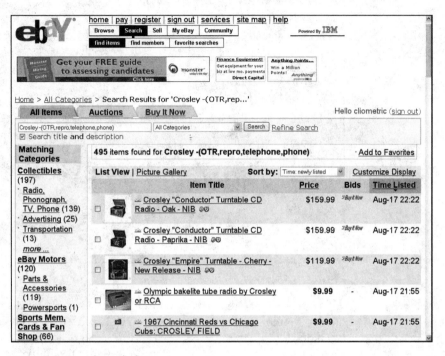

Figure 3-2: Search results list

As you can see, each item in the list has a title, a price (which is the currently bid price), and the time left before its auction ends (in days, hours, and minutes).

Some auctions in search results lists have small photos or other images displayed to the left of the item title. These photos are known as *gallery photos*, and are extra-cost options that sellers can use to catch the buyer's eye. If an item has no gallery photo, but photos are included within its listing, a small camera icon appears to the left of the item title. Gallery photos are displayed in larger format when you choose the Picture Gallery view (by clicking that link on the top-left side of the search results list), as shown in Figure 3-3.

To view any item in a search results list, click its title, gallery photo, or camera icon.

NOTE *When you find an item of interest, don't jump in and bid on it right away. Instead, click the "Watch this item" link, located just above the Seller Information box. This places it on a list on your My eBay page.*

Figure 3-3: Search results list in Picture Gallery view

At the left of the first several items in the search results list is a box labeled Matching Categories, as shown in Figure 3-4. This box will contain breakdown of the main categories and subcategories in which items on the search results list appear. Next to each category title in parentheses is the number of items in that category.

Figure 3-4: Matching Categories list

The search results list offers additional useful controls and features for sorting, filtering, and viewing only certain items.

NOTE *A link labeled Customize Display, located to the right of the Sort by menu, leads to a page where you can set the search results page to display the results in the Picture Gallery or List view every time you view a list, set separate default sort orders for search results lists, set the time display, show or hide item numbers, and convert prices to U.S. dollars.*

Sorting and Filtering Search Results

Using the Sort by pull-down menu at the top of the search results list, you can rearrange the order of the list. As shown in Figure 3-5, you can sort items by auctions ending soonest, items newly listed, highest priced items first, lowest priced items first, or by distance, with the items nearest to you first.

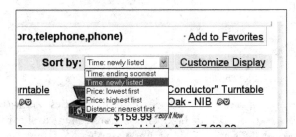

Figure 3-5: Sort by menu

NOTE *If you're looking for entertainment and enlightenment, try sorting a category to display the highest prices first, and look for items that have been up for a few days and have no bids. When you take a look at specific items and their sellers, patterns sometimes emerge. Many of the highest priced items will have been posted by sellers with low Feedback scores—and who have a lot to learn about selling on eBay. Some may be posted by sellers who normally don't sell the kind of item they have overpriced; a quick look at the other items they're offering (and items they've sold) will tell you if this is the case. (Chapter 5 has information on determining what an item is really worth.)*

Selections in the Search Options list on the left side of the search results page, beneath the Matching Categories list, let you show only specific items. As you can see in Figure 3-6, you can choose to view only PayPal items, Buy It Now items, gift items, items listed in groups or lots, and completed listings (a valuable tool for buyers and sellers alike, as you'll learn). Via a pull-down menu, you can view listings that started today, end today, or end within five hours. Additionally, you can choose to see only items priced (or bid) within a certain range. These options can be combined to speed up searching.

Figure 3-6: Search Options list

Where appropriate, you will see an Item Specifics box with a list of links beneath the Search Options box. This is an excellent tool for filtering out unwanted results. Figure 3-7 shows an example of an Item Specifics list.

Figure 3-7: Item Specifics list

Finding eBay Store Items

Beneath the Search Options and Item Specifics lists, you will often find a More on eBay box. This offers links to eBay stores that, in the judgment of the Search system, stock items similar to what you're seeking.

You will sometimes find a link at the bottom of the search results list labeled "See Additional Buy It Now Items." This transfers your search to eBay stores. If there are only a few items in eBay stores, the Search system displays those items here.

Saving Searches

You can save any search you create by clicking the Add to Favorites link at the top of the search results list. Once you've done that, you can run the same search any time you wish, without needing to enter and select all the parameters.

Now that you know how to use a search results list, let's examine the many powerful features eBay's Search system offers.

Conducting Refined Searches

The place to begin learning about the power of eBay's Search system is on the Search: Find Items page, frequently referred to as the Search page, shown in Figure 3-8. You can get to this page by clicking **Search** on the main menu, by choosing **Buy** on the Search submenu, or by clicking links on other eBay menus.

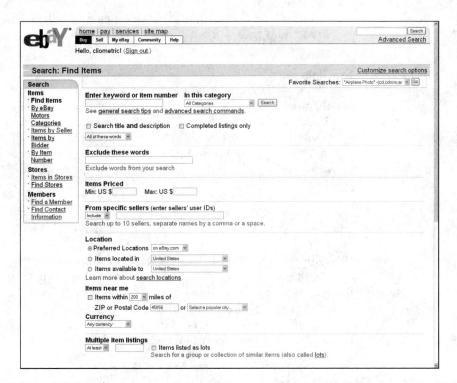

Figure 3-8: Search page

The Search page offers quite a range of options to use in finding items. In general, searching on eBay is just like using your favorite search engine, such as Google or Yahoo! The format of your search will determine how targeted or how vast your search results will be.

You can search by keyword(s)/item number, by category (eBay searches all categories by default), or by item description. You can also limit the results returned by setting certain filters, such as searching only completed listings.

NOTE *The Search system searches only the titles, not the descriptions, of completed items.*

Just beneath the "Search title and description" check box is a pull-down menu with three options that apply to the words entered in the "Enter keyword or item number" text box:

All of these words

This choice means that the Search system will return only items whose titles and/or descriptions contain each and every word you enter, though not necessarily in the order in which you entered them. Thus, if you enter the words *motor* and *car* and *American*, you will get a list of only those items whose titles or descriptions contain all of those words.

Any of these words

If you select this option, the Search system will return a list of items whose titles and/or descriptions contain any one of the words you've entered.

Exact phrase

This selection returns only auctions whose titles or descriptions contain the words you entered in the exact order in which you typed them. Thus, if you enter *American motor car*, you will get a different list of results than if you entered *motor car American*. One list will include every item that has "American motor car" in its title or description, and the other will include every item with "motor car American."

Another helpful way of narrowing your search to a manageable list of results is to use the "Exclude these words" option. For example, if you are searching for airplane photos and want only real photographs, you might enter *CD* as a word to exclude, so that the search results list does not include CDs with scans of photos. This tool is also useful for filtering items that contain irrelevant keywords, which some sellers include in their descriptions to force people who aren't looking for what they're selling to view their items. (Sellers who do this are known as *keyword spammers*.)

Use the check boxes under "Show only" to find only items that you can buy immediately, gift items, and/or pay for with PayPal.

Using Other Search Pages

eBay has several additional Search pages for finding items by seller, bidder, or item number; searching the eBay store stock; and searching for specific eBay stores. Each of these pages is accessible from the Search submenu on eBay's main menu, as well as through links on the small Search menu at the left side of any Search page, as shown in Figure 3-9.

Figure 3-9: Search page menu

Searching by Seller

The Search: Items by Seller page, shown in Figure 3-10, finds current and completed items. You can specify how far back to search (eBay auctions are usually available for a month after they end). This page also has a results per page setting and, for the named seller only, an option to display the bidders' email addresses.

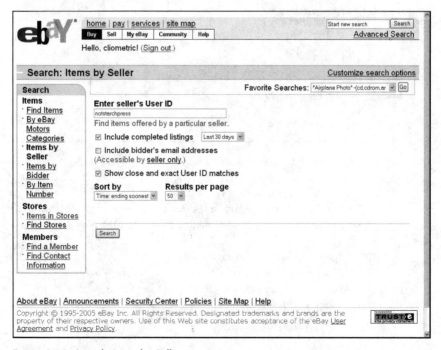

Figure 3-10: Search: Items by Seller page

Why search by seller? A seller from whom you've bought in the past may offer similar items in the future. If you are a seller, you may want to keep an eye on another seller who offers the same kind of merchandise you sell, in order to avoid posting the same or similar items at the same time.

Searching by Bidder

The Search: Items by Bidder page, shown in Figure 3-11, lets you see all the items a member is bidding on and everything that person has bid on for the preceding month. Enter a member's ID, select whether you want the search to include completed items, choose whether to include only items the bidder won, and specify the number of items to display on each results page.

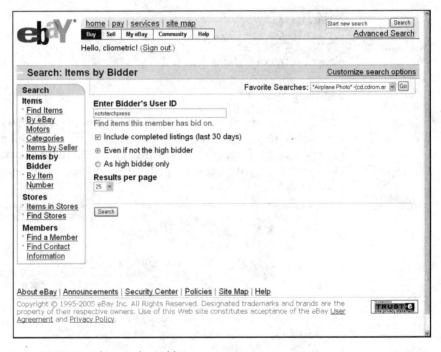

Figure 3-11: Search: Items by Bidder page

If you're a seller, you can use this feature (in conjunction with reviewing Feedback) to examine a bidder's history and performance. It may also be useful to know what other things the bidder is interested in.

NOTE *You aren't supposed to engage other eBay members with a sales pitch outside of auctions. However, if you see that someone has a record of buying items similar to the ones you want to sell, you can ask him if he is interested in your item, and then post an auction listing and notify him.*

If you have more than one eBay ID (one for selling and one for buying, for instance), you can use this feature to check the status of items you're selling or auctions you're bidding on with your other ID, without needing to log out and log in again.

Searching in eBay Stores

The Search: Items in Stores page, shown in Figure 3-12, works like eBay's main Search page, described earlier in this chapter, but with a few differences. First, it searches only items that are in eBay stores. This, however, includes store-only stock *and* store items that are being offered on regular eBay auctions or fixed-price items. You can limit the search to store stock only and ignore auctions and fixed-price items by clicking the "Search Store Inventory items only" check box.

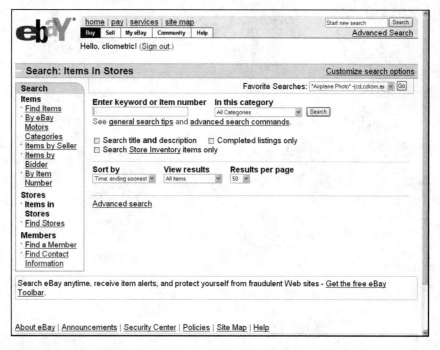

Figure 3-12: Search: Items in Stores page

The tools covered in this chapter should get you started finding stuff on eBay. The next chapter expands on the basics, showing you how to implement eBay search techniques for maximum results. You will also learn about an alternative approach to searching called *browsing*.

4

FINDING STUFF ON EBAY: HIGH-POWER SEARCHES

With a little knowledge and advance planning, you can develop strategies to find anything that exists on eBay, even things that other people can't find. If you're a seller, you can greatly enhance the probability that everyone who might be interested in what you have to sell will find your items. All it takes is an awareness of how various buyers search and a willingness to use that knowledge in your listings. The preceding chapter covered the fundamentals of searching eBay. In this chapter, you'll learn how to combine basic search techniques with Search commands and unconventional techniques to conduct truly high-powered searches.

Search Commands

In Chapter 3, you learned that you can limit how eBay searches for words with a pull-down menu on the Advanced and Basic Search pages. With this menu, you can direct eBay to find listings that contain all the words you enter, in any order; to find listings that contain any of the words you enter; or to search for the words you enter as a phrase.

The searches you can set up using the selections and menus on eBay's Advanced Search page are fairly simple. You cannot, for example, use the selections and menus on eBay's Advanced Search page to direct eBay to find listings that contain the phrases *new book* and *Stephen King*, along with the word *ordinary*, plus either the word *phrase* or the word *forgotten*. However, you can set up this sort of search if you use eBay's Search commands.

Search commands are specific characters that instruct eBay to treat the words you enter in a certain way. Search commands let you set up complex searches that you cannot set up using selections on eBay's Advanced Search page, such as the one described in the previous paragraph. The symbols you can use in Search commands are shown in Table 4-1.

Table 4-1: Search Command Symbols

Symbol	Function
" "	Specifies that the words you enter be treated as a phrase
-	Excludes words or phrases
,	In a group of words, designates the end of one word or phrase and the beginning of another
( )	Sets off a group of words or phrases to be searched for or excluded on an "any of these words" basis

For example, here's the Search command to find only those listings that contain the phrases *new book* and *Stephen King*, along with the word *ordinary*, plus either the word *phrase* or the word *forgotten*:

"new book" "stephen king" ordinary (phrase,forgotten)

You can conduct four basic kinds of searches using the Search commands just described:

- All words (also known as an AND search in other contexts)
- Any word (also known as an OR search)
- Phrase (all words in the order given)
- Exclude this word or words (also known as a NOT search)

Here's how to use the Search commands in each type of search:

Search for all words (AND)

To require that *all* words you enter in a Search box be found, simply type in the words, separated by spaces. This will return items that contain every one of your keywords, though not in any order. For example, **Revell model airplane** will return listings that contain the words *Revell* AND *model* AND *airplane*.

Search for any words (OR)

To tell eBay's search software to find items that contain *any* of the words you enter, separate the keywords with commas and enclose them in parentheses. For example, **(Revell,model,airplane)** will return listings that contain the words *Revell* OR *model* OR *airplane*. (The search results list will be larger than that returned by an AND search.)

Search for a phrase

To specify that a series of words be searched for as a phrase, enclose the words in quotation marks. For example, **"No Starch Press"** will provide a list of items with the phrase *No Starch Press* in their descriptions (which would be a list of books published by No Starch Press).

Multiple phrase search (AND)

You can search for multiple phrases (an AND search) simply by entering the phrases in quotation marks, with no other punctuation. For example, **"Analog Magazine" "Michael A. Banks"** will return one or more listings containing both phrases (or, viewed another way, listings that offer issues of *Analog* magazine with stories by Michael A. Banks).

Any phrase search (OR)

To specify a search for items that contain any of several phrases, place quotation marks around each phrase, a comma between each phrase and the next—*outside* the quote marks. Enclose the whole entry in parentheses. For example, **("de soto","de sota","de soda","de sodo")** will return items that contain *de soto* OR *de sota* OR *de soda* OR *de sodo*.

Exclude words from a search (NOT)

To exclude a word or words from a search, separate the words with commas and enclose them in parentheses. Place a minus sign before the first parenthesis. For example, **–(army,navy,military,force,fighter)** will exclude those words from the search.

Exclude phrases from a search

To exclude phrases, place quotation marks around each phrase, and a comma between each phrase and the next—*outside* the quotation marks. Enclose the phrases in parentheses, with a minus sign before everything. For example, **–("de soto","de sota","de soda","de sodo")** will give you a list of eBay listings that do not contain any of these phrases: *de soto* OR *de sota* OR *de soda* OR *de sodo*.

Exclude words and phrases

You can exclude a combination of individual keywords and phrases by separating the excluded items by commas. For example, **car –("ford motor",Chevrolet,"Straight eight")** searches for all listings that contain *car* but do not contain *ford motor* OR *Chevrolet* OR *Straight eight*.

All the various kinds of keyword, phrase, and exclusionary searches can be combined in any way you wish. For example, if you wanted to find all items with the words *Revell* and *model*, and the phrase *new in box*, but without the words *boat*, *car*, and *ship*, you would enter this:

Revell model "new in box" –(boat,car,ship)

Now that you know the mechanics of using Search commands, let's consider how you can conduct effective searches.

IT'S ALL IN HOW YOU LOOK AT IT

When you're conducting a search, remember not everyone thinks as you do. For example, some people think of a magazine as a book. Others consider a catalog to be a magazine or a book.

Thanks to this sort of thinking (and a lack of information on the seller's part), I found one of my finest treasures on eBay. I don't remember what I was looking for, but my eye happened across an auction titled "2 1920s maps and car book." The maps weren't of interest to me, but I decided to look at the listing in case the book might be a history I hadn't seen or an early motorist's magazine. When the listing came up, I was surprised to see that the "book" was a small 1918 catalog from an automotive company whose history I had been researching. I bid on the items and won. I did end up spending more than I wanted, because someone was bidding against me. But it turned out that he was after the maps only, so I sold those to him later.

Had the seller been a car fanatic or more knowledgeable about her auction item, she might have stated in the description that the "car book" was a pre-1920 catalog from a certain automobile company. That may have drawn a few more bids, depending on who happened to be looking around eBay that week.

The point is that you should consider how an uninformed or novice seller might describe a particular kind of collectible or class of merchandise he knows little about. On the seller's side of that coin, this demonstrates how a little research can be to your profit.

Search Factors

Simply typing a name or a few words of description into a Search box is no guarantee that you'll find what you're seeking. The item you're looking for may elude you, even if you enter a precise description. This is because of variables in how a seller may describe an item. These include spelling, synonyms, plurals, possessives, historical terminology, and regional uses.

Spelling

You'll see a lot of misspelling on eBay (and on the Internet in general). Sellers misspell common words like collectible (as collect*able*), and buyers search for Volkswag*on* when what they're looking for is a Volkswag*en*. Similarly, a VW Beetle may become a *Beatle*, while the music group the Beatles magically metamorphoses into the *Beetles*. Many people simply don't bother to look up a word's spelling; instead, they write it as it sounds to them (phonetically).

Which words are most likely to be misspelled? Proper names are often misspelled, simply because they aren't used very often. Thus, the knowledge-able would-be buyer who is searching for a Duncan Phyfe chest can't find it because a seller who is unfamiliar with fine furniture posted it as a Duncan Five chest.

Brand names are often misspelled. This is an important consideration, since so many items sold on eBay involve brand or trade names. Consider the name De Soto. In addition to being the name of a sixteenth-century Spanish explorer (Hernando De Soto), De Soto was the name of an automobile pro-duced by the Chrysler Corporation between 1928 and 1961 (not to mention a motorcar manufactured in Indiana during 1913 and 1914). On any given day, hundreds of history and automobile buffs are likely to be searching for something De Soto-related. And hundreds of sellers will be offering De Soto items of all sorts, ranging from reference books to hood emblems. Some of the sellers will find buyers, but many won't, because they spelled De Soto as De Sota, De Soda, Da Sota, or some other phonetic variation.

Another problem stems from the contemporary trend to run words together because they LookCool or AreMemorable as TradeNames. The pervasiveness of such words can confuse your search strategy. Desoto (or Desoda) is one example that appears frequently on eBay. Interestingly, searches I conducted using both *De Soto* and *Desoto* showed that four times as many people go for the SmashWord version as use the correct version.

Being familiar with the correct name, the typical collector in search of a De Soto hood emblem will most likely enter **De Soto** as his search phrase. If that is the only search he does, there is a good chance he'll miss a set of De Soto wheel covers because they're listed using the wrong spelling.

As a buyer, you can turn this to your advantage. Stop and think of all the ways De Soto can be misspelled. Then do an "any of these words" search, as described in the previous section using all the variations, perhaps like this:

emblem ("de soto","de sota","de soda","de sodo",desoto,desota,
desoda,desodo)

Or, since some people think of a hood emblem as a hood ornament, you might expand the search thus:

(ornament,emblem) ("de soto","de sota","de soda","de sodo",desoto,
desota,desoda,desodo)

These are extreme examples, to be sure, but they indicate just how far you may have to go to find every listing that *might* offer what you want.

Synonyms

Synonyms can complicate searching, or they can give you an advantage over others looking for the same thing. Depending on who is posting or looking for an item, an automobile may be called an auto, motorcar, motor car, motor vehicle, or just car. A vending machine might be called a vendor or a dispenser. Sellers should think of all possible ways to name an item they're selling.

NOTE *Sellers should include alternate spellings and terminology in the narrative of a description, instead of a list of words at the end, because eBay sometimes views a long list of words as keyword spamming—something that can get your listing canceled. You can use a line like this: "This Volkswagen (which some people insist on spelling 'Volkswagon' and which others abbreviate to 'VW') tail light (tailight) or stop light (stoplight) lens is in new condition." This way, you catch all the searchers.*

You can direct eBay to include synonyms in most searches but putting the words in parentheses and separating them by commas, as described earlier in this chapter. For instance, if you're searching for photos of airplanes, you might set up the search this way:

> photos (airplane,airplanes,airship,airships,plane,planes,aeroplane, aeroplanes,aircraft)

This will find all listings that contain the word *photos*, plus any one of the words in parentheses.

A synonym dictionary or thesaurus can be a secret weapon in searches. Microsoft Word, among other common applications, has a thesaurus feature built in, or you can visit websites like Merriam-Webster online (www.m-w.com) or www.thesaurus.com.

Plurals and Possessives

Even if you want only one airplane photo, you should include the plural form of the noun when you search. If you are looking for something in the plural, such as engines or tires, you should also search on the possessive (engine's or tire's) because a large portion of the world's English-speaking population doesn't know the basics of punctuation.

eBay's Search system recognizes **engine's** without quotation marks around it the same as **"engine's"** (with quotation marks). If, however, you want to include those words as part of a phrase, eBay's search system will not view them as the same. Thus, **"engine's horsepower"** will return a different list of results than **"engines horsepower"**.

eBay is gradually adding *automatic search expansion* of plural and singular forms to a variety of commonly used keywords. This means that a keyword search for a plural or singular form of a keyword will return listings that contain both plural and singular forms of that word, provided the word or phrase with the keyword is not in quotation marks. For example, if you search for **book**, the search results will include listings that contain either *books* or *book*. If, however, you search with the exact phrase **"Harry Potter book"**, the search results list will contain the singular version only. eBay's system selects the words to expand, not you, so it is still a good idea to use both plural and singular forms in searches, if you are seeking both forms.

Abbreviations

Just as in the classified ads, sellers often use abbreviations (official and invented) in eBay auction titles because space is limited. And they're used in auction descriptions because not everyone can type well. Although you may rarely use abbreviations in searches, it's a good idea to familiarize yourself with common usages.

You can usually figure out what an acronym means by its context. For example, New in Box is abbreviated to NIB, and New Old Stock is NOS. Single-word abbreviations are created by truncating words or by removing vowels, such as Ed. (Edition) or RSRV (Reserve).

Some categories (particularly hobbies and collectibles) have their own special terminology. Radio control for cars, boats, and airplanes is referred to as RC or R/C. Stamp collectors often seek MNH (Mint, Never Hinged) stamps, while numismatists look for BU (Brilliant Uncalculated) coins.

A number of abbreviations are in common use on eBay, some of which are peculiar to auctions. For a list of commonly used abbreviations, see the appendix.

Historical Usage

If you are looking for older items, be aware of usage changes. In the nineteenth century, *car* meant a railroad car. Those lucky enough to have a refrigerator in its early days referred to it as an *icebox*. In the 1970s and 1980s, video game cartridges were often called *roms* or *tapes*. These are just a few examples. Sellers are advised to use both the old and new terminology when describing antique or older items.

Regional Usage

You are probably aware that a soft drink is referred to as a *soda* in some parts of the United States, while it's called *pop* in other areas. A paper bag is called a *sack* or a *poke* in some places. What's known as a *wrench* in the United States is a *spanner* in England, while a vacuum tube is a *valve*. You can learn about such variations by reading the listings for items similar to what you're seeking or selling.

Search Flukes

For some unknown reason, in some instances, eBay's search system cannot find a phrase *as a phrase*. But it will find the phrase when you do an "any of these words" search.

For example, I was once looking for something from a 1930s New York institution called the Aviation Country Club. Without thinking, I typed **Aviation Country Club** into a Search box and clicked **Search**. eBay turned up a booklet about the Aviation Country Club. (Yes, I had clicked the "Search titles and description" check box.)

Then I noticed that I had not included the quotation marks. I thought I might find even more matches if I added them. The result was no matches. eBay did not find the item I had just viewed, even though the phrase "Aviation Country Club" was right there in the text of the description. I went to the main Search page, entered the words, and selected exact phrase from the pull-down menu. Again, no search results were returned. But when I removed the quotation marks, the system found the listing again.

Why this happened, I can't say. Some glitch in the system may have caused the listing to be stored with an invisible character between two of the words. Whatever the cause, it was certainly fortunate for me, as I was the only bidder on the item.

The moral of the story is that if you're really intent on finding an item, spend some extra time using unconventional search techniques. Your diligence may be rewarded.

I am fairly sure that other types of searches miss items on occasion, too. It could be a technical glitch, or you may have run your search just a few seconds before a new matching item was posted. You can pick up just-posted items by reloading the search results list (click your browser's **Refresh** or **Reload** button), or by changing the sort order to display new items first. You might also try running the same search a few hours or days later.

Search Tips

Along with the suggestions presented in the previous sections, here are a few more tips for your eBay searches:

Double-check the results using your browser's search feature
No matter how bright and alert you are, there's always the possibility that you will miss something. Sometimes, it's easy to skim right past the exact item you're seeking in a long search results list. But you will never miss a word or phrase if you use your browser's Find or Search command to search the page for it. (Be sure to search for possible misspellings and synonyms.)

Change the search results list sort order or parameters
Changing the sort order of a search results list can also help you notice items that didn't jump out at you before. You can do the same thing by altering the search parameters—narrow the search with a new keyword, perhaps.

Search completed items
Periodically, do a search of completed items. If the item didn't sell, you may be able to convince the seller to sell it to you or repost it. I've done this several times, and the seller in each case obliged by posting the item with a Buy It Now price that suited us both. The only risk was that someone else might spot the item and get it first (which did happen to me once). See Chapter 14 for a more detailed discussion on this subject. A completed item search can also identify sellers and other bidders who have or are interested in the sorts of things you seek.

Search the sellers
When a seller has something you want, don't ignore the possibility that she may have more items of the same kind. You can view a list of what a specific seller is currently offering via the View Seller's Other Items link on any item page. Or you can use the Search: Items by Seller page. (See

the preceding chapter for more information about these Search pages.) The latter is probably the better choice, since the results will include the seller's items from completed auctions (some of which may not have sold).

Check out other bidders

You can often get help with your searches from other bidders—without their knowledge of such assistance. If you find an item that you want that has already attracted bids, make a note of the bidders. Then use eBay's Search: Items by Bidder page to see what else they're bidding on. The odds are good that one or more of them have already done the legwork to find similar items and have bid on them. Be sure to include completed items in the search. You may find a buyer who won a multiple-item lot and is willing to part with something in it.

Favorite Searches and Categories

As well as saving searches from the search results list, as explained in Chapter 3, you can also manually add searches to the My eBay Favorites page, as shown in Figure 4-1. (To get to My eBay, click **My eBay** on eBay's main menu.)

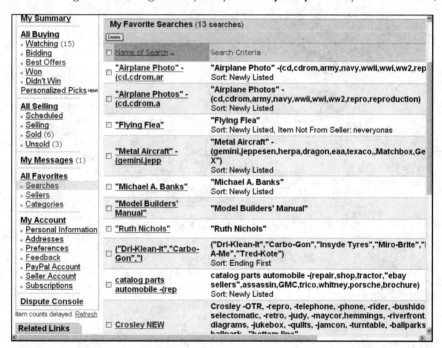

Figure 4-1: My Favorite Searches page

You can also set up a favorite search to send you an email alert whenever a new matching item meeting is posted. This speeds up the search process considerably, and all you need to do is to remember to check your email. I suggest being judicious in creating such search notifications, however. If you have too many active at a time, you could end up with hundreds of email messages.

If you prefer to browse or search specific categories, you can eliminate some drudgery by adding those categories to your Favorite Categories list from your My eBay Favorites page. To add a category or categories to your Favorite Categories list, go to My eBay, and click the Categories link in the Favorites section on the left side of the page. This will display your My Favorite Categories page. Click the Add a Favorite Category link near the top of that page to go to the Add or Modify Your Favorite Category page, as shown in Figure 4-2. Click the category and subcategory names to specify the desired category, and then click **Save** to save your selection. Use this method to add as many categories as you wish.

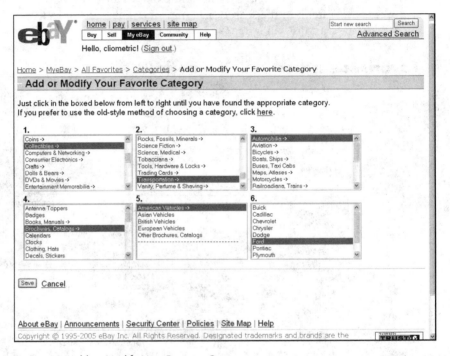

Figure 4-2: Add or Modify Your Favorite Categories page

You can also add a category to your favorites list with an Add to My Favorite Categories link that appears at the top of each category page when you are browsing that category (see Figure 4-4 for an example of a category page).

Browsing

Browsing simply means looking at items by category. You can browse a category by clicking a category name wherever you see one on eBay's home page, or by clicking on the Buy link on eBay's main menu. Figure 4-3 shows a Browse page.

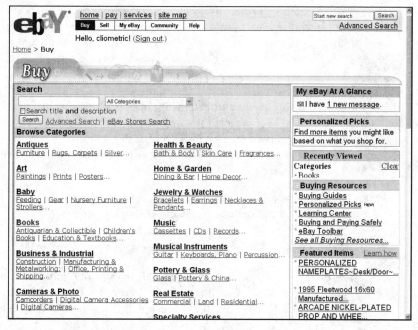

Figure 4-3: Browse page

Using the Browse Results List

Click a category or subcategory name on the Browse page, and you'll see either more subcategories or a browse results list, like the one shown in Figure 4-4.

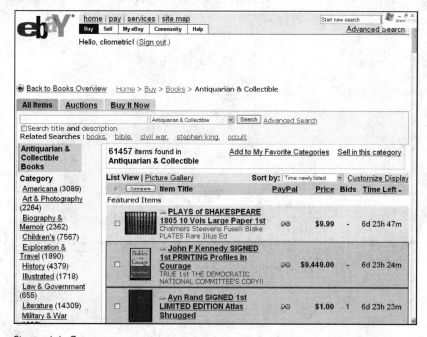

Figure 4-4: Category page

A category browse list looks like the search results lists shown in Chapter 3, but it will be much longer, because it lists *every* item in the current category. Displaying the entire category may take dozens and dozens of screen pages.

From the category page, you can do sorts, additional searches, or anything else you can do with a search results list. You can also begin a search from a browse list.

Browsing can be entertaining, but it can also be useful. Sometimes, you can find items that won't turn up in a search, especially if you use the Search Options box or Item Specifics box (both available when you are browsing) to filter a browse results list. Just scanning a list will sometimes give you an idea for a new search.

NOTE *If you click a category name from a search results list or within an item listing, the category list will still be limited to whatever search is active.*

Browsing and Searching eBay Stores

You cannot browse the stock of all stores simultaneously. If you click one of the category names in the Stores Directory list on the left side of the eBay Stores home page, shown in Figure 4-5, you will see a list of stores that stock items in the category in question.

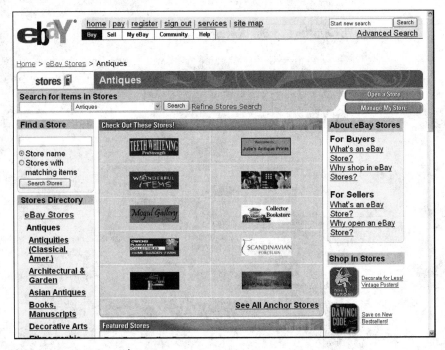

Figure 4-5: eBay Stores home page

You can browse the stock of a store by category by going to a store's main page and clicking a link in the Store Categories list. Figure 4-6 shows an example of a store's main page.

Figure 4-6: Main page of an eBay store

Using the tips and techniques you've learned in this and the previous chapter, you should be able to find anything that any seller posts on eBay. Once you find it, you'll want to know what it's worth. The next chapter describes some ways to determine an article's value.

5

WHAT IS IT WORTH?

Determining an article's value can be tricky for buyers
and sellers alike. Without venturing into economic
theory, let's agree that a thing is worth what someone
is willing to pay for it. The amount a given buyer is
willing to pay is determined by his finances, the
condition of the article up for grabs, its scarcity, and other variables,
many of them transient. Logic isn't necessarily involved. Still, there are
ways to arrive at a reasonable asking or final selling price, whether you
are the buyer or the seller.

In this chapter, we'll consider the relationship between value, price, and
demand, and look at some methods for calculating prices. I'll also introduce
you to some resources you can use to research prices and demand for both
individual items and categories of merchandise.

Why Prices Don't Always Reflect Value

Minimum bids, reserves, and Buy It Now prices do not necessarily indicate
the worth of an object. Minimums and reserves are often reflections of seller

expectations and hopes. They can also reflect seller ignorance. An uninformed seller may ask far too much for an item. Or a seller may set a ridiculously low minimum or Buy It Now price, thinking the item isn't worth much. And on occasion, a seller will put a low minimum or Buy It Now price on an item because she needs money fast.

While it would seem that an item's final sale price would be a reliable indicator of value, this isn't always true either. Competition, stubbornness, need, or desire can motivate a bidder to drive the price of an item far past its real value to an amount that no one else will ever bid again. I've done this myself—once because I felt a strong competitive urge, and several times because I absolutely had to have the item in question for research or a gift. (Obviously, "need" and "desire" cover a lot of territory!)

On occasion, a particularly stunning description can persuade bidders to go beyond what they would otherwise pay for an item. I've spent more than the usual amount of time crafting a description I hoped would persuade bidders that the item was so totally alluring and desirable that they simply had to buy it—which they did, and at my price. (Unfortunately, I can't do this every time.)

Sometimes, sellers figure they can price an item based on the prices of similar items sold recently, but that's not an entirely reliable gauge either. Circumstances and priorities change, as does the pool of available bidders. An item can sell for far less than its counterpart brought just weeks earlier, because the item is, for all practical purposes, worth less than it was in the past.

For example, I've bought quite a few items on eBay for research. Often, I buy a book only to check a reference or scan a photograph. I usually resell such items. Most of the time, I break even, but I've frequently bought items and resold them at a loss, even though they were hotly contested when I bought them. Obviously, to me and to the bidders I battled, these items were worth what I paid for them. Later, though, they were worth far less. Perhaps the previous bidders found what they wanted somewhere else or spent their money on a different item. Many conditions can reduce an item's value on the eBay market. If I lose money like this, I just chalk it up as a cost of doing business there.

Then there are the anomalies: buyers who are willing and able to pay $1,000 for a $100 item. These buyers wreck the value scale. I've bid against such people a number of times, raising the bidding to a level that I was certain no one else would be willing to meet, like $200 for a $20 item, only to get trounced by a $220 bid. Then I watch the poor seller scramble to put up something similar with a $100 minimum bid—only to find that the people who were willing to spend that kind of money are gone, or they are not interested in the specific item he is offering. I've also bought an item or two that I later sold to the losing bidder at his high bid after I had finished with it.

All of this adds up to this lesson: selling prices are not the final arbiter of value. eBay is a land of extremes, with the potential for fantastically high or incredibly low sale prices lurking behind every auction. At the same time, you can't ignore final sale prices in trying to make a determination of value.

Researching an Item's Value

You can use various criteria and resources to judge an item's value. Along with the described condition and grade (if a grading system exists for that item), you can compare prices and consult experts.

Condition and Grading

Condition can be a very subjective quality, or it can be very precise. Some elements of condition are obvious. An article offered as "new" is either new or it isn't. A lamp either works or it doesn't. A guitar may have a warped neck, or it may be easy to tune and deliver a sweet sound. Still, so many of the qualities that define an object's condition are a matter of opinion.

The seller can be relied on to provide only a very basic summary of the item's condition. The article works or it doesn't work. It has all its parts or it is missing parts. The automobile is a certain color. The color is faded or bright. There is rust or there is no rust. There are no tears, folds, or smudges, or the magazine is ripped nearly in half. The tires are new or they are worn. These are fairly obvious elements of condition.

More subtle elements of condition may take a practiced eye to recognize, escaping the attention of uninformed sellers. Consider comic books as a case in point. To a seller who is not familiar with comic books (or, more to the point, unfamiliar with the rules on quality and the temperament of comic book collectors), a comic book with a shallow, near-invisible crease 1/32 inch long at the bottom of the cover in no way detracts from the comic book's appearance or value. This seller would call the condition excellent. If you are a comic collector, however, you might feel that this tiny mar downgrades the comic's condition to good. You might also think the seller is trying to defraud buyers. Not at all! The seller doesn't know as much as you do about the comic book grading system, nor does she understand your subjective requirements.

NOTE   *The appendix includes a list of acronyms used on eBay to describe item condition.*

Subjective requirements and observations are very important, even when a precise grading system is involved. Despite the existence of an accepted grading system, recognized authorities on comic book condition still argue about this or that book's condition. This being the case, you should not expect a seller who has little knowledge to grade a comic book according to *your* standards. All the seller knows is its publication date, its title, and whether there are any gross defects such as missing pages. *You* are the buyer, so it's up to you to be a savvy consumer and determine the item's worth, and to ask the right questions.

NOTE *Well-established grading systems exist for books, postage stamps, coins, comic books, and a variety of other collectibles. These are usually explained in collector price guides (one instance in which price guides are definitely worthwhile), as well as at websites and in magazines devoted to specific collectibles.*

Even if a seller understands condition and grading, descriptions can still be inaccurate. Some sellers just don't pay attention to what they're selling, and describe things as being in better or worse condition than they really are. Some sellers don't like to type, so they write the briefest descriptions possible.

The point is that you should pay close attention to descriptions and photos, and ask questions. Here are a few tips:

- To examine a photo, you can copy it, paste it into a graphics viewing program, and enlarge it.

- Ask specific questions, even if the seller is a seasoned dealer who uses an appropriate grading system.

- If it's important, travel to view the auction item. Or, if you know someone who lives in the same area as the seller, ask her to take a look at it for you.

To avoid being disappointed, you need to do everything you can to determine an object's condition.

Price Histories, Guides, and Other References

You probably feel like anyone else when you buy something and then find out you overpaid—you hate it. You can avoid this situation by doing some comparison shopping. When you find a likely item, look for more of the same, even if you think you've found the only one in the solar system.

Some resources for researching recent selling prices include online auctions, experts, the Web, retailers, price guides, and appraisal services.

Online Auctions

Search eBay and other auction sites such as Yahoo! and Amazon.com auctions. Current bids can indicate the relative demand for a piece, and final sale prices can help you determine its approximate value.

But don't rely on the information you glean from online auctions alone. As I explained at the beginning of this chapter, auction prices are affected by more than actual value. If you can find several auctions for the item or type of item you're considering, ignore any bids or selling prices that are very high or very low. Generally speaking, a group of prices that are within 25 percent of one another can be employed to calculate valid median or average prices. Thus, if you are faced with seven sale prices of $240, $118, $38, $90, $100, $84, and $120, you can eliminate the $38 and $240 as aberrations. The rest—a range between $84 and $120—are good indicators of what the item is worth and, more important, likely to sell for at auction.

Expert Opinions

If you know or can find someone who deals in what you're considering buying, it may be worth a phone call or visit to get an opinion on the item's value. You can also find dealers, collectors, or other experts online—beginning with eBay. Winning bidders of past auctions are likely to know something about the kind of article you're evaluating. (Losing bidders probably won't want to share any information with you, since they could end up bidding against you or buying from you.)

Contact a winner or two, and ask what they think the item is worth, and any other questions you might have about it. You may not get any answers at all, but it's worth a try; people are often flattered to be asked for their expert opinion.

The Web

You may also consider collecting price information on the Web. Search engines can lead you to a variety of retail, wholesale, and collector sites. Yes, there *are* still people who aren't selling on eBay, preferring instead to just put up a "For Sale" sign at a website, and let people find their merchandise however they may.

Prices asked at websites may be higher than prices realized on eBay. This is because eBay sellers are usually motivated to sell quickly, while those just offering something on a web page are probably content to wait for a buyer who is willing to pay a premium price. But if you're lucky, you may find the same item for sale at a website for less than the eBay auction's minimum bid. I've done this several times, and even resold some items for a tidy profit.

While website asking prices may be misleading, final sale prices aren't. Some web merchants—especially those dealing in specialized products, antiques, or collectibles—keep an item posted even after it sells. This helps the sellers because it confirms that prices asked are realistic in comparison with prices obtained.

Retailers

List prices you'll find in brick-and-mortar stores may or may not give you an indication of how much an item normally goes for, depending on the particular item.

When you're researching a collectible, you'll often find that people selling in retail establishments may know what they want to get for an item (as much as possible), but they have no idea of what it is worth. Their typical pricing strategy is to match or exceed the highest price they've seen elsewhere for the item. (They do, after all, have a higher overhead than the typical eBay seller.) Or they may set prices based on the size or age of an item, or whether they've seen one before. This sort of practice is why you see articles languishing in antique malls and shops for years.

When it comes to new merchandise, retail prices have a definite effect on what you can get for items on eBay. Since most people are located near enough to a department store (or whatever kind of store carries what they're after), you need to give them some incentive to buy online instead. After all, if they buy the item at a local store, they don't need to wait for the auction to end, nor do they have to worry about whether their item will be lost in the mail or if an unscrupulous seller will victimize them.

The usual buyer incentive (sometimes called a *value-added element*) is lower cost. If the latest Niklod ZowiePix digital camera sells in discount stores for $395, and I have a chance of getting it online for $280, I'm going to bid on that auction (or buy it, in the case of an eBay store or Buy It Now sale). Provided, that is, I'm not in a hurry to get that camera.

NOTE   *Be sure to cross-check retailers' in-store prices with their online prices, because sometimes they differ ("Web specials" are popular). Also, check online-only retailers' prices against brick-and-mortar store prices. Ignore the ultra low-end operations, however, because these tend to be rip-offs or fly-by-night operations, and their prices don't have much relation to reality.*

Price Guides

Whenever I think of price guides, I'm reminded of an eBay listing I once saw for a monstrous console radio made in the 1930s by a well-known manufacturer. Judging from his recent auctions, the seller had never sold anything like this, and it was obvious that he thought he had a gold mine on his hands. After describing the radio in some detail, he roared into a sales pitch based on what he had read in a price guide. "THIS BOOKS FOR $3000 IN THE PRICE GUIDES!!!" he shrieked, "SO YOU KNOW IT IS A STEAL AT $2800!!!" The seller continued in the same vein for several more lines, making obvious his firm belief that everyone was obligated to accept price guides as the last word in value. The radio failed to sell through two listings, and then disappeared from eBay forever.

This seller should have learned that, for the most part, neither sellers nor buyers adhere to price guide listings. Price guides offer *approximations*. Some are based on current prices charged by dealers or recent auction sale prices, but many are not. Worse, there are multiple guides for some kinds of antiques and collectibles, so the buyer or seller must find a halfway point between warring standards. Quite a bit of educated guessing is involved, too. And some price-guide authors cater to the sales side of the market by bolstering prices.

It is also true that price guides cannot reflect market fluctuations. Factoring in publishing lead times, the information in a guide can be two years old or older.

Stamp and coin price guides are among the few such books worth consulting. These are used daily and accepted as standard references by just about every serious collector and dealer in the business. You will find the same to be true of the National Automobile Dealers' Association (NADA) and Kelley Blue Book price guides for automobiles. Issued quarterly, NADA guides are based on the actual sale prices of thousands of motor vehicles over the three months preceding each issue's date.

To sum up, price guides aren't the absolutes that sellers and their publishers would like you to think. So don't get fooled into believing you must pay the price guide value. If data in a price guide convince you that a high minimum bid or reserve on an auction is reasonable, it doesn't mean anyone will pay that price. Before accepting a guide's valuation, take the time for a reality check with real-world prices.

Authentication, Grading, and Appraisal Services

If you have any questions about the authenticity or value of collectibles, fine art, jewelry, autographs, or antiques, you can hire a service to give you an opinion or full evaluation. eBay recommends several companies that provide these services. See eBay's Authentication and Grading Overview page, which you can get to by clicking the Services link at the top of most eBay pages.

Classified Ads

Classified ads in magazines, newspapers, and "trading post" type papers may help you determine appropriate prices for a lot of items. Be a little wary, however, of online classified ads, which can be as much as four or five years old. (Some people just never get around to updating their sites.)

eBay's Comparison Guide

eBay's comparison tool allows you to compare up to 25 items side by side. After you do a search, simply check the boxes of the items that you want to compare in the search results list, and then click the **Compare** button. The items will be displayed together on a new page, similar to the one shown in Figure 5-1.

From this display, you can do the following:

- View an item.
- Bid on it (or buy it now).
- If you've chosen more than four auctions to compare, expand the view to include all items selected.
- Export the data on the page to Microsoft Excel, by right-clicking with the cursor on a blank part of the page and choosing this option from the pop-up menu.

Add one of the items or all of the items to your watch list (on your My eBay page), by clicking the "Watch this item" link above the Seller Information box.

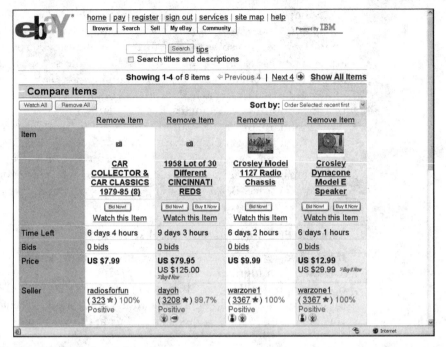

Figure 5-1: eBay's Compare Items page

NOTE   *If you don't plan on using eBay's comparison tool, you may wish to remove the comparison check boxes from your search results lists. To do so, click Customize Display at the upper-right side of the search results list page and choose to not display those check boxes.*

Finding Out What's Hot and What's Not

All sorts of general variables (that is, other than the subjective, like desire and fierceness of competition) affect demand and prices realized. These include the season, the availability of an item, cultural trends, and fads. And it often happens for no reason at all that a lot of people decide they want to buy a certain thing *right now.*

It's not always possible to predict increased demand. Nor will you, as an individual, necessarily notice an increase in demand for a certain product right away, if ever.

So, how *do* you find out about consumer and cultural trends and fads—especially those that result in unexpectedly high demands for short periods—and their effects on prices? You can guess, or you can scan thousands of listings looking for patterns, or you can use eBay's What's Hot feature.

You access What's Hot through a selection on eBay's Seller Central page. Click the Seller Central link on eBay's home page or any seller page, and then click the What's Hot link. You will see the page shown in Figure 5-2.

Figure 5-2: What's Hot page, with links to lists of "hot" auctions

The links on this page lead to listings of groups of categories (such as Computers, Consumer Electronics, Cameras, Photos, Cell Phones). Clicking any of those category links will display a PDF file with details about the kinds of products in the categories listed. (These and similar lists are updated frequently.) As you can see, high-demand items are singled out in the lists. You can view lists of the hottest categories by clicking the Hot Items by Category link.

Clicking this link loads a lengthy PDF file that includes all categories. A sample portion of this list, displaying hot items from the Toys & Hobbies category, is shown in Figure 5-3.

NOTE *To view PDF files, you must have the latest version of Adobe Reader, which is available as a free download at www.adobe.com.*

You may find it faster to download the PDF file rather than read it online. This also lets you save the file for future reference. To save the list, right-click the link and select **Save As** from the pop-up menu. Figure 5-4 shows a portion of the Antiques category listing from the What's Hot list, as viewed offline with Adobe Reader.

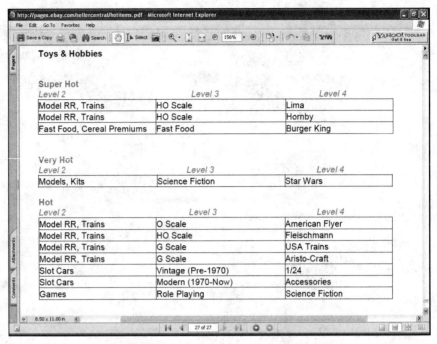

Figure 5-3: What's Hot listing for the Toys & Hobbies category

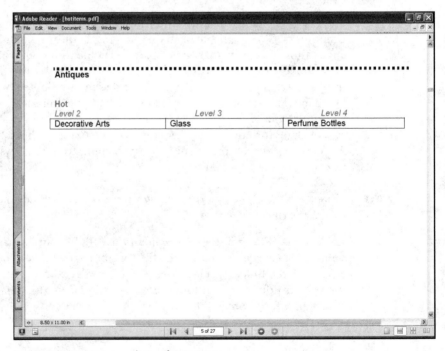

Figure 5-4: Hot Category listing for Antiques

The information about what's hot in categories can help sellers decide whether they should increase or decrease minimum bids or sale prices. Buyers on a budget can use this information to find out what sorts of items to avoid, at least for a brief time, since the increased demand will drive up prices.

The Merchandising Calendar, another link on the What's Hot page, displays lists of merchandise calendars that will be featured on eBay's home page in coming months. Being featured means eBay will display banners promoting the listed categories. Sellers can take advantage of this by paying to have links to their items featured on the home page or simply posting items in the featured categories.

Tracking What People Are Searching for and Buying

In addition to the What's Hot lists and the Merchandising Calendar, eBay offers several tools that you can use to view the most popular keywords being used in eBay searches. To access these lists, click the Buy link at the top of any eBay page, and scroll to the bottom of the Buy page, where you'll see the Other Ways to Browse box, as shown in Figure 5-5. You can view both popular eBay keywords and common searches by clicking their respective links.

You will find two additional selections in the Other Ways to Browse box especially useful: eBay Pulse and Popular Products.

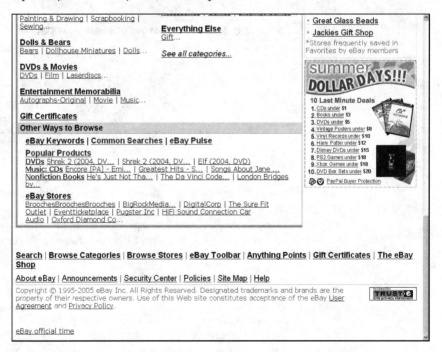

Figure 5-5: Other Ways to Browse box on the Buy page

eBay Pulse

eBay Pulse shows you eBay's most popular searches, stores, and products, along with the most watched items and highest prices. The data are updated daily. You can get to eBay Pulse through the link in the Other Ways to Browse box near the bottom of the Buy page (see Figure 5-5), or use the URL http://pulse.ebay.com. Figure 5-6 shows an example of an eBay Pulse page.

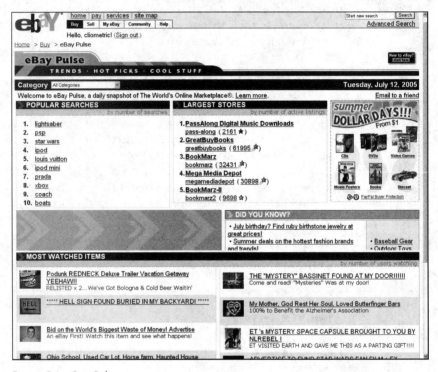

Figure 5-6: eBay Pulse page

This tool helps you identify trends and chart the popularity of specific items, as well as classes of merchandise. You can quickly collect organized price information with the search and store links.

The search listing lets you track potential demand not only for items currently available on eBay, but also for items that aren't being offered by other sellers.

Popular Products

Popular Products is a "bestseller list" of the most popular products on eBay. Click the link in the Other Ways to Browse box on the Buy page (see Figure 5-5) to see products listed by title and category. Categories included video games, DVDs, CDs, and books, as shown in Figure 5-7.

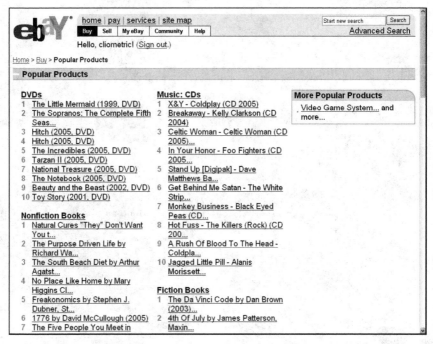

Figure 5-7: eBay Popular Products (partial listing)

Clicking any product name in the Popular Products list initiates a search for that product. With this tool, you can identify popular products, pinpoint those that are in short supply, *and* collect valuable price information.

Using Third-Party Price Research Data

Research services such as Andale, Terapeak, HammerDrop, and Sellathon can provide current and historic prices for online auctions. You can get price reports for specific items or categories of merchandise, and view the data in a variety of ways.

Andale's Price Finder, for example, searches eBay auctions for the item and returns a list of closed and current auctions. It also provides a detailed analysis of sales, which includes the average selling price and even a graph showing how well the item sold. The analysis is more suited to sellers interested in how well a specific product performs than for general pricing, but the data collected by this service are probably more complete than what you can track down manually. Figure 5-8 shows an example of pricing data gathered by Price Finder.

As you can see in the example, the data provided include the full range of prices as well as the average price for items. Such a report can cover specific items or items of a type, depending on the keywords used.

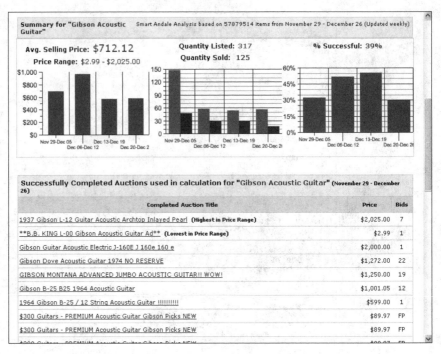

Summary for "Gibson Acoustic Guitar"   Smart Andale Analysis based on 57879514 items from November 29 - December 26 (Updated weekly)

Avg. Selling Price: $712.12   Quantity Listed: 317   % Successful: 39%
Price Range: $2.99 - $2,025.00   Quantity Sold: 125

Successfully Completed Auctions used in calculation for "Gibson Acoustic Guitar" (November 29 - December 26)

Completed Auction Title	Price	Bids
1937 Gibson L-12 Guitar Acoustic Archtop Inlayed Pearl (Highest in Price Range)	$2,025.00	7
B.B. KING L-00 Gibson Acoustic Guitar Ad (Lowest in Price Range)	$2.99	1
Gibson Guitar Acoustic Electric J-160E J 160e 160 e	$2,000.00	1
Gibson Dove Acoustic Guitar 1974 NO RESERVE	$1,272.00	22
GIBSON MONTANA ADVANCED JUMBO ACOUSTIC GUITAR!! WOW!	$1,250.00	19
Gibson B-25 B25 1964 Acoustic Guitar	$1,001.05	12
1964 Gibson B-25 / 12 String Acoustic Guitar !!!!!!!!!!	$599.00	1
$300 Guitars - PREMIUM Acoustic Guitar Gibson Picks NEW	$89.97	FP
$300 Guitars - PREMIUM Acoustic Guitar Gibson Picks NEW	$89.97	FP
$300 Guitars - PREMIUM Acoustic Guitar Gibson Picks NEW	$89.97	FP

Figure 5-8: Andale's Price Finder price history report

Data analysis of this kind will give you accurate information about *possible* sale prices. You cannot count on such information to predict *exactly* what an item will bring (nor, from the bidder's viewpoint, how much you'll end up paying for it). But you will at least gain a solid idea of how much the item is worth.

Given the resources discussed in this chapter, you can determine the value of just about anything you see up for auction. Add your specific situation and needs to the mix, and you have a good indicator of how much you might bid if you're a buyer or the price you may ask for an item if you're a seller.

PART II

EBAY FOR SELLERS

6

SELLER DO'S AND DON'TS

The ideal eBay seller describes his merchandise accurately and unequivocally, ships quickly, doesn't pad selling prices with "handling" charges, and leaves Feedback for buyers as soon as they pay, rather than waiting to see what sort of Feedback he receives. The ideal eBay buyer pays promptly and is happy with her merchandise because she made sure she knew what she was bidding on.

This chapter takes a look at how you can fit the profile of the ideal seller, and how to handle those less-than-ideal buyers you may encounter. The next five chapters provide more detailed how-to information on the ins and outs of selling.

eBay Seller Rules

As you might expect, eBay's rules for sellers are less restrictive than those for buyers. This is because eBay is seller-driven; that is, sellers pay the bills.

eBay seems to enforce the rules lightly at times, but this doesn't mean that sellers can do as they please. Break the wrong rule at the right time, or break a rule too many times, and you'll find your account suspended.

The Prime Directive

While it's not exactly set forth in this manner, one rule for eBay sellers outweighs all others: *You must pay your eBay seller fees.* Not surprisingly, failure to pay eBay will get your account suspended faster than *any* other rule infraction.

NOTE *If your account is suspended for not paying your seller fees, the fastest way to get your account reinstated is to use an alternate means of payment. Use a different credit card, PayPal, or your checking account instead of the credit card, or vice versa. This way, there's no chance that your payment will be rejected. Be prepared to wait as long as two or three days after you make your payment for reinstatement.*

Prohibited Items

The next most important rule from eBay's viewpoint has to do with items you are not permitted to sell. Prohibited or banned items include firearms, live ammunition, and dangerous toys like Jarts (a two-player outdoor game that involves tossing large, metal, potentially lethal darts at a target), fireworks, Freon, illegal drugs, drug paraphernalia, body parts, and hundreds of other items. To see a full list of prohibited items, go to http://pages.ebay.com/help/sell/questions/prohib.

If you post a prohibited item, eBay will catch the listing within hours, if not minutes, of its posting. When a prohibited item listing is discovered, eBay ends the listing and removes it from the Completed Listings database as well. The listing fee is refunded to the seller.

NOTE *If eBay's staff doesn't catch a banned item right away, it will probably be reported by a member. Finding and reporting listing violations is a hobby for many eBay users.*

On occasion, a potential buyer may spot a prohibited item before it's canceled and place a bid. But unless you're hovering over the listing, watching it from minute to minute, it's unlikely you'll even see the bid or find out who the bidder was.

If you repeatedly post prohibited items, eBay may suspend your account. There is no evidence that eBay keeps a tally of how many times a member posts a prohibited item, but that doesn't mean eBay monitors aren't tracking you.

NOTE *Unfortunately, quite a few prohibited items are in great demand, and some sellers may be tempted to post items that are prohibited but not illegal (such as Jarts sets). There are a couple of avenues available for those sellers. One is to try another auction site. Another is to post it as a Buy It Now item or as a regular auction, and check it frequently to see if you have any bidders (whom you can contact by email to close the deal, even if your item is canceled). Just be aware that you are putting your seller account at risk.*

Ironically, legitimate items are sometimes canceled as prohibited. This probably happens because people monitoring the site cancel items based on the presence of certain keywords and phrases alone, rather than investigating what the item really is. If this happens to one of your listings, all you can do is relist the item.

Excessive Shipping and Handling Charges

It is against eBay policy for sellers to extort money from buyers with inflated shipping and handling charges. eBay is particularly sensitive to this because the practice costs the company money in lost final value fees.

eBay doesn't set a ceiling for handling charges, but it's easy to detect when a seller is shaking her customers down for extra cash. If you try to pull this on bidders, someone (probably several someones) will complain, and eBay will act.

In addition, you will lose bids and never know it because hardheads like me will refuse to do business with you. Be honest and build your costs and your desired profit into an item's minimum bid or asking price.

NOTE *More and more buyers are expressing unhappiness with the idea of handling charges. Some regard it as an illegitimate way to raise the price on an item. To avoid problems, include what you feel is a fair percentage of your costs in your auction minimum or sale prices. Say it costs you $5 to make a round trip to the post office once a week to do your mailing, and you pay 1½ cents each for shipping envelopes. If you ship 40 items a week, adding 15 cents to each auction will more than cover those expenses—the real cost for handling—without alienating buyers. Add 50 cents to each item for the tiny amount of time you spend handling it, and you're way ahead of the game.*

Good Business and Common Sense

The remainder of eBay's rules and policies for sellers involve being honest and doing what you say you will do. Basically, eBay requires the following:

- You don't misrepresent what you're selling.
- You ship the items you've sold (no substitutes) in a timely manner.
- You provide accurate contact information.
- You don't engage in shill bidding (see Chapter 16).
- You do not indulge in Feedback extortion.

It's all fairly basic, but there are those who miss the point or are intent on ripping off buyers in one way or another. Because of this, eBay has posted an exhaustive discussion of rules for sellers. To see the rules, go to eBay's main Help page, type **rules for sellers** in the Search box, and click the **Search Help** button. You will see the screen shown in Figure 6-1.

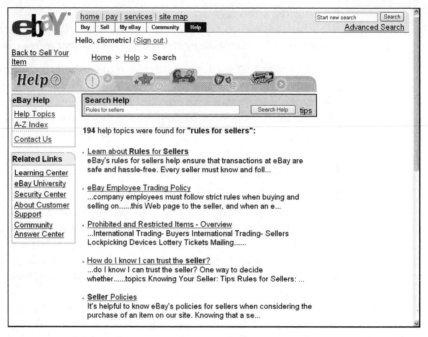

Figure 6-1: Rules for Sellers page

Communicating and Closing the Deal

Assuming that you aren't planning to deceive buyers and want to get all your deals done as quickly as possible and without problems, you'll want to follow certain steps after an auction ends.

More often than not, the buyer will be waiting to hear from you. Send the buyer a note, thanking him and advising him of the total amount due and the payment methods you accept. eBay recommends that sellers contact winning bidders within three days of the end of an auction. (Again, this is a *recommendation*, not a rule.) The majority of eBay sellers contact buyers within 24 hours. If you are like most sellers, you will probably send email invoices advising buyers of their totals and payment options. (Several services can do this for you.)

NOTE *It is against eBay rules to require buyers to pay cash.*

Most of the time, winning bidders will reply to let you know of their intent regarding payment. They might let you know they're using eBay's Pay Now feature to pay immediately with PayPal, or that they will be paying with a check, using a money order, or by other means.

If you don't hear from a buyer the same day an auction ends, don't get nervous. He may be traveling or indisposed for one reason or another. If you don't hear back within two days, send a polite note advising him that you need a shipping address, so you can pack his item and send it as soon as payment arrives. (This beats the heck out of "I ain't heard nuttin' from you yet—you gonna pay or not?")

Sometimes, the buyer initiates contact, which is fine. This kind of buyer is usually anxious to pay for and receive what he has won, so you should make it a point to reply to him as quickly as possible.

Once you've heard from the buyer—directly or through an automated system—it's polite to acknowledge the contact and let the buyer know you'll be shipping his item as soon as you receive payment. This also reassures the buyer and may spare you from subsequent follow-up inquiries.

If you have a stated shipping policy, such as "I ship only on Thursdays," remind the buyer of that in your email. And make sure it's a *reminder* of something you already stated in your auction listing. Don't spring a funky shipping schedule on a buyer *after* he wins an auction.

Most buyers don't expect notification when a seller ships their items, and most sellers don't send notes to buyers advising them that they've shipped an item. Thus, it's usually a nice surprise if you go the extra mile to provide such added service. Good communication creates good will, which can result in repeat customers *and* make handling any problems easier.

What If the Buyer Doesn't Contact Me?

If four or five days go by and you don't hear from your winning bidder, you might consider contacting her by phone, snail mail, or an alternate email address. You can usually find such information through the Find Contact Information page, shown in Figure 6-2. (To get to this page, go to the Advanced or Basic Search page and click on the Find Contact Information link in the Members box on the left side of the page, near the bottom.)

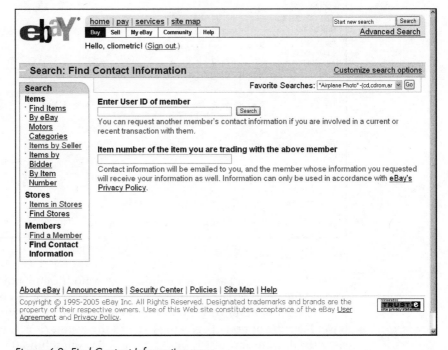

Figure 6-2: Find Contact Information page

Filing a Payment Reminder

If you cannot reach the member by phone, or don't want to spend the money for a long-distance call, you have two options: wait and hope to hear from the buyer or file a Payment Reminder.

As with most kinds of conflicts, bringing in a third party usually gets the other person's attention and prompts him to resolve the issue. Filing a Payment Reminder brings in that third party, in the form of eBay. Whether the buyer has flatly refused to pay (due to buyer's remorse or whatever) or just hasn't contacted you, filing a Payment Reminder will most likely bring about a resolution.

How long you wait to do this is up to you, and will probably depend on the amount of money involved, how many bids the item received, and how much apparent interest there was in the item (gauged by the number of views and watchers). But by eBay rules, you must wait until ten days after an auction ends to file a Payment Reminder. This is to ensure that the buyer has plenty of time to contact you.

You can file a Payment Reminder from the Dispute Console (shown in Figure 6-3), which is accessible via a link on your My eBay page.

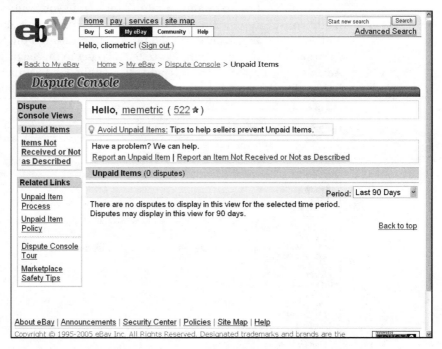

Figure 6-3: Dispute Console

When you file a Payment Reminder, eBay notifies the buyer by email. And for the next 14 days—or until the buyer contacts you—a pop-up window is displayed whenever the buyer signs on to eBay. At this point, you and the buyer have the option of agreeing to abort the transaction. If you do this and close the dispute at your Dispute Console, eBay will refund the final value fee charged for the auction. If the buyer doesn't respond to the email or pop-up window within seven days, you have the option of closing the dispute and receiving a final value fee credit. See the "What If a Buyer Doesn't Pay?" section later in this chapter for more on Non-Paying Bidder Disputes.

Packing and Shipping

Whatever you sell, pack it carefully. Use bubble wrap, tissue, newspapers, boxes in boxes, and/or padded envelopes as necessary. Overpack—it's better to pay for a couple of extra ounces of postage than to deal with an item damaged in transit. Buyers appreciate good packaging almost as much as fast shipping, even if your packaging makes the item difficult to open.

The main consideration in shipping is time. It is helpful for sellers to remember that the "clock" starts running in the buyer's mind the day he sends payment. Take this into consideration when replying to an anxious seller's query as to the status of the item.

Most buyers get uncomfortable if they need to wait for an item more than a week. So, if you don't plan on shipping until several days after an item is paid for, make a point of letting the buyer know when you do ship the item, so he can "reset" his mental clock. You may want to do this even if you ship the item the day you receive payment; the wait will seem far shorter to the buyer.

For the same reason, if you ship an item by Parcel Post, Media Mail, or another slow delivery service, advise the buyer that the item will take some extra time to reach him. Better yet, head off potential buyer anxiety by using the fastest available shipping method that the buyer is willing to pay for. For example, books can be shipped First Class less expensively than Priority Mail, and they will arrive much faster than items shipped as Media Mail.

International shipments should go by airmail. This is true even of shipments between the United States and Canada. The nature of the Canadian postal system is such that items sent by regular surface mail from a point in the United States only 200 miles away can take a couple of months to arrive. If you ship to Japan or Europe and use surface mail instead of airmail, you can encounter extreme delays. (One package I sent to Belgium from the United States took five months to get there!)

NOTE *I am told that customs officials in some countries or ports simply allow international surface mail to back up until the pile is too big to ignore. In countries where political unrest is common, internal delays can result in even airmail taking months to be delivered.*

Also, be sure to fill out any required customs forms when you send packages out of the country. Your local post office will have these forms on hand, or you can complete a customs form online at http://webapps.usps.com/customsforms.

Dealing with Problems

After the auction, things might not go all that smoothly. The buyer might not pay, or she may say that your package didn't arrive.

What If a Buyer Doesn't Pay?

If a buyer doesn't reply to your contact attempts or simply doesn't pay, don't waste a lot of time dunning her and making threats. You can send invoices and wave the phrase "binding contract" all you like. "I'm reporting you to eBay!" is unlikely to get money out of a recalcitrant buyer. And the additional threats of filing a Non-Paying Bidder Dispute (three of which *may* result in the buyer being suspended) and posting Negative Feedback won't carry a lot of weight if a winning bidder doesn't have the money to pay, is suffering from buyer's remorse, or is angry at you because you've threatened her.

Why are threats unlikely to work? For openers, Feedback is less important to buyers than it is to sellers. (The only time most sellers check buyer Feedback is after an auction closes.) And having your buyer account suspended is not the disaster it may seem. A suspended member can easily open a new account with alternate contact information. A buyer who has accumulated a large number of Negative Feedback ratings won't mind a fresh start with a clean record if she is forced to ditch her account for a new one.

All that aside, you rarely know what is happening on the other end. The buyer may have problems that make your demands laughable. It may be that the buyer died. That has happened to me. I heard nothing from one buyer for nearly two weeks. After three messages requesting the buyer to pay, I gave up. A few days later, his widow sent a brief note advising me of his passing.

The point is that a nonpaying bidder isn't worth a lot of effort. Make a Second-Chance Offer to the backup bidder (see Chapter 14) or repost the item (see Chapter 11). If the final value fee is significant (more than, say, 30 cents), leave Negative Feedback and file a Non-Paying Bidder Dispute (also known as a Non-Paying Bidder Alert), as shown in Figure 6-4, so you can recover the fee later.

NOTE   *An Unpaid Item Strike does not affect a buyer's Feedback profile, but eBay keeps track of Unpaid Item Strikes, and if a buyer accumulates too many in too short a time period, she may be suspended from buying or selling on eBay. (eBay doesn't publicly define the number or time frame.)*

After that, move on to something constructive. Don't waste your time sending email messages, making phone calls, and complaining on bulletin boards. All that will get you is elevated blood pressure.

What If a Buyer Says the Item Didn't Arrive?

Mail can be lost or stolen, but it's relatively rare in my experience. (Since the 1970s, three items I've mailed didn't reach their destinations, three sent to me didn't arrive, and one item was stolen from my mailbox.)

If someone complains that an item didn't arrive, you may be skeptical, but the first thing you should do is check your records. Make certain that you did, in fact, ship the item.

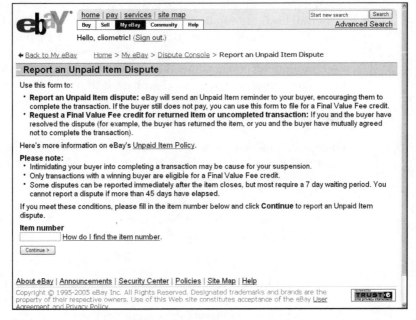

Figure 6-4: Non-Paying Bidder Dispute page

NOTE *You* are *keeping records of your eBay shipments, aren't you? You'll need them for tax purposes, as well as to track what you've sold and shipped.*

If there hasn't been enough time for the item to arrive, wait a couple of days before you reply. In the majority of cases where someone has griped about an item not arriving, it showed up a day or two after the complaint.

If you use delivery tracking (an extra cost for U.S. Postal Service shipments but free with services such as United Parcel Service and Federal Express), you will have little problem verifying an item's location. You may want to offer this (and insurance) as an option to buyers in your listings, accompanied by a *caveat* that you will not be responsible for nondelivery. Or you may want to make it your policy that *all* items sent by U.S. mail must have delivery tracking, paid for by the buyer.

If an item still hasn't been delivered in a reasonable time frame, it's not necessarily lost forever. Ask the buyer whether someone else at his house (or apartment building) might have picked up the item inadvertently. On two occasions, I learned that the buyer's brother or spouse had picked up the mail and forgot to tell the recipient that he had a package. Also, be aware that weird things happen all the time—in post offices, in mail-handling centers, and in delivery vehicles—that can delay mail. Small packages or envelopes can slip in between the pages of a magazine (I've received someone else's mail this way a couple of times), or fall beneath a cartload of mail, only to be found and put back on the path to the addressee days later. So, give the postal mail system at least a month to make the delivery, keeping in mind that the wait is going to be more difficult for your buyer than for you.

If the item can't be found, it is up to you to decide if you want to accept responsibility for nondelivery and refund the buyer's money. Ideally, you will have included a note in your listings stating that you are not responsible if an item doesn't show up, unless the buyer pays for delivery confirmation or insurance. In the end, it comes down to two things: whether you can afford the refund, and how important Feedback is to you.

What If a Buyer Is Trying to Con You?

Of course, some people will try to defraud sellers by claiming an item didn't arrive and demanding a refund. If you think someone is trying to con you, you have several options:

- You can ignore the complaint, if you don't mind taking a hit with Negative Feedback or an Item Not Received dispute (see Chapter 12).

- You can cave in and send a refund.

- You might offer a replacement or substitute item.

If none of those options appeals to you, try this trick, posted on a Seller Central bulletin board: Ask the buyer if he would like for you to phone his postmaster for help in tracking down the item on that end. According to the seller who posted the tip, this flushes the frauds every time. If the buyer is lying, the item mysteriously arrives the next day.

Sometimes, a buyer will try to con a seller into giving him a full or partial refund by saying that his item arrived damaged. The simplest way to handle this is to ask the buyer to return the item. If the buyer wants to keep it despite the damage, he is probably lying about the damage.

To avoid both of these problems, include a statement in your item descriptions that you are not responsible for items not delivered or damaged on delivery, unless the buyer purchases insurance. You might also require delivery confirmation on all postal shipments.

Yet another con involves the buyer complaining that an item is not as you described it and wanting his money back. If this happens to you, tell the buyer you will refund the item's selling price as soon as he returns the item to you. (Don't offer to refund shipping either way; you shouldn't have to pay for the buyer's having the privilege of viewing the item.) If the buyer is lying to you, he will usually decide to keep the item. On occasion, a crooked buyer may ask for a partial refund but still keep the item. Don't fall for this; offer a full refund (minus shipping fees) only if the item is returned to you intact.

Watch out for buyers who try to "bargain" after an auction ends, by saying something like "I don't think the item is worth the $20 I bid, but I'll give you $12." (This does happen.) Tell the buyer that he is committed at his high bid, and that you will file a Non-Paying Bidder Dispute if he does not pay you the full amount due.

NOTE   *State your refund policy in your auction descriptions. Whether it's "no refunds" or "refund minus shipping costs," set a time limit, such as two weeks after receipt of the item, after which you will not allow a refund.*

If you suspect a buyer of trying to con you out of money or merchandise, you can report your concern using the eBay contact form shown in Figure 6-5. You can find a link to this form on just about any Help page.

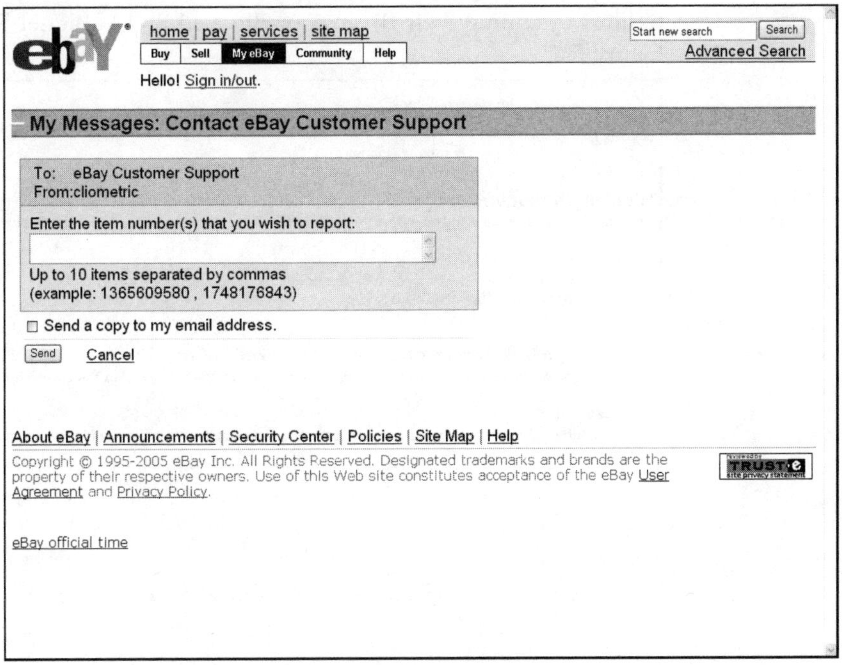

Figure 6-5: Contact eBay page

What If Shipment Is Delayed or You Can't Ship?

Circumstances may come up that prevent you from shipping an item immediately—or at all. Perhaps you misplaced the item. (Some of you who run an eBay business from your home know how easy that is, especially when you've filled up the garage and all your closets with merchandise!) Or you might have put it on the floor and stepped on it. (I did this with a rare, 55-year-old plastic model kit—*ouch!*) It could have been stolen or accidentally sold to someone else.

Whatever the reason, let the buyer know right away if there is going to be a delay, and explain why. You'll find that it's better to tell the truth than to make up a complicated excuse like having to go in for brain surgery on short notice.

If you must refund your customer's money because you lost or damaged the item, get the money out *immediately*. Then write to the buyer and tell her that the refund is on the way.

Most buyers will understand, as long as you don't compound the problem with additional delays. The few times this has happened to me, the buyers were so relieved that I handled the problem in a straightforward fashion that they had no problem with leaving me Positive Feedback.

How to Block a Bidder

A bidder who is guilty of any of the crimes just described is not someone you want bidding on your auctions again. Fortunately, you can block undesirable bidders by adding their IDs to your Blocked Buyer/Bidder list, as shown in Figure 6-6.

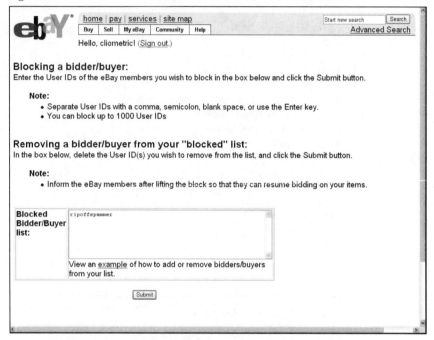

Figure 6-6: Block or Pre-Approve Bidders page

To reach this page, click the Selling Resources link near the bottom-left side of your My eBay page. This displays the Selling-Related Links page. Click the Block or Pre-Approve Bidders link in the first column of this page, which will take you to the Buyer/Bidder Management page, where you will find the appropriate link. (eBay may make this link easier to find—perhaps by adding a link to the Buyer/Bidder Management page on the My eBay page.) As you can probably figure out from the name of the link, you can also use this page to pre-approve select bidders for your auctions.

Feedback for Sellers

Feedback is important for sellers, because eBay buyers are the first to extend trust by parting with their money. If the seller doesn't deliver, the buyer loses his money. Thus, buyers are more likely to check sellers' Feedback than sellers are to check buyers' Feedback. In addition, maintaining a high level of Positive Feedback can qualify you for certain added-value programs, such as eBay's PowerSeller program and PayPal's Buyer Guarantee, described later in this chapter.

Posting Buyer Feedback

As a seller, you should leave Feedback for your buyers as soon as you receive payment from them. If payment is prompt and in full, leave Positive Feedback. If the buyer doesn't pay for five weeks or tries to get you to accept only partial payment, leave Negative or Neutral Feedback, as you feel is deserved. But make it a policy to leave honest Feedback as soon as you receive payment. After all, once you've been paid, the buyer has done everything she is required to do by eBay rules and by law.

Handling Feedback Extortion

Some eBay sellers practice something called *Feedback extortion*. They withhold Feedback from buyers until the buyers have posted Feedback for them. This is done under the guise of giving the seller a chance to "make things right." In reality, the seller is using the threat of Negative Feedback to extort Positive Feedback from the buyer. I hope you won't be trying to pull this low-life trick yourself.

Feedback extortion is commonly associated with sellers, but buyers have been known to try it, too. A buyer may tell you that he is not going to leave Feedback until after you do—and that he will leave the same kind of Feedback as you leave for him. Some buyers also use this threat to avoid a Neutral or Negative Feedback rating in the wake of a troublesome deal (one in which they pay late, demand a partial refund, or cause other problems). Others do it as a matter of course.

Whether you give in to Feedback extortion is up to you. You can leave Positive Feedback and hope the buyer does what he promised. Or you can leave Neutral or Negative Feedback if it is deserved, and prepare to take the hit—Negative Feedback and probably a nasty comment. If you do get Negative Feedback on this basis, be sure to post an explanatory reply to the Feedback that the buyer left for you.

If you want to leave Negative Feedback without fear of retaliation, wait to leave Feedback for the problem buyer until just before midnight on the ninetieth day after the auction in question ended. No one can leave Feedback for a transaction that is more than 90 days old, and the odds are good that the buyer will have forgotten about the dispute by then—leaving you free to post the kind of Feedback the buyer deserves without fear of retaliation. (At least one online auction service, AuctionHawk.com, will do this for you.)

Added-Value Programs for Sellers

As a seller, it behooves you to conduct yourself properly. Along with boosting your sales, good conduct opens the door to some added-value programs. Sellers should do everything possible to earn Positive Feedback—from describing items accurately, to maintaining good communications, to shipping promptly.

eBay's PowerSeller Program

The PowerSeller program is an elite club for sellers who maintain at least $1,000 per month in sales and a high Feedback rating (98 percent or better Positive Feedback is required). Membership is by invitation only, and PowerSellers are identified by a special PowerSeller icon in their listings.

PowerSellers get prioritized customer support by mail or phone, access to an exclusive discussion board, and access to special promotions and online tools. Most sellers consider PowerSeller status to be an advantage.

PayPal's Buyer Guarantee

PayPal allows sellers with a high level of Positive Feedback to offer a money-back guarantee with qualifying listings. The guarantee provides potential bidders with some extra assurance that a seller will be good to do business with, and thus encourages bids. See Chapter 15 for more information about PayPal.

Now that you know something about dealing with your eBay customers, let's take a look at your first step to becoming an eBay seller: figuring out what to offer for sale.

7

FIGURING OUT WHAT TO SELL

So, you're going to become an eBay seller, make tons of money, buy a new car, quit your job, and live happily ever after? Well, *maybe* that could happen.

While anyone with Internet access can be an eBay seller, how well you do depends on a number of variables, the most important of which are product, pricing, and presentation. Of those, product is the most significant. A fantastic price, wonderful description (assuming it's honest), and stunning photos won't make people buy a useless and unappealing item. But, given a good product for which there is a market, the other factors can influence your sales.

This chapter is all about helping you decide what you are going to sell. We'll examine how your personal and professional interests, what you own, and your business contacts can influence the kind of merchandise you offer. Of course, you also need to consider whether what you intend to offer (or can get at a good price) is likely to sell. Finally, I'll offer some guidelines for figuring out whether you are making the best use of one of your most important assets: time.

Will People Really Buy *Anything?*

Other than the prohibited items described in the previous chapter, you can sell basically anything someone is willing to buy. Your wares can be old or new, homemade or factory-fresh, created by professionals or amateurs, working or not. As long as it's not illegal and not on the banned list, you can sell it, or at least offer it, on eBay.

You can sometimes sell things that you might not even think of selling elsewhere, such as an empty Coca-Cola can—something that actually *was* sold on eBay. And I'm not talking about a Coca-Cola can that once touched the lips of Elvis Presley. Nor was this a collector can. It was an ordinary Coke can that someone smashed up and posted on eBay. It sold for more than $20.

Why would anyone buy an empty, smashed-up Coca-Cola can from an eBay seller? The most likely answer is that the buyer bought it to have a story to tell. eBay members love to swap stories about outrageous bargains and silly buys. You can imagine the Coke can buyer talking with his friends:

"I got this new Sony PlayStation for a hunnert dollars!" Ben said. "What'd you get?"

"That's nothing," Alphonse replied. "I bought a 2004 Ford Explorer for eight grand!"

Smiling with pride, Ruben held up his latest eBay treasure. "I got you both beat: I bought a smashed-up Coke can for twenty bucks!"

Some similarly unlikely items I've seen offered on eBay include hair strands from famous people; a bag of dirt from Texas; a fantasy life (a couple of pages detailing some imaginary situations for those who have no imagination); 1950s douche bags; and even pieces of race cars, airplanes, and buildings.

Not all of those items sold; just posting something doesn't mean it will sell. But you're free to *offer* anything for sale, as long as it doesn't violate eBay's rules or federal or state laws. And there *is* a market for weird stuff—provided it's the right kind of weird stuff. That's why eBay created a category called "Weird Stuff," although weird stuff can appear in other categories, too.

NOTE *The fad of selling advertising space on a body part—forehead, arm, and so on— originated on eBay early in 2005. Since then, ads have been offered just about anywhere you can imagine. Most don't sell.*

If you approach eBay as a business, you aren't likely to be wasting time with such silly items (unless you perceive or can create a market for them). But the range of products, services, and additional items you can sell is still broad—as broad as eBay's category list.

What Will You Sell?

To decide what you will sell, first, think about the category or categories of merchandise you would like to sell. Then take inventory of what you have to sell. Finally, take inventory of what you know in terms of product knowledge and sources.

What Do You Want to Sell?

Given some idea of what you *can* sell, what do you *want* to sell? Even if you're not selling yet, you probably have some idea of what you'll offer. Maybe it's something you have on hand in good supply or something you create, like an arts or crafts item. Perhaps you want to sell a certain type of antique or collectible because you have knowledge of that merchandise. Or you might want to offer some sort of information or service. How many of what kind, and for how much? It's up to you.

Most items that you might want to sell require some sort of investment, which is to say that as an eBay seller, you will probably find yourself in the business of buying things for resale. This is what most eBay sellers do, and their strategy is to buy as low as possible, and then sell high (but not so high an asking price as to discourage sales).

Whatever you decide to offer, don't limit yourself to one kind of item, or even to one category. If you do, you may be locking yourself out of a lot of potential profit. Keep an open mind. At the same time, don't go around buying items—individually or in lots—just because they're cheap. As you learned in Chapter 5, what someone pays for an item often has no relation to its value on eBay.

What Do You Have?

It may be that you want to sell a little bit of everything. Perhaps you've gone to a few too many flea markets and yard sales and accumulated some boxes filled with junk and some mystery items that look salable.

Many sellers have started out just wanting to get rid of unwanted junk cluttering up their homes, but then they got hooked on eBay. What sorts of things do you have that you don't need, but might bring a few dollars on eBay? Perhaps you've cleaned out your basement or a storage space and have furniture, decorative items, books, or who-knows-what to get rid of. Possibly you're ending a domestic partnership and want to convert co-owned possessions to cash. Or maybe you're a collector (of comic books, baseball cards, autographs, or First Day Covers) and you've accumulated duplicates as you upgraded your collection over the years. eBay lets you dispose of these items and finance new acquisitions.

If you look around, you'll probably be surprised at the amount of "junk" in your garage, basement, or attic—much of which could be more valuable than you think. Dispensing of unwanted items that hold no value for you can actually be a good way to get practice as a seller.

What Do You Know?

If you have specialized knowledge of fine art, antique toys, old magazines, or any of dozens of other collectible categories, you can turn what you know into profit. Such knowledge will enable you to spot salable items that others might miss at flea markets, yard sales, and elsewhere, and help draw bidders with informative, credible descriptions. Consider selling items that fall within the realm of your expertise.

Expand your knowledge by researching items in your category on eBay. Find low-cost sources for such items (auctions, flea markets, and dealers), and you're in business!

You might also put your knowledge to work creating salable articles. Many eBay sellers manufacture their own products—jewelry, artwork, pottery, computer components, automobile accessories, and other items.

Similarly, you might be able to sell knowledge you've earned from your job, education, or hobby, in the form of a small book or video. If you are a singer or musician, you could try selling audio CDs of your work.

NOTE *The problem with selling homebrew information or entertainment products is that many people consider it okay to steal your work. Or, even worse, to make and sell copies of it. Copyright provides some protection, but it is difficult for a small-time publisher to enforce. The best way to discourage theft by copying is to make copying difficult. If you're dealing with text and graphics (as in a how-to manual), publish it as a book, rather than on CD. The second-best way to discourage copy theft is to provide a value-added element to those who buy your product from you—perhaps a color poster, a booklet of lyrics, or something else not easily duplicated.*

What Can You Get?

Okay, so you don't have a lot of junk lying around, you're not an expert on anything, and you have no talent. Can you still get into selling on eBay? The answer is yes, if you keep your eyes open, have a little money to invest, and make "Buy Low, Sell High" your driving principle.

My friend Charlie is a good example of someone who was able to make good money on eBay with little specialized knowledge. A few years ago, he went to a university surplus auction, looking to pick up some office furniture and maybe a computer. He ended up buying neither, but did come home with a load of 4,000 empty videocassette boxes, for which he paid $10 (he was the only bidder). With that price, he was sure he could turn over the boxes for a profit. (This was before CDs and DVDs.)

The only thing Charlie knew for sure was that there was a demand for the empty boxes; he had bought more than a few himself. And here was an opportunity to get a large quantity of them for next to nothing (a quarter of a cent each, to be precise). At that price, he could sell the boxes for a fraction of what they sold for in stores and still make a profit. This made it easy to draw in customers.

Over the next several months, Charlie sold these videocassette boxes on eBay (usually in lots of 10 or 20) and made back many times his original $10 investment—more than $1,000, in fact. Still, he was lucky; he might just as easily have found himself with a white elephant.

Of course, you can always educate yourself about what's in demand. A couple I know, Bill and Rita, got into selling household items on eBay to get rid of two families' worth of pots and pans, knickknacks, and small appliances they had accumulated over 20 years of marriage. They knew there was more money to be made, but how? They spent a number of hours looking at what sorts of items regularly went for high prices. But they didn't look at everything. They focused on merchandise that was small, easy to pack and ship, and which—per their online research—moved quickly. Furthermore, what they sold had to be available in their area and at a price that would allow them to make a profit.

Already dealing in household items, it was natural to start looking at decorative collectibles. To make a long story short, Bill and Rita ended up dealing in pottery—specifically Roseville and Rookwood. They remembered seeing quite a bit of these kinds of pottery at flea markets, auctions, and yard sales where they live in southwestern Ohio, near where Rookwood pottery was made in the late nineteenth and early twentieth centuries. After purchasing several books about these collectibles to further their education, they cautiously bought a few pieces. They found that they could easily get 10 to 20 times what they had paid for a piece of name-brand pottery.

Once they had the basic education, they expanded their line, picking up additional brands of collectible pottery that they found to be in demand and relatively easy to buy in their area.

Demand and Market

Before you decide to sell something (either one item or a category of merchandise), determine whether a market exists for it and how great the demand for it is. Markets exist for all sorts of items—from plain white socks to high-fashion shoes—but substantial demand is usually what drives high prices and fast turnover.

So, whatever the product or commodity you plan to sell, make sure the demand is there and that the market isn't saturated. Online research will usually tell you what you need to know about demand and market, as described in Chapter 5.

Don't let wishful thinking or enthusiasm for a certain kind of item blind you to lack of demand. Similarly, think twice before buying a lot of something just because the price is low. If you have your eye on some merchandise but don't know if it will sell for a good price, research the item before you make the purchase. If you have to, pass up whatever the deal is; another will come along later.

Also, avoid going for merchandise simply because you like it. This is an easy way to end up with a lot of items that you'll never sell or will sell only at a low profit. For example, just because you think old CDs with smiley faces painted on them are the coolest things ever doesn't mean that people will be waiting in line to buy them. Remember that you're not the buyer. Ask yourself, "Do hordes of people really want this stuff, or is it just my personal taste?"

Knowledge and Research

Not to advise you against doing what Bill and Rita or Charlie did (whose stories I told earlier), but it is usually easier to deal in something you already know than something you need to research. Sometimes, however, it makes sense to test uncharted waters. If you decide to get into a new line because you have a good, low-cost source, be sure to research the product thoroughly.

Say you find several new Tag Heuer watches at a flea market offered for what seem to be low prices. You check eBay and find that these watches are actually quite expensive. Do you rush back and buy the watches? Not unless you know something about this kind of watch, such as which specific models are in demand and if the watch is a popular item for counterfeiters. Or, you may notice that old tube-type radios made by the Crosley Corporation often draw several bids. Does this mean you should start looking for Crosley radios? Again, no, because after 1945, Crosley radios were made by a company called Avco, and most are of little value to collectors.

The fact that a certain item or brand is selling on eBay doesn't mean that similar items will sell. You need to gather more information about the item to determine if it will sell.

How Much Is Your Time Worth?

Unless you're researching a book about eBay, or just want to unload a bunch of junk you've accumulated, you're probably in the eBay business to make as much money as you can. It's only logical that you want to minimize the amount of time you spend researching, finding, and buying stuff to sell, as well as the time you spend selling and shipping items.

Your goal is to make a decent profit on each item you sell. Given a choice of two jobs doing the same kind of work, one paying $5 per hour and the other paying $50 per hour, anyone would choose the $50 per hour job. It's a no-brainer. But thousands of eBay sellers are doing the equivalent of choosing the $5 per hour job by electing to sell items on which they make only a dollar or two, justifying the decision by saying they can sell low-priced items in greater quantities, just as discount stores do.

It just doesn't work out that way. As an eBay seller, you don't have the same kind of overhead structure that brick-and-mortar stores have, so they can make more money selling an item for a dollar or two. Plus, time is critical to eBay sellers, who spend far more time on each deal than they imagine, and unlike retail stores, don't have staff to handle the many small and large tasks associated with running a successful business.

Consider this example: You find 50 different issues of *TV Guide* from the 1960s at a flea market and buy them for $1 each. Then you sell each for $2 on eBay, which nets you $50 on your investment.

But how much time did you spend making that $50? Say an hour to locate and obtain the magazines, and another hour to sort through them, for a total of 120 minutes. Adding another 3 minutes to scan the cover and write a description of each of the 50 magazines puts you at 120 minutes + 150 minutes = 270 minutes, or 4½ hours.

That puts you at $11 per hour—not quite lawyer money, but maybe enough for you. But don't forget the minute or so you spend posting each magazine. That's 50 minutes + 270 minutes = 320 minutes, or a bit over 5¼ hours.

Whoops—now you're at $9.52 per hour. Okay, that's still more than you make asking "Would you like fries with that?"

But wait—you still need to process your orders, and pack and ship each item. Processing includes getting shipping addresses and transferring them to labels (or copying them by hand). Even if you spend only 30 seconds per item (including sending an email message to the auction winner), and 30 seconds packing and labeling each of the 50 magazines, that still adds another 50 minutes, which brings your running total to just over 6 hours.

Figure another hour getting this stuff to the post office and adding postage, and maybe a half hour dealing with email from people wanting to know where their magazine is (because they didn't allow for typical delays in postal shipping), and you have invested 7½ hours in this project. Your hourly earnings come to $6.67, *before* you subtract eBay's posting and final value fees.

"Would you like fries with that?"

Of course, this example assumes that you sell each magazine to a different person. The magazines could sell in lots, which would cut your processing and shipping time. You might also spend less time writing the descriptions by using the same one for each magazine, with minor alterations. But you probably still won't make $10 per hour.

This example underscores several important points. The most important one is that you won't get rich with small per-unit profits on eBay. There is a definite limit to how much you can make, and it's tied to the time you have available to devote to your eBay business. If you're netting a dollar per sale, you won't have enough time in a week to make decent money. Using the hourly figure from selling old magazines, even if you worked 15 hours per day, 7 days a week, you would bring in less than $700, before taxes and overhead. And that's assuming you sold everything you posted.

You might pad your income with "handling" charges, but you won't get rich that way either. Adding $3 or $4 to an item that sells for $2 is going to turn off quite a few buyers. (For that matter, many buyers would object to a $3 handling charge on a $200 item.) Chapter 10 goes into detail about the pros and cons of handling charges, but the most important thing to remember about handling charges is this: When you add a handling fee you are, in effect, charging the buyer more than she agreed to pay for the item. Thus, you reduce your sales, which, in turn, reduces your net profit.

So, you probably want to deal with items that give you a higher per-unit profit. If, instead of the 50 old magazines that bring you $1 per sale, you sell 50 items and make $10 on each one, you net $500. This would put your hourly rate at $66.70—everything else (the time required for posting, packing, and so on) being equal.

You have several ways to achieve that $10 profit level. The most obvious way is to buy something for $1 and sell it for $11. But you're not going to get $11 each for back issues of *TV Guide*, which means you need to offer something different. With luck, you can make that kind of profit on old comic books or pulp magazines.

Another way is to move up to bigger ticket items, dealing in items that you can buy for $90 and sell for $100, or more. Ideally, these items would take no longer to post, handle, and ship than the magazines or comic books in the previous examples. You might sell collectibles of another kind, or maybe consumer electronics.

Or, you can work the opposite end of the equation by reducing the time you put into each unit. If all the issues of *TV Guide* were the same date, you *could* save time by cutting and pasting descriptions, but that's penny-ante stuff. A realistic approach would be to sell the 50 magazines in lots of 10 or 20 (as my friend Charlie did with his videocassette boxes), or as one lot of 50. That would kick up your hourly rate considerably, with the added benefit of giving you more time to spend finding and posting additional items (which, hopefully, bring in far more than $1 per sale).

The moral is that an item's worth to a seller is measured by how much net profit it brings in, not by how many are sold. Making $50 on one sale is *always* preferable to making $50 on 50 sales.

Having determined what you will sell, the next step is to find sources for your wares. That is the subject of the next chapter.

8

SOURCES OF ITEMS TO SELL

Once you know what you want to sell, your next step is to locate items at a good price—a "good price" being low enough to allow yourself enough profit to make your time and effort worthwhile. For more information about pricing, see Chapters 5 and 9. Sources for eBay merchandise are almost endless, ranging from flea markets, eBay and other online auctions, wholesalers and, sometimes, retailers. In this chapter, I'll suggest how you might go about finding items to sell on eBay.

Flea Markets, Yard Sales, Rummage Sales, and Auctions

The most common sources for collectibles and used merchandise are flea markets, yard sales, rummage sales, and auctions. New merchandise, and even wholesale lots, can turn up in these venues as well.

Flea Markets

Flea markets can be found in any part of the country. While they are most prevalent during the summer months, you'll find indoor flea markets a permanent fixture in some areas.

The merchandise at flea markets tends to be portable, and it may be old or new—like most of the items on eBay. In my experience, the majority of flea market sellers who do not specialize in new merchandise are people who cruise auctions, yard sales, and other flea markets in search of items to buy for resale. (Not unlike eBay sellers.)

NOTE *The end of the day can be the best time to go to a flea market, as most of the sellers have made their money and don't want to have to lug home more merchandise than necessary. Thus, they are often willing to bargain.*

Yard Sales

Yard sales (also known as garage sales or bundle sales) are held primarily during warm-weather months and can yield some surprising finds. My most memorable yard sale find was a rare, transparent slide rule (used as a teaching aid), which I bought for $1 and sold for $366 on eBay. Another memorable yard sale coup was a friend's purchase of a pocket ashtray for 25 cents, which she sold for more than $25. I've also found a number of rare books, and even autographed record albums, at yard sales. Usually, people are unaware of the bargains they're offering, or sometimes they just don't care. The latter was the case when I bought a rare Swiss music box mechanism for 50 cents. It went for $80, to a collector who also rebuilt music boxes.

On occasion, desperate store owners or failed antique mall sellers will use yard sales to unload merchandise in a hurry, resulting in some very unusual bargains. The possibility of stumbling upon an unexpected treasure is one of the things that makes yard sales interesting.

One drawback to yard sales is the fact that they eat up time. You need to go to 10 or 12 yard sales to see half as much merchandise as you might find at an auction, flea market, or thrift store.

NOTE *Enterprising individuals in some communities have built up a good stock of eBay items by offering to haul away old household items for free. This usually involves cleaning a basement or attic, or an entire house. My sources tell me that they have made good money culling through other people's "junk."*

Rummage Sales

Churches and other organizations often hold rummage sales, where you can find some real bargains. Most of the goods offered at rummage sales are donated by members of the sponsoring organization, so the majority of the merchandise is likely to be personal items, clothing, and housewares. You can often find interesting books and collectibles at such sales.

I attended a rummage sale at a temple once and found some 40-year-old board games in pristine condition, priced at a couple of dollars each. Apparently, an older couple had decided to "clean house" and donated some of the toys their children had owned decades before. On eBay, several of these toys brought 20 times their purchase price.

Auctions

Auctions are year-round events, held frequently during the summer months, and diminishing greatly in number around the winter holiday season. They are held when people retire or move, to liquidate estates, or when companies go out of business, to dispose of surplus merchandise or merchandise that retailers or wholesalers just can't move. You can find just about anything if you go to enough auctions.

With a little luck, you can make some amazing buys at auctions. The "luck" centers on not getting into a bidding war with someone else. If you seek items that the average person doesn't consider valuable (such as some of the paper ephemera that I buy), you can walk away from an auction with stunning bargains.

NOTE   *Many of my best auction bargains have come in boxed lots, like a lot of two boxes of "junk" that I bought for a bid of 50 cents. In addition to books, knickknacks, and paper odds and ends, I've found a 1920s brass candlestick telephone and a letter from a famous nineteenth century writer to an equally famous judge.*

For more commonly known or recognized items, you can enhance your chances of winning without spending too much by attending auctions in remote or inconvenient locations, or finding auctions that are going to be lightly attended for other reasons (auctions held on a weekday or in bad weather qualify).

I know of several people who run quite profitable eBay resale businesses by buying big-ticket items, like antique furniture, at auctions in their areas. The most successful of such operations are partnerships. Two members of one team I know attend separate auctions to maximize their buying potential. Both are equally well versed in the kinds of items they handle, and every weekend during the summer, they buy more than they can sell in a week. As a result, they have rented warehouse space and sell from the accumulated stock, while still buying new items at auctions.

A husband-and-wife team I know split their efforts between large auctions and eBay research. He uses a cell phone to call her from auctions when he sees an intriguing item; then she researches it online to determine whether it's worth bidding on and how much to bid to ensure maximum profit.

Thrift Stores

Thrift stores offer used and new merchandise in many categories. Largely dependent on donations from the public, the stock of a typical thrift store consists mainly of clothing, personal items, and housewares. However, at times, a thrift store will feature new merchandise, which is usually bulk lots of slow-moving stock donated by manufacturers, wholesalers, or retailers for tax write-offs.

The big bargains tend to be in small things like books and collectibles (especially china and pottery) or vintage electronic items. On several occasions, I've bought books for 50 cents in thrift stores and later sold them for $30 to $50 on eBay. I know people who regularly find valuable china selling for a few dollars in thrift stores.

Some eBay sellers shop thrift stores (as well as yard sales) for clean, little-worn clothing—especially designer label merchandise—for resale and do quite well with this. Others cruise thrift shops in search of jewelry and watches at bargain prices.

Antique Malls and Shops

Despite the mindless proclivity of antique mall sellers to overprice things, you can find profitable bargains at some of these malls. The trick is to shop for the right kinds of items. In general, you should avoid shopping at antique malls for anything likely to show up in a price guide. Most antique mall dealers are amateurs, and they get their prices from price guides (and wishful thinking). Second, look for small—but not too small—items. Unknowledgeable people tend to attach value to large objects and to small, shiny articles like medals, jewelry, and coins. (In addition to pricing by size, these dealers often price by age.)

Most important of all, shop for things about which you have knowledge. I've lost count of the times I have spotted valuable books and paper ephemera (two areas in which I have extensive knowledge) priced at a dollar or two in antique malls. I've also found toys of the kind that don't show up in price guides selling for absurdly low prices. These sorts of discoveries have helped enlarge my collections, and they can add to your bank account as well.

Right after New Year's and midsummer are times when antique malls experience sales slumps. During these periods, you'll find that many dealers reduce prices by anywhere from 10 to 70 percent.

You can apply the antique mall strategy to antique shops, even though the proprietors are usually better informed about values. No one can know everything, so there is always the chance that a store's stock will include items that you know are valuable, but about which the owner is clueless. Also, since most antique dealers expect customers to bargain, you can often bring a price down to a level that will guarantee you a nice profit. (Bottom-line pricing in most antique shops is often determined by how much the proprietor paid for the item in question.)

eBay and Other Online Auctions

I have made tidy profits on items purchased from online auctions on several occasions. I've bought Tootsietoy and Midgetoy die-cast cars and trucks from

Yahoo! Auctions, where they aren't very popular, and sold them on eBay, where they are popular and bring high prices.

I've also bought items on eBay and resold them on eBay, either because no one else happened to find them or because they were poorly described. An example of the latter was a hard-to-find collectible called a poker slide rule. Made in the early 1960s, it was a wooden slide rule without a cursor and marked with poker cards and hands. The device was used to calculate the odds of being dealt a certain hand in draw poker games. I had just sold one for $48 in an auction with three bidders when, on a whim, I decided to see if there were any more of these around. Searching for "poker slide rule" didn't yield anything, but when I searched using the words "poker," "ruler," and "wood," I found another poker slide rule, posted with the title "Card Game Ruler." (These are the only two examples I've ever seen.) I bought it for $10, including shipping, and had it posted (using the other seller's photo) and resold for $42 before it arrived in my mailbox. This sort of thing doesn't happen every day, but obviously, it is possible to score some great resale merchandise in online auctions.

I know of several sellers who buy pre-1960 toys on eBay to refurbish and resell. These sellers will typically buy broken toys, but sometimes they will go for toys that are in good shape but worn. As they accumulate multiples of the same toy, they take the best parts from each and combine them into a near-perfect item. Then they take the next-best parts and create a toy in good condition. These are, for the most part, high-end toys, which can be sold at a large enough profit to justify the investment in the broken toys and parts.

Wholesalers and Manufacturers

If you want to deal in new merchandise, you may think it prudent to buy from wholesalers or directly from manufacturers, in order to get the lowest prices and thus beat out the competition while maximizing your profit. This is a fine idea, but not as simple as it may sound. Buying wholesale often requires that you purchase more of an item than you can easily dispose of. Many manufacturers will not sell to individuals or even to small businesses. Here, I'll discuss these and other reasons that buying direct can be more difficult and less appealing than it seems.

"I Can Get It for You Wholesale!"

Among the uninformed, there is a certain cachet to terms such as *bulk lot* and *wholesale*. The implication is that there exists some sort of magical entity that will provide merchandise for next to nothing, if only one knows where to look and how to ask. This is far from the truth. A conventional wholesaler sells to businesses in quantity after buying in even larger quantities from manufacturers, or, in some instances, from other wholesalers, who buy in still greater quantities and at even lower prices.

To look at it another way, wholesale is like a good news/bad news joke: The good news is it *is* possible to buy a portable CD player for $3; the bad news is that you have to buy 100,000 of them to get that price.

Wholesalers serve those who want to buy in smaller quantities than a manufacturer is willing to sell, as well as those to whom a manufacturer will not sell.

Most wholesalers will not sell to just anyone. The majority sells only to licensed businesses with tax IDs (so the wholesaler does not need to bother with paying sales taxes, among other reasons). Some wholesalers will not sell to small businesses (like the many one- or two-person operations that sell on eBay) at all, because a small business cannot afford to buy enough to make it worth the wholesaler's time. The wholesaler may want to deal only with businesses that can guarantee consistent repeat business—something possible with a brick-and-mortar store, but not always with an eBay merchant.

Yet, you can find some wholesalers from whom you can buy merchandise at (relatively) low prices, provided you have a tax ID number, are willing to buy in quantity, and you can pay up front. There is nothing mystical or magical to it. And, as a rule, the greater the quantity you buy, the lower the per-unit price.

NOTE *If a "wholesaler" asks you to pay a membership or another up-front fee before you can buy from him, take your business elsewhere. True wholesalers are in business to make money from quantity sales of items they've bought at a low price. (One reason that Sam's Club was ordered to remove "Wholesale" from "Sam's Wholesale Club" was the fact that the operation charged a membership fee.)*

Where Are Wholesalers?

Wholesalers are pretty much everywhere. I know of two toy and hobby wholesalers, a book distributor, an auto parts wholesaler, and a candy and confections wholesaler within 30 minutes of where I live, and there are similar outfits near where you live. But you don't need to live near wholesalers to do business with them; you just have to find them.

To track down wholesalers, look through the appropriate industry directories at your local library. Check your local yellow pages. Ask retailers where they get their merchandise. Write or visit the websites of industry organizations, and read trade journals (some of which are online). You'll find thousands of companies that sell at wholesale.

When exploring opportunities to buy wholesale, take your time and shop around. You have no way of knowing whether wholesalers bought the goods they offer directly from the manufacturers at super prices, or if they dealt with the third or fourth wholesaler down the line from the manufacturer. The companies nearest the manufacturer tend to have the lowest prices, but the only way to find out which company has the lowest prices for the quantities you seek is to do comparison shopping.

NOTE *If you can't afford to buy enough items to please a wholesaler, or can't quite get it together to buy enough items to reach the discount level you would like, consider teaming up with another eBay seller. You can realize a lower per-unit cost without needing to overload yourself with merchandise.*

eBay Wholesalers and Secret Wholesale Sources

Now and then, you will find eBay sellers offering bulk lots of items at "wholesale" prices. These sellers are doing nothing more than buying merchandise in quantity from a legitimate wholesaler and marking it up. The quantity price they offer is less than retail, but it's not the lowest wholesale price you can find. They rely on your belief in the mystique of the Internet as the source of secret bargains to help you sell yourself on their claims.

NOTE   *If a "wholesaler" doesn't require you to have a state tax ID number, you're not dealing with a wholesaler.*

Don't buy lots offered at "wholesale" on eBay if you plan to resell them. You can get better prices by doing some research and buying from the same wholesalers these sellers are using.

THE WELDING SHOP BOUTIQUE

The prospect of buying wholesale appeals to so many people that con artists are racking up thousands of dollars daily from would-be eBay entrepreneurs. One example of this was a scammer who set up a "wholesale" website offering to sell "brand-new" jeans, blazers, and other articles of clothing at prices that would allow anyone to make "up to 500%" profit reselling these items. Buyers were promised brand-name merchandise, "100% guaranteed."

Several eBay sellers thought this was a grand idea and placed orders, with payment in advance. Unfortunately, they missed some warning signs that should have told them the site wasn't quite what it professed to be. There was no minimum order, and the "wholesaler" did not require buyers to have tax IDs. In many respects, the site was hastily done, with errors in spelling and grammar, and statements that made no sense. The site also bragged that the "new" merchandise was free from tears, rips, or stains.

In the end, it turned out that what the site was selling was used clothing. Each buyer received at least one brand-name item, albeit used, but not every item was from a brand name. As for the guarantee, the wholesaler promised a "full refund" to anyone who returned his or her orders—less shipping and a 15 percent "restocking charge."

The scam was quite simple. The seller was buying used clothing for pennies, calling it "new," and offering it at alleged wholesale prices that were almost pure profit. As for the refunds, the seller was counting on the fact that many buyers wouldn't even bother asking for refunds. If he gave refunds to those who asked, he was still coming out ahead with the restocking charge. (It is likely that no refunds were given, and the site simply folded after doing a few thousand dollars in business—after which the scammer set up a new "wholesale" operation.)

While I won't name the website here (it is probably gone by now), I will note that the physical address for the business turned out to be the site of a welding shop.

In various eBay categories, you will find for-sale lists of "secret wholesale sources" of items at prices that are so low that they can't be mentioned. Some such offers claim to have wholesale sources for things like new laptops for a dollar, or whatever the current glamour product may be for less than a tenth of what it costs at your local Wal-Mart. (You can find the same offers in tiny ads in the backs of "income opportunity" magazines.) Some lists are sold as "e-books," as a part of a "business opportunity kit," or something similar. Many of them claim to be selling information about sources that "eBay doesn't want you to know about."

Are these for real? No, they're not.

First, there are no *secret* wholesale sources. The concept of secret wholesale sources is a fiction, created to prey on your gullibility. The illogic of this scam should be evident to anyone who can count to ten: *No business with merchandise to sell is going to keep itself a secret from potential customers.*

Second, eBay doesn't care if you know about wholesale sources. In fact, eBay *wants* you to know about sources of wholesale goods! The more people who can buy merchandise in bulk lots at wholesale prices to sell on eBay, the more eBay makes. If eBay didn't want you to know about something that's posted for sale, eBay would cancel the posting.

At the same time, not every wholesaler (or business of any kind) is going to advertise where *you* will happen to see their ads. The people who offer lists of so-called secret wholesale sources have merely spent some time searching the Web and browsing in "income opportunity" magazines, as well as industry directories, to collect the addresses of companies that sell in quantity to business or even individuals. You can save money by doing this yourself.

Some of the lists of secret wholesale sources are outright scams. What you get is a text file or a few sheets of paper with instructions on how to resell those same instructions to people looking for "secret" wholesale sources. In other words, you end up trying to resell the scam.

If you have any doubts as to the legitimacy of the information an "opportunity" seller is offering, take a look at her Feedback. Write to five or six of her customers (preferably those who left Negative or Neutral Feedback) and ask what the seller sold them, or at least whether it was a scam. You should get at least one reply from a buyer who is disgusted with his purchase. (And when you're checking the seller's Feedback remember that buyers don't always leave Positive Feedback because they're satisfied; sometimes, they leave it to avoid getting Negative Feedback or because the seller made a deal with them to leave Positive Feedback for a refund.)

Buying from Manufacturers

In only a few instances is it possible for a small retailer (such as an eBay seller) to buy directly from a manufacturer. This is because many manufacturers restrict their sales to brick-and-mortar stores. Some operate exclusively through a system of franchises and sell only to their franchisees. This is how automobile, airplane, recreational vehicle, and boat manufacturers operate.

A good number of manufacturers work only through distributors and wholesalers, who, in turn, sell to retailers. The book publishing industry operates in this way, although it sells to retailers and to consumers, too, albeit at higher prices. For appliance makers, clothing manufacturers, consumer electronics companies, and most hard goods manufacturers, selling in large quantities to wholesalers is preferable to dealing small quantities directly to retailers. This is because it generates a cash flow matching the manufacturers' scale of operations. The wholesalers operate on a different scale and can find profit in selling smaller lots to retailers and to lower-volume wholesalers.

Manufacturers that sell directly to resellers (like you) are often startup operations that have yet to get connected with the system of distributors, wholesalers, and retailers that serve the markets for the kinds of products they make. Or they are small enough that they can still profit from selling in quantities that would not interest larger operations.

You will find manufacturers who sell direct advertising in trade journals or magazines for entrepreneurs. Those same magazines may publish lists of such companies. And a few books for entrepreneurs list companies that sell directly to resellers. Beyond these guides, you can learn whether a given company will sell to you as a business in the quantities you want to buy by contacting the company's sales or marketing department.

Drop-Shipping

Like the term *wholesale, drop-shipping* has a semi-magical aura to it. In concept, drop-shipping is simple: you sell an item, send the money to a manufacturer or wholesaler, and the manufacturer/wholesaler sends the item to your customer.

It sounds like the perfect business—all you need to do is take orders and send in the money. You don't need to worry about details, and no heavy lifting is involved!

But selling drop-ship items is not as ideal as it may seem. In most cases, you won't get the best prices. You need to consider shipping charges, and the drop-shipper will tack on a "handling" charge. You may need to pay a "membership" fee. If you check around, you will probably find that you could get a much better price by buying in quantity from a wholesaler.

The fact that order fulfillment is out of your hands can create problems. You have no way to assure the quality of the items you sell. If the supplier runs out of items, messes up your order, or goes out of business, you are stuck with the obligation to the customer. After all, you took his money, and it's not as if you can just reach up on the shelf and grab another item to send him.

Then there are the scammers. The idea of working with a drop-shipping arrangement is so attractive that it's relatively easy to get people to sign up for it. Some scammers create fancy catalogs and send them out to people who agree to be their "resellers" or "representatives." The resellers, in turn, spend money on advertising (or post items on eBay), and begin sending in orders to the scammer. By the time the resellers begin getting customer complaints, the scammer has abandoned his post office box or mail drop and is setting up a new scam.

As with the wholesale business, you will find some unscrupulous people trolling for easy money by selling "plans" and lists of companies that drop-ship items. Ignore these; you can use the same sources recommended for finding wholesalers to find companies that do drop-shipping. You won't find many manufacturers who drop-ship, however; the overwhelming majority of manufacturers are in business to make big money on large orders. Few legitimate operations are willing to fool around with one-item orders, whether they are from a reseller or the end user.

Finally, if you're asked to pay a membership or other up-front fee by an alleged drop-shipper, forget about doing business with him.

Retailers

So you stop by your local Kmart or Sam's Club, where you notice that blank DVDs are on sale in packages of 20 for a dollar. You immediately buy $50 worth, figuring that you can make a killing on eBay by selling these at 20 for $5. You rush home, write up descriptions, post the packages of DVDs, and wait for the bids to come in.

But the bids don't come in. Nor does anyone bid the second time you post the DVDs. What's going on?

If you bothered to check listings for DVDs, you might have found quite a few sellers offering 20 DVDs for $5—or even $4 or $3. Which would seem to explain the lack of bids. But you might also notice that very few of those offerings are drawing bids. Why not?

Everyone in North America can go to the local Kmart or Sam's Club and buy a package of 20 blank DVDs for a dollar. Remember that you bought them at a *chain store*, which was able to sell 20 DVDs for a dollar because the store buyers bought enough to get a price at which they could make a profit selling them for a dollar. And, of course, the chain is offering them at more than one store.

Another example: a chain of used bookstores called Half Price Books, which also handles remaindered books, has several stores near where I live, not to mention more than 80 stores in 13 states. Whenever I visit Half Price Books, I make a mental note of the latest new books at bargain prices. Almost every time I see a book in large quantities at Half Price Books that's selling for less than $5, I can count on seeing that same book being offered on eBay by a dozen or more sellers, most of them offering more than one copy. All the copies are priced near cover price.

So, a dozen eBay sellers in cities with Half Price Books stores saw that same book on sale and said, "Ah-ha! Here's my chance to make a killing . . ." Of course, most of the potential buyers for those books also found them at their local Half Price Books store, or at other stores that handle remaindered books. The greedy sellers ended up waiting a year or more to unload the books they bought, mostly at prices far below what they thought they would get.

The moral of the story: Don't assume that bargain sale prices on mass-produced items are limited to one city or region.

Determining what you're going to sell is only the beginning, of course. Now you need to figure out *how* to sell an item, which involves more than simply posting it as an auction or fixed-price item. The next chapter will help you with the many issues involved in listing your items.

9

LISTING ITEMS: WHEN AND HOW

You need to do several things before you list something on eBay. These include such obvious measures as getting an image of your item, setting a price, writing a description, and selecting a category. But there are certain additional considerations involved in creating a successful auction. You'll learn about them in this chapter and the next.

Look Before You List

So, you have a widget to sell, and you have some idea of what it's worth. But don't click the Sell link yet! Several tasks await your attention, not the least of which is finding out whether others are selling the same, or very similar, widget. If another widget is listed, listing yours at the same time is likely to reduce the final selling price for both items, so you may want to delay posting your widget. If the other widget has more than one bid, at least you know that there will be a market for yours after that auction ends.

If, however, you are in a real hurry to sell your item, you can turn this situation to your advantage. Simply post your widget with a Buy It Now price equal to or lower than the current bid on the other widget. It's likely that one of the currently losing bidders will notice your listing and buy your widget.

NOTE   *Do* not *contact anyone bidding on the other auction. That is interfering with a sale, which is against eBay rules. That doesn't mean you can't do it, but you won't like it if the other seller finds out and complains to eBay.*

Study the descriptions in the other widget auctions. You may learn something you didn't know about the widget or find a better way to describe it. Don't steal the other seller's description, though. Not only does eBay discourage this, but it's tacky as well as potentially in violation of copyright. Worse, you may copy some elements of the auction that you don't want in yours—the other seller's PayPal link, for example.

Note in which categories the other auctions appear. Perhaps those offered in a particular category have more bids than those in other categories. Remember that not everyone uses eBay's Search feature all the time. Some buyers simply browse categories, scanning headers for something interesting. According to eBay, more than 30 percent of auctions are located by browsing.

Don't neglect completed auctions and eBay stores in your search. Multiple completed auctions without bids could mean that there is no demand for widgets, other sellers have priced their widgets too high, or the sellers placed them in the wrong categories.

NOTE   *Not checking for the presence of an item you are listing can result in embarrassing situations. I recall one instance in which there were nearly two dozen copies of a book about the assassination of John F. Kennedy titled* Four Days *posted by several sellers. Among these listings was one by a seller who had obviously not done this bit of simple research. His listing was headed "RARE COPY OF KENNEDY BOOK!!!" To compound the error, the minimum bid was five times that of the highest priced competitor.*

When to List Your Items: The Importance of Timing

The time of day that you list an item for sale can affect the number and amount of bids the item receives. This is also true for the day of the week and the time of year. Hence, you will want to pay attention to both the calendar and clock when you list items.

What Time Is Best?

Two auctions for the same item are posted on the same day. One is posted at 3:30 AM Eastern Daylight Time (EDT); the other at 10:00 PM EDT. Which will receive the highest number of bids?

As will be obvious to some readers, the 10:00 PM auction will receive the most bids, and also usually higher bids. This is because an auction ends at the same time of day that it was posted, and when it's 10:00 PM EDT, it's 7:00 PM Pacific Daylight Time (PDT), 8:00 PM Mountain Daylight Time (MDT), and 9:00 PM Central Daylight Time (CDT). The majority of the nation's population will still be awake and active at those times—something that's not true when it's 3:30 AM EDT, 12:30 AM PDT, 1:30 AM MDT, and 2:30 AM CDT. This translates into more people being online and putting in last-minute bids when your auction ends.

If you're selling in time zones other than those used in the example, adjust your schedule accordingly.

Which Day Is Best?

Because the last few hours of an auction are generally when the most bids are made, you will probably want to have your auctions end on a day when a lot of people are home and online. Do auctions for specific types of merchandise do better if they end on a certain day? Are Sundays in the winter better for ending auctions than Sundays in spring?

There is no single answer to these questions because they involve so many variables. The type of merchandise, the time of year, and even what's showing on television—not to mention a thousand and one other factors—can affect bidding.

At first glance, you might assume that either Saturday or Sunday would be the best day (or evening) for auctions to end, because the majority of people aren't at work. But if they're not at work, most folks are out and about, taking care of things they can't do on workdays. Plus, both Saturday and Sunday are holy days for various religions, and you can expect a large number of people to be involved in activities at their temple or church during the morning, afternoon, and evening.

Okay, what about weekday evenings? Most folks are home from work, right? But wait—weekday evenings are favorite times for people to take classes or go to club meetings, at least during the winter. In the summer, the days are longer, so people are likely to be out and about until at least 9:00 PM.

Many sellers swear by Thursday, because it's the day before payday. Others say that Sunday evening is best, because there's little else to do besides surf the Internet. Saturday is a good candidate in the minds of some sellers, because that's when people are used to spending most of their money (or is that Friday evening?).

A recent poll conducted by AuctionBytes (www.auctionbytes.com) indicated that Sunday is the best day of the week to end an auction, with 64 percent of the vote. Monday was a distant second with 11 percent of the votes, and Saturday was third, with 8 percent.

AuctionBytes has been conducting the poll for several years, and uses this and other data to drive an Interactive Auction Calendar, which provides free forecasts of whether a given day in the current month is a good one for starting an auction. You can access AuctionBytes' Interactive Auction Calendar at www.auctionbytes.com/Email_Newsletter/calendar/calendar.html.

Data gathered manually or from your own eBay sales reports can give you answers that are perhaps better suited to the kind of selling you do. However, eBay sales reports are limited, in that they provide information about only your own sales. For a more comprehensive look at how a specific item or category of item has done, use data from a product like HammerTap's DeepAnalysis, which refines huge amounts of sales data from eBay and presents it in reports such as the one shown in Figure 9-1.

Research Report Index

Item Description	Number of Auctions	% of Total Auctions	Auctions with Sale	Auction Success Rate	% of Total Auctions w/ Sale	ASP per Auction	$ Sales	% of $ Sales
Ending Day								
Sunday	68	13.60%	16	23.53%	14.81%	$7.13	$114.02	6.78%
Monday	62	12.40%	19	30.65%	17.59%	$15.52	$294.97	17.54%
Tuesday	132	26.40%	15	11.36%	13.89%	$17.28	$259.20	15.41%
Wednesday	61	12.20%	16	26.23%	14.81%	$15.01	$240.12	14.28%
Thursday	73	14.60%	15	20.55%	13.89%	$25.40	$381.01	22.66%
Friday	69	13.80%	17	24.64%	15.74%	$14.77	$251.10	14.93%
Saturday	35	7.00%	10	28.57%	9.26%	$14.11	$141.13	8.39%

Figure 9-1: DeepAnalysis report focusing on auction scheduling

As you can see, DeepAnalysis delivers comprehensive data that you could never get on your own. A detailed analysis of this type can be filtered or sorted by type of product, price range, keyword, and other parameters. The sample report shown in Figure 9-1, sorted by day of the week, indicates that auctions that closed on Tuesday had the highest number of sales, while auctions that ended on Thursday had the highest average price.

Other services, such as Andale's Price Finder (described in the "Getting Price Research from Auction Services" section later in this chapter), allow you to zero in on very specific items.

Such data can also be extremely useful in isolating trends, judging the effectiveness of Reserve and Dutch auctions, and getting information such as the average duration of auctions that ended with Buy It Now. There is no guarantee that the answers you derive from such reports will accurately predict the future, but this kind of information puts you several steps ahead of competing sellers.

Is It in Season?

The values of a variety of goods are affected by seasons—or, to put it more accurately, the time of year, since there are several kinds of seasons. Climactic seasons, school seasons, holiday seasons, hunting seasons, and others increase or decrease the demand for certain kinds of clothing, travel, books, automotive accessories, recreational equipment, and various other goods.

The seasonality of a given category of merchandise is usually obvious, though it is a good idea to stop and think about whether the time of year could have an effect on what you are selling. Large, illustrated books of the "coffee table" kind, for example, tend to sell well just before Father's Day and Mother's Day, in addition to the Christmas/Hanukah/Kwanza holiday season. Calendars are hot immediately before and after the New Year. The demand for auto accessories increases in the spring, as many drivers start thinking about summer travel.

NOTE   *eBay's Pulse, at http://pulse.ebay.com, offers the latest information on what's selling on eBay, with data compiled directly from eBay's listings and updated daily.*

In addition to seasons, events can drive demand for merchandise. Just before the United States got into World War I, automobile accessories manufacturers took advantage of the surge in patriotism and made millions of dollars selling small flag holders that clamped onto automobile radiators. In more recent years, the sales of flags increased dramatically in the wake of events related to international conflict. An event that focuses media attention on a specific locale, institution, product, or person can spark a demand for products. For example, the death of an important political figure or celebrity sparks a demand for related books or mementos.

NOTE *Natural disasters and other tragedies focus intense interest on the people and places involved. Unfortunately, some sellers think it appropriate to try to profit on such events. Out of respect for victims and to maintain decorum, eBay will end auctions that are obviously in poor taste or exploit human suffering. eBay staffers also keep an eye out for bogus charity efforts in these situations.*

How About Holidays and Anniversaries?

In addition to the gift-giving aspects of holidays, you may want to consider what people *do* on holidays. Many people take three-day treks for Memorial Day, Labor Day, and other holidays—which means they won't be browsing eBay listings. If what you have to sell will benefit by maximum exposure time, don't post it within a week of a national holiday.

During other holidays, like Christmas and New Year, people tend to do things that keep them away from their computer. So you don't want to have an auction end on the day of the holiday itself, and probably not for a day before and after the holiday.

Anniversaries can also create demand, the American Bicentennial being a prominent example. In similar fashion, the hundredth anniversary of the founding of the Ford Motor Company in 2003 focused attention on anything to do with the company, including Ford collectibles, relics, and books—all of which were sold on eBay.

Unlike historic or otherwise noteworthy events, anniversaries are predictable. You can consult calendars, "today in history" lists, and perhaps a few history books to become informed. As I write this, eBay sellers might be preparing for several anniversaries:

- The fiftieth anniversary of the classic 1957 Chevrolet (2007)
- The fiftieth anniversary of Sputnik, the first artificial satellite (2007)
- The fortieth anniversary of the first lunar landing (2009)

Of course, there are many more, including city and state anniversaries, the founding of corporations, and the discovery or invention of a variety of places and things (2012 marks 135 years of the telephone).

Can You Predict Fads and Trends?

Fads based on products are almost impossible to predict. By the time most people are aware that a fad like Beanie Babies is afoot, the people who can make big money on the fad have been pushing the product for weeks or months, leaving only bits and pieces of the market for latecomers. In addition, big business tends to move in quickly to institutionalize such opportunities, so the best you can hope for is to make a few dollars around the edges of the fad.

Trends, on the other hand, tend to last longer than fads, and are often easily predicted. The current sustained interest in space-related toys, games, and entertainment that started in the late 1970s was easy to foresee: *Star Wars* touched off a boom in science-fiction movies and television, increasing interest in space exploration as well as science fiction. The success of the American space shuttle program accelerated the trend and continues to do so.

The cellular phone trend caught some people by surprise, but others saw it coming and jumped on the bandwagon, just as happened with CB radios in the 1970s. Also as with the CB radio trend, there were opportunities for small businesses early on, but the small operators were soon squeezed out by corporate operations. The cell phone trend is here to stay, of course, but unlike the trend in space-related items, there is little opportunity for individuals or small businesses to make money.

The trick with trends, then, is to get in on them early. No matter how long a trend lasts, the best opportunities are found at the beginning.

How to Create Your Listing

When you've decided the time is right and you're ready to sell, click the Sell tab at the top of any eBay page. You'll see the Sell page, as shown in Figure 9-2.

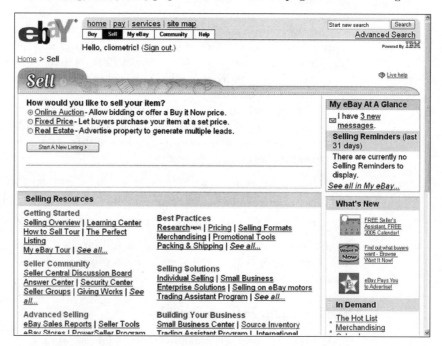

Figure 9-2: The Sell page

Click the appropriate radio button to select Online Auction or Fixed Price, and then click the **Start a New Listing** button. (See Chapter 2 for an explanation of eBay auction formats.)

Select a Category

The next page you will see will be the first of two Select Category pages. This page displays a list of all eBay's main categories. Figure 9-3 shows part of this listing.

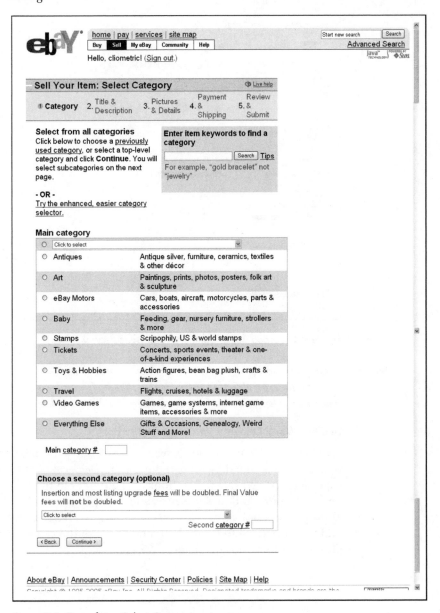

Figure 9-3: First of two Select Category pages

Click the button next to the category you wish to use, or select a previously used category from the drop-down menu under Main Category. At the bottom of the page, select a second category if you wish, and then click **Continue**. On the next page, shown in Figure 9-4, select your subcategory. Take some time to consider your selection here, as described in the following sections. After you've finished selecting categories, click **Continue**.

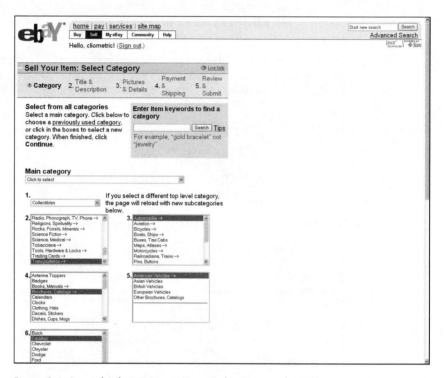

Figure 9-4: Second Select Category Page (subcategory selection)

NOTE *If you post your listing in the wrong category (list a music CD in the Books/Magazines category, for example), your listing will be moved. If your listing belongs in the Mature Audiences category and is placed elsewhere, it will be ended.*

Deciding Which Category (or Categories) to Use

As you can see, actually specifying a category and subcategory for your listing is fairly simple. The difficult part is deciding *which* category to use. Most items suggest their own categories: books should be sold in the Books category, antiques in the Antiques category, and so forth—each with placement in an appropriate subcategory. However, the obvious choice is not always the best, and it may pay you to think about and research the categories in which you choose to offer your merchandise.

An example of an item not going to the obvious category would be an owner's manual for a 1915 Model T Ford. At first glance, it would seem that this item should be sold in the Automotive–eBay Motors category, and specifically in the Manuals & Literature subcategory of the Parts & Accessories category (also known as Automotive/Parts & Accessories/Manuals & Literature).

But consider exactly who is likely to buy an item of this kind. Are your potential buyers only people who own 1915 Model Ts? Not really—that would be limiting the market a bit too much, because although many people are interested in the Model T Ford automobile, few own one (and fewer still own a 1915 Model T). But many automotive buffs collect ephemera such as car manuals. Therefore, you would do best to list your Model T owner's manual where collectors and automotive fans look—in the Collectibles category.

I just ran a search for Model T manuals on eBay, and the results were typical and repeatable. While I found 15 manuals listed in the Automotive category, none of them are getting bids. However, of the 5 manuals listed in various subcategories of Collectibles, 3 have bids. Zero percent of the manuals listed in the Automotive category are selling, while 60 percent of those listed in the Collectibles category are selling.

If you had a Model T Ford manual to sell, I think your choice of categories would be obvious. Either list it in the Collectibles category, or—if you think there might be some hardcore shoppers who look only in the Automotive category—in both Collectibles and Automotive.

I've used this theory to sell any number of items in the "wrong" categories. In one instance, I had a catalog of model airplanes from the 1940s. This may seem like an item for Toys & Hobbies/Models, Kits/Air or Books/Children's Books. But the people who buy these old catalogs aren't children, and they're hardly using them for contemporary hobby activities. They want the items for their historical value or as mementos of their childhoods, which makes them collectibles.

What about that ugly old wood and brass wall clock? Should you try to find a place for it in Home & Garden/Home Decor, or just sock it into an Antiques category and hope for the best? Or is it one of those really ugly items that some might consider to be a collectible? In that case, it should go in Collectibles/Clocks.

When you think about the best category for your item, consider who might be buying it and why. Then choose the category or categories they would search. In other words, think of your customers first. You want to make it easy for them to find your items.

If you have any doubts as to the appropriate category, do a search across all categories, as I did with the Model T Ford manual. Go with the category that draws the most bids.

Don't forget to look at completed auctions as well as current auctions. Also, remember that the Matching Categories box to the left of a search results lists shows how many items are listed in each category, as shown in Figure 9-5.

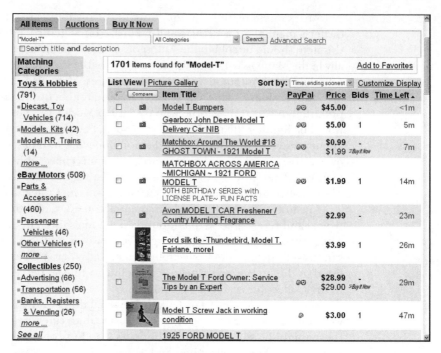

Figure 9-5: Matching Categories list with numbers of items in each category

Posting in Two Categories

As you can see in the accompanying images, eBay allows you to post your item in a second category if you wish. This doubles your listing fee, but not your final value fee. Whether it's a good idea to use two categories is basically a judgment call. However, if you have an item that would appeal to buyers in two different main categories, you might consider it. An example of this might be a book about auto repair, which could be listed in a Books category as well as an eBay Motors category.

The amount you expect to receive for the item also has some bearing on your decision. Listing a $500 item in two categories is worthwhile, but listing a $10 item isn't, since a significant percentage of your final price will go to listing in the second category.

List with Pre-Filled Item Information

If the category you choose is one that offers the option, you will next be given the opportunity to list with pre-filled information or list the conventional way. If you use the pre-filled listing option, certain information about your item is entered in the listing form for you. All you need to do is enter a product identifier (such as an ISBN for books or the UPC code or product brand name), as shown in Figure 9-6.

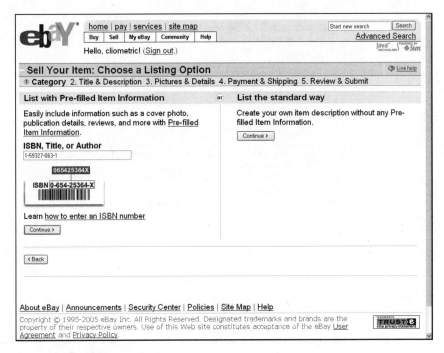

Figure 9-6: A Pre-filled Item Information option

The pre-filled information feature then automatically fills in details that are specific to the item you're selling (also known as Item Specifics). For example, if you are offering a book and enter the ISBN, the system will put in the title, author, date of publication, and publisher, and supply a stock image of the book's cover.

There is no charge for this service, which is offered for books, videos, game cartridges, and selected other items. You can add your own image, as well as your own description and subtitle if you wish. (Charges for the subtitle and extra photos still apply.) An advantage of using this option is the fact that Item Specifics can be used as search and sort criteria within a subcategory.

NOTE *Additional information about your listings, such as the kinds of payment and whether you offer refunds (and how many days the buyer has to return an item) can be filled in using check boxes on the listing form.*

Describe Your Item

The Describe Your Item page, shown in Figure 9-7, is up next. Here you enter your item's title and its description.

Chapter 10 has guidelines and advice for creating titles and descriptions that sell. I recommend that you read the entire chapter before you create a title and description.

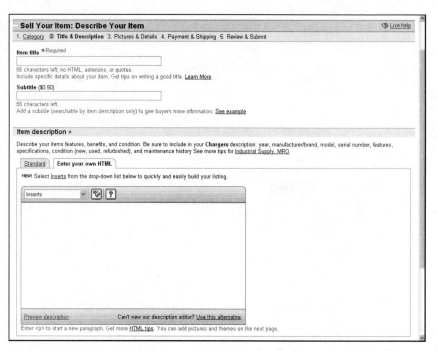

Figure 9-7: Describe Your Item page

Note that you can also enter a subtitle on this page (for an extra charge). You probably won't use this option, unless you feel that the main title's 55-character limit is not enough for you to make your best first impression.

Only plain text can be entered in the Item Title and Subtitle fields; HTML tags will have no effect. You can, however, use HTML in the Item Description. Basic HTML coding is fairly simple, and you can find a number of free websites, such as http://clockworkwebsites.com/HTML, devoted to helping computer users learn to use HTML.

NOTE *Creating your Item Description, with or without HTML, is best done with your word processor. You'll be able to work faster, and do a complete spell check and grammar check if you wish. After you've completed the description, you can copy and paste it into the Item Description box.*

After you've entered your title and description, click **Continue** at the bottom of the page.

Set the Minimum Price

Next, you'll see the Enter Pictures & Item Details page, the first part of which is shown in Figure 9-8. The first field asks for your starting price (minimum bid).

As I'm sure any buyer will agree, the most frequent cause of items not selling on eBay is overpricing. As you learned in Chapter 5, determining the value of an item can be a tricky business, and value is not always indicative of how much buyers are willing to pay.

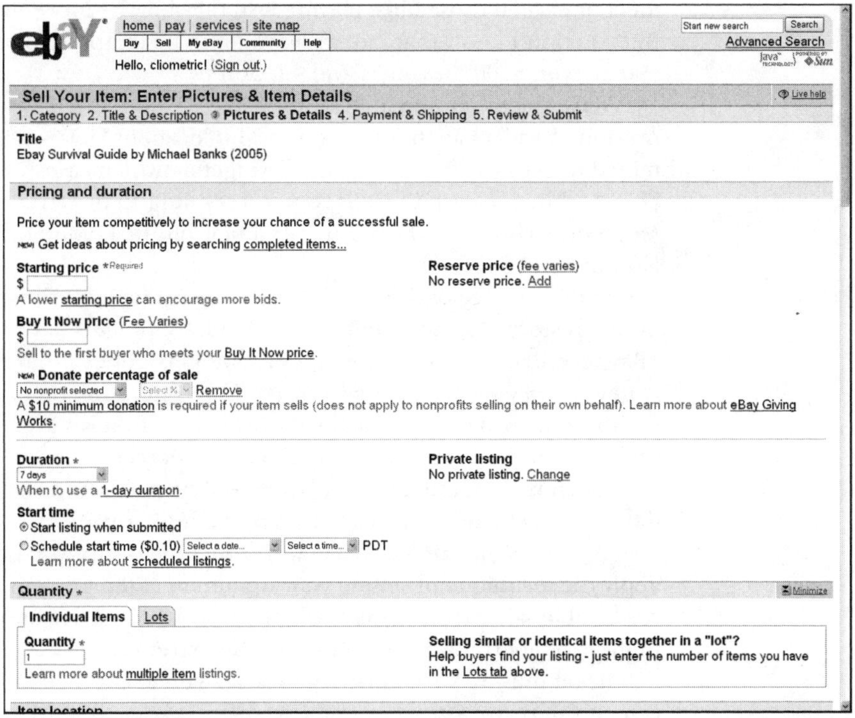

Figure 9-8: Enter Pictures & Item Details page

So how do you set your minimum price? If you know the absolute lowest price you'll accept for the item, sometimes it's easiest just to make that your minimum. But there's always a chance the item will actually sell for that amount, simply because potential bidders missed it in their searches or happened to be on vacation that week. So, you're left with only one interested bidder who might have actually paid more, if you had only set your minimum higher.

The question "How do I set my minimum price?" then becomes "How high can I set the minimum price without discouraging bidders?"

With collectibles, antiques, and rare or unusual articles, you can use historical price data to determine your minimum. This does *not* mean that you look up the prices that a 1927 Model T-widget brought over the past few weeks, and then set your minimum at the highest price you observed. Prices realized by an item in the past are not a forecast of what it will bring in the future; all they tell you is the maximum each person was willing to pay to win the item in an auction. The person who made the highest bid among all the auctions may well be the only one willing to pay that much.

Suppose that three T-widgets sold for $100, $72, and $87 in the past two weeks. That doesn't mean that your T-widget will sell for $100, $87, or even $72. The bidder who was willing to pay $100 already has his T-widget. Ditto for those who were willing to pay $72 and $87. This is not to say that a losing bidder or bidders from the previous auctions won't loosen their purse strings and meet or exceed those bids. Having lost, they may be more strongly motivated. But you don't know that. So, while you may be tempted to put a minimum of $90 or even $100 on your T-widget, don't.

Make the minimum at least ten percent under the lowest winning bid on previous T-widget auctions (in our example, about $65)—unless you are determined to get at least $85 for your T-widget; in which case, set the minimum at $85. And just in case there is someone willing to pay $100 for the T-widget (someone who is tired of losing or a new bidder), you might add a Buy It Now price of $92.

In the absence of direct historical data on auction prices, you can fall back on the history of similar items. If no Model T-widgets have been offered on eBay recently, perhaps some Model A-widgets were sold. If you're offering issues of *Newsweek* magazine from 1937 but find none on eBay, look for comparable magazines, like *Time* or *Business Week*. Take an average of all sales of similar items and set your minimum at ten percent less.

When researching eBay and other online auctions doesn't yield enough data to make a decision regarding price, look for sales in other venues: dealers/stores, private sales, real-world auctions. Once you have some prices, apply the technique of setting your minimum at ten percent below the lowest reasonable sale price. (There will probably be low-price anomalies as well as high-price aberrations, so factor out the extremes.)

If you must resort to price guides, it's safe to cut their estimates by 25 percent at the very least.

NOTE *While this text mostly disparages price guides, some people do think highly of them, and they may be bidding on your items. For the benefit of those people (and your pocketbook), quote the highest price you've found in a price guide, along with the source, in your item description. This often carries weight with potential buyers, especially those who use price guides.*

If you are dealing in new retail merchandise, setting prices will be much simpler. Look at the prices charged by brick-and-mortar stores and online merchants. Then check out the minimum prices in online auctions, if any. Set your minimum price noticeably lower than the lowest of these. Be sure to allow for shipping cost; most buyers take this into consideration, and if your price is not lower than the competition after the shipping cost is added, you'll lose sales.

In the absence of any outside price information, you can use what you paid for an item as a reference. For articles that cost a few dollars, double the amount you paid and make that your minimum. For high-priced articles, add 50 percent. If you have nothing in the item, or bought it in a lot, follow your instincts. Some things just look like $50 items, while others seem like $100 items. Shave a bit off that gut price, and you'll be safe.

For example, I picked up a very early radio antenna coupler in a leather case—possibly a one-off—in a box of junk at a yard sale. The hardware used in making this collectible artifact indicated that it was made in the 1920s. I put it up for sale with a $40 minimum, and it went for $60 in two bids.

As another example, a 1904 *Williams City Directory* for Dayton, Ohio, cost me $10 at a flea market in 2003—the hundredth anniversary of flight. Dayton was, of course, Wilbur and Orville Wright's hometown, and the directory had listings for all the Wrights, plus their businesses and listings for other interesting folks. "This," I said to myself, "feels like a $100 item." So I posted it for $85 with a $110 Buy It Now, and it sold for $110 a few hours later.

Getting Price Research from Auction Services

Several online auction services offer reports that show the minimum, maximum, and average prices for a given item, as well as the quantity of that item sold and the percentage of items offered sold. Andale's Price Finder (www.andale.com) is one of several services that offer price research. Figure 9-9 shows an example of an Andale Price Finder report covering Gibson guitars. (This is only a partial report; the full report presents several additional views of the data, covering several screens.)

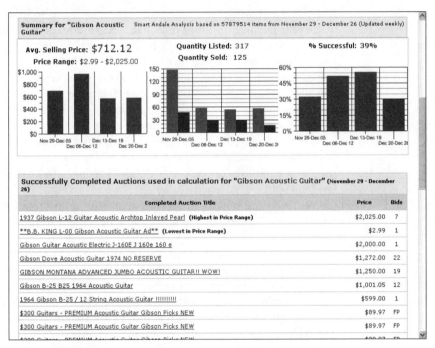

Figure 9-9: Item pricing report from Andale auction research service

As you can see, this report provides the prices realized by various Gibson acoustic guitars in numbers and in graph form. It also provides access to the listings used to generate the report.

Andale Price Finder reports can be refined to zero in on a specific model, size, or color item, so it is possible to find out exactly how much people have been willing to pay for the item you want to sell. You can use this data to come up with a minimum bid (ideally, one that is significantly lower than the average), a Buy It Now price, and even a reserve price.

A Penny *Can* Make a Difference

Most of us tend to think in whole numbers. And some of us disparage pricing something at $49.99 rather than $50 as a cheap department store trick, intended to make the buyer equate the price with $40 rather than $50. So, for one reason or another, many eBay sellers will post an item for $50 rather than $49.99—and lose money in the process. How? By letting eBay charge a higher listing fee. The listing fee for an item with a minimum price of $49.99 is, as of this writing, $1.20, while the listing fee for an item priced at $50.00 is $2.40.

So, stop and think (and consult eBay's price list) before you set a minimum bid, because a penny saved can be worth several dollars.

For your reference, the prices at which eBay's fee increases are: $1, $10, $25, $50, $200, and $500. List an item with a minimum price of 1 cent less than any of these amounts, and you save money.

"Buy This Car for $1?" Ultra-Low Minimum Bids

If you've spent much time browsing eBay listings, you've seen plenty of listings with absurdly low minimum bids, like a late-model pickup truck for $10 or a new laptop computer for $1. Before you even looked at such listings, you probably guessed that the minimum bids were come-ons. In nearly every instance, you'll find that the item has a reserve. A reserve might just as well be called an "invisible" minimum price. It is a way to require that bids exceed a certain amount before anyone can win the auction. See the discussion of reserves in the next section for more information.

Of the few low-minimum items without reserves, some had huge shipping costs attached, like, "Okay, kid—you can buy this laptop for $1, but shipping and handling comes to $600." This is against eBay rules, but some sellers try it anyway.

Still, you will find $1 minimum items with no reserve and no exorbitant handling or shipping charges. Are the sellers really willing to let the items go for $1?

The answer is yes, although the sellers don't *expect* to sell the merchandise for a dollar. Most items posted with absurdly low minimum bids and no reserve are in very high demand. Consider a laptop offered for $1. Potential bidders are pulled in by the low minimum, and place bids "just in case." At first, there are plenty of bids, with one bidder after another bidding first $1, then $10, $15, $32, $44, $50, and $64 for a new laptop.

Then the bidding slows down, but it doesn't stop because this laptop sells for $995 in discount stores and, while it would have been a real steal to get it for $75, getting it for $580, $600, or even $850 isn't so bad. Enough people think this way that no matter how many laptops are posted, none will go for less than $725. Quite a few people who weren't thinking of spending over $500 for a laptop—or buying a laptop at all—are persuaded to jump into the affray by the prospect of a bargain and all the excitement being generated.

The sellers, who have maybe $350 invested in the laptop, aren't going to lose any money. The high demand is as good a guarantee as a reserve, and the seller doesn't need to pay a reserve fee or look like a jerk for setting a reserve.

This illustrates the only practical use of an absurdly low minimum bid: to draw attention to an auction. How intense the demand for an item must be for this to be effective is difficult to say, but it works more often than it doesn't. I have seen all sorts of things sold at high prices using the low minimum come-on to generate interest, including laptops, automobiles, rare books, collectibles, cameras, and more. This often works with relatively low-cost items, too; a $25 best-selling novel with an opening bid of 50 cents will often close at $12, while the same book posted with an opening bid of $10 will get no bids at all.

There is always a risk that you can end up losing, and having to sell your laptop or pickup truck or new digital camera for $50, but the likelihood of this happening decreases in direct proportion to the demand for an item.

After you enter a starting price, you have two additional pricing options to consider: reserve and Buy It Now prices.

Set a Reserve Price

A reserve price prevents anyone from winning an auction with a bid below the amount you specify. The amount of the reserve is not displayed to others, but you can post it in your listing if you wish. The cost of posting a reserve price depends on the amount of the reserve, and it is refunded if your item sells.

As I pointed out earlier, putting a reserve on an auction isn't the best thing you can do to help sell an item. It costs money, and it annoys some potential bidders. It's also somewhat sleazy. Here you are telling potential bidders that you have a great bargain for them (the minimum bid displayed next to your auction's title in a search list). Then, when they look at your listing, they're blasted with "Reserve not met," essentially telling them that your minimum bid is a lie. Some will wonder what other kinds of tricks you have up your sleeve. Either be honest with a real minimum or bet on demand to generate a decent price for your items as discussed earlier.

Set a Buy It Now Price

Buy It Now is one of eBay's most-used options. Until eBay added fixed-price listings, it was the only way to sell items for flat prices—and instantly. It still serves these purposes, giving bidders the option to ace out the competition by jumping in and paying your price. The Buy It Now option stays active until the price you set is met or exceeded by a conventional bid, or someone uses Buy It Now. Buy It Now costs between 5 and 25 cents, depending on the amount of your Buy It Now price.

If you are serious about selling with Buy It Now, it is best to keep the price within 25 percent of your minimum bid (unless you have a ridiculously low minimum bid and are using a reserve). Otherwise, make it what you would really like to get for your item. If you go much higher, most buyers will opt to take their chances battling it out with bids.

Set the Auction Duration and Scheduled Start Time

After you have set your Starting, Reserve, and Buy It Now prices, scroll down to the Duration section of the page. Here, you can specify the duration of your auction and its start time, as shown in Figure 9-10.

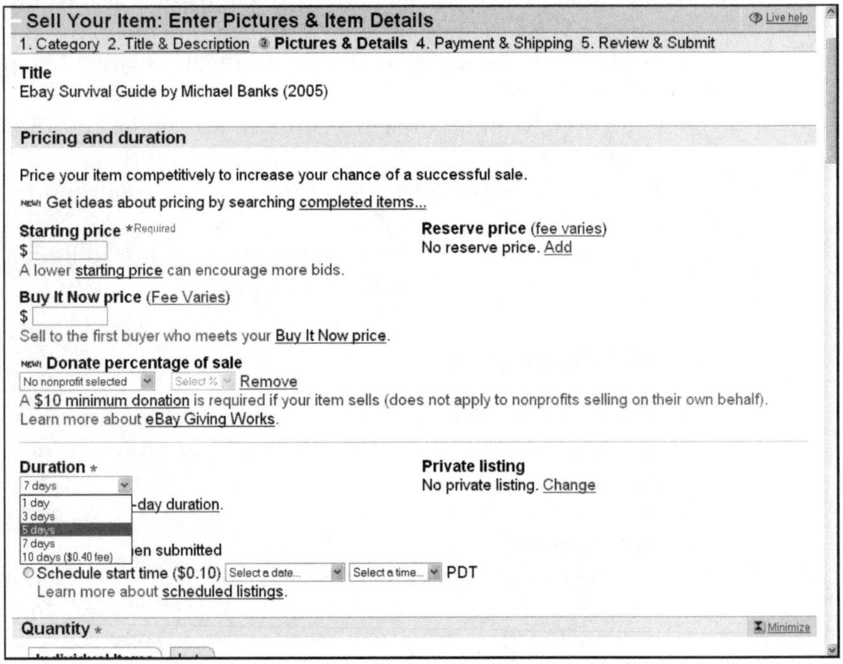

Figure 9-10: Setting auction duration and start time

eBay allows you to specify that your auction will last one, three, five, or seven days, without incurring any extra fees. If you want the auction to last ten days, there is a small fee. If you want to stir things up, you can post your auction for one or three days; people who see such a short listing will often get caught up in the excitement generated by the short deadline and jump in with bids.

If you want to give your item maximum exposure, list it for ten days. Otherwise, list it for seven days; this is the most common period for an online auction.

By default, all eBay auctions begin the second you post them. For a fee, you can schedule an auction to start up to 20 days in the future. In addition to setting the auction's starting date, you can also set the hour it ends, which is the most frequent application for this feature. Some sellers use auction scheduling when they plan on traveling, so an auction can start when they're away and end when they return.

Have a Private Auction

If you are selling a really big-ticket item, you and your bidders may be more comfortable if no one other than you can see who is bidding on the item. If this is the case (or you have another reason for not wanting bidders' IDs shown), you can make the auction private by choosing the Private Auction option on the Enter Pictures & Item Details page (see Figure 9-10).

Sell Multiple Quantities or Lots

As explained in Chapter 2, you can sell multiple items in several ways: as a group, in a multiple quantity (Dutch auction), or as a lot. These options are also specified on the Enter Pictures & Item Details page, as shown in Figure 9-11.

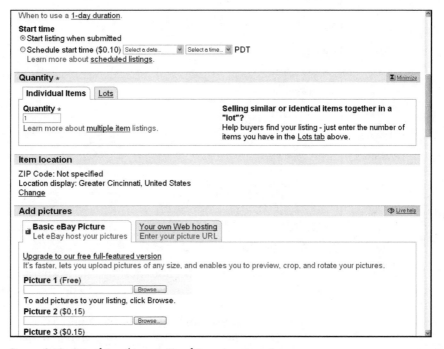

Figure 9-11: Specifying the quantity of items in an auction

You must click the Lots tab if you plan to sell a lot. This will display a different set of controls in the Quantity section of the page.

NOTE *It is against eBay rules to list multiple items as a conventional auction without offering the entire group for one bid. To post five items and permit bidders to buy only one for their bid is called "Dutch auction avoidance," and can get your auction canceled and/or your account suspended. So, don't list five collector coins and say, "Buy 1 or more, paying your bid amount for each" or "You choice of these items for your bid."*

After you finish entering the number of items or lots you have to sell, scroll down to the Add Pictures section of the page.

Add Pictures

You add pictures and select picture options in the Add Pictures section of the Enter Pictures & Item Details page, as shown in Figure 9-12.

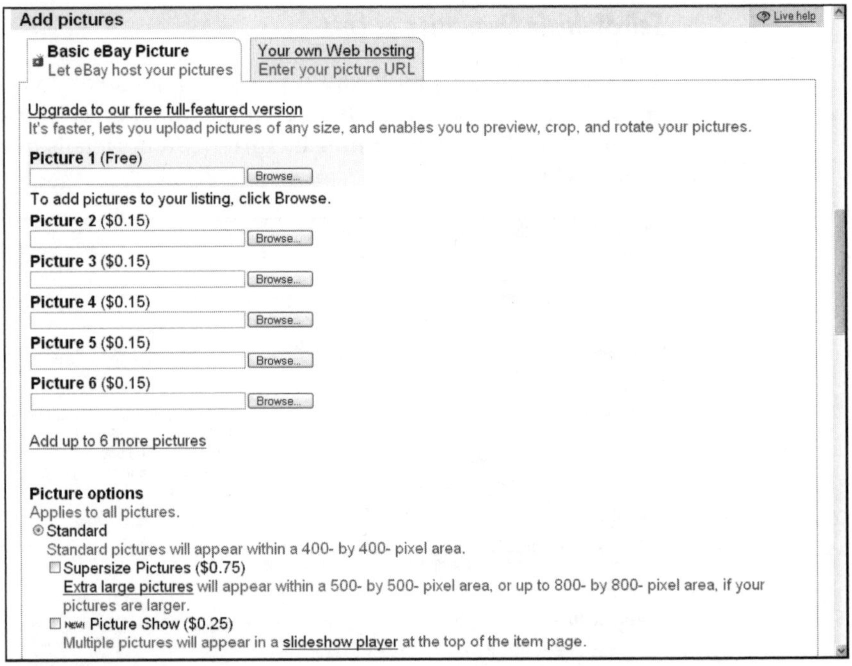

Figure 9-12: Add Pictures options

If you plan to use eBay's photo hosting, this is where you upload your photos. You can enter as many as 12 pictures. The first picture is free, but there is a small charge for every photo after the first.

The images you use can be color or black and white, and come from a digital camera, scanner, or any other source of digital images. The format must be JPEG (files whose names end in .jpg, like image1.jpg) or GIF (files whose names end in .gif, like image1.gif).

NOTE   *Don't steal someone else's photo. This can get you suspended from eBay if the seller (or website owner) from whom you copied it complains. It's likely that your item looks different from one already posted, anyway.*

eBay will automatically resize your photos to 400 pixels by 400 pixels. A photo this size will measure 5½ by 5½ inches if printed out, but the size of the display is about half that. (The actual size depends on your monitor's resolution.)

Since eBay reduces the size of your photos, their original size doesn't affect how they are displayed with your listing. However, if you upload extremely large photos (like 1 MB), you'll find that the upload time is correspondingly increased. If you have photo-editing software, it is a good idea to reduce the size of your photos before uploading them. Doing this will also allow you to view the photos as they will appear with your listing.

While the photos or scans you use with eBay listings don't have to be works of art, they should depict your item clearly. Ideally, an auction photo will focus on the article for sale, and not be cluttered with other objects. Use close-up photos to show the important features of large items. Photograph small objects, such as jewelry, close-up and in focus. If your camera doesn't do well with close-ups of small items, place the item on a scanner.

If your photos don't come out the way you would like, you can improve them with graphics programs like PhotoShop, Paint Shop Pro (highly recommended), or editing programs that come with digital cameras and scanners.

Uploading Photos

eBay offers direct uploading of photos, which means you don't need to bother with FTP or other file-transfer programs. Simply click the **Browse** buttons shown in Figure 9-12 (beginning with Picture 1), and eBay will guide you through the upload process. You simply locate the image you wish to upload on your hard drive and click its name.

Editing Pictures Online

If you use eBay's enhanced uploader (available as a free download), you can perform simple edits on photos after uploading them. Edit options are crop, rotate, and brighten. Figure 9-13 shows a picture being edited with eBay's enhanced uploader.

NOTE   *eBay's enhanced uploader is available only for PCs with Microsoft Windows.*

For a fee of 75 cents, you can have eBay display your photos in either of two "supersize" formats (a good idea if you want to show details of an item). These are 500 by 500 pixels or 800 by 800 pixels.

If you have multiple pictures, eBay will display them in slideshow format (one at a time) for a fee.

An eBay special called Picture Pack lets you add up to 12 photos to a listing, all at supersize, and in the slideshow format. You also get a gallery photo with this option, the price of which varies depending on the number of photos you add.

Using the eBay Picture Manager

For those who have a high volume of listings or repeat listings, eBay provides something called eBay Picture Manager. This tool lets you store photos and other images on eBay as long as you wish, and add these images to your listings at no extra charge beyond the monthly fee eBay charges for Picture Manager, which is based on the amount of storage space you use.

Figure 9-13: Editing a picture with eBay's enhanced uploader

Using Your Own Photo Hosting or Third-Party Hosting Services

As a rule, you will get the best results with eBay's photo hosting system. It's designed to operate with eBay's pages, and the price for multiple photos and other options is reasonable. There are less costly alternatives that may be of interest to those who are high-volume sellers. These include hosting at your own website and using hosting services.

To include a photo from your website in a listing, all you need to do is place a link to the photo at the appropriate location in the listing text. To provide that link, insert this line in the point in your listing where you want the photo to be displayed:

`<img src=http://www.yoursite.com/myimage1.jpg>`

`<img src=` is the command to display a photo, `http://www.mysite.com/` is your website, and `myimage1.jpg` is the name of the image. The character `>` completes the command.

As with photos uploaded to eBay, photos you host at another site must be JPEG or GIF format. eBay recommends that you use photos no larger than 50 KB, to minimize the time the photos take to be displayed. (I've used photos as large as 100 KB with no appreciable delays.)

NOTE *If you wish, you can provide a link to a web page where you have one or more images stored. Many sellers use this technique to make extra-large images available to buyers who may want to see them. The link to do this would look like this:* `<a href="http://www.yoursite.com/myimage1.jpg"> </a>`, *where* `<a href=` *is the command to link to the*

page, `"http://www.yoursite.com/">` *is the URL for the page, and* `</a>` *completes the command. You would put the link in the middle of the text instructing the reader where to click, like this: To see a photo,* `<a href="http://www.yoursite.com/ myimage1.jpg">click here</a>`.

You will find dozens of third-party photo hosting services on the Web. The majority (those offering the best performance) charge monthly fees, usually for unlimited service. A few of the more popular are Andale.com, ePier.com, Ezlister.net, Imagecave.com, Inkfrog.com, Photobucket.com, and Vendio.com.

A FEW WORDS ABOUT IMAGES

Here are a few tips regarding photos:

Light

Light is what images are all about. The better the lighting, the better your item looks and the more detail is shown. You can often save yourself a paragraph or two with a good image that depicts important elements (or flaws) in an item that may be difficult to describe in any event. The best light is outdoors. Avoid direct sunlight, though, because it can create shadows. Indoors, light your item from more than one direction. Don't rely on your camera's flash to handle all the lighting; like direct sunlight, a flash can create shadows that detract from the image quality.

Clutter

The item you're selling should be the star of your photo. Avoid taking a photo of the item with a cluttered background. Too many sellers simply place an item on a desktop, kitchen table, or garage floor and start taking photos. This usually results in a picture of the item in the middle of all sorts of distracting junk. A fine piece of Rookwood pottery ends up surrounded by a nest of old rope and jumper cables. Or, a computer hard drive is shown on top of a pile of newspapers. Find or make a clear spot. If possible, shoot your item against a plain backdrop.

Backdrops

Backdrops are easy to create. A sheet, towel, piece of velvet cloth, or a large piece of poster board—any of these can be laid on a table or propped against the back of a chair to create a neutral background. Either black or white is the best background color, although red, yellow, or green can work, too, depending on the color of your item. Clear or translucent items (such as cut glass or patterned vases) photograph best on dark backgrounds.

Editing

Just about any photo can be improved by judicious editing. Something as simple as copying and enlarging a portion of the item's image can enhance the chances of a sale. Even the simplest photo-editing programs will allow you to do this. You can also lighten or darken a photo, or increase its contrast to better display your item's attributes. You can even save money by making a photo collage that shows your item from several different viewpoints in one image (thus eliminating the need to use more than one image with a listing). Most photo-editing software will also allow you to add text to images, which you can use to call the viewer's attention to certain features. Experiment with your images to see how you can improve them.

Use the Listing Designer

Scrolling down from the Add Pictures section of the Enter Pictures & Item Details page will take you to the Listing Designer section. If you would like a more aesthetic display of your listings than offered by eBay's basic listing layout, you can use eBay's Listing Designer to improve the visual appeal of listings. Figure 9-14 shows the Listing Designer's options.

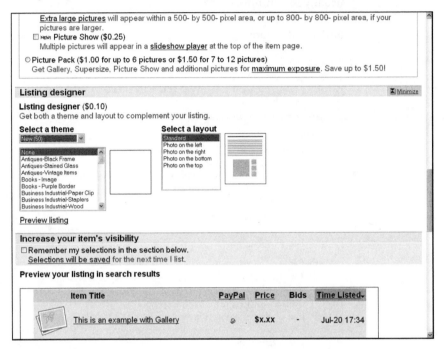

Figure 9-14: eBay's Listing Designer

The Listing Designer lets you choose from several themes (top and bottom borders with color backgrounds) and varying layouts of pictures and text. There is a fee involved.

Whether adding a design actually impresses buyers or increases bids is debatable. While a border of baby icons and a pastel background may seem fitting for baby items, these won't have any effect on the number or amounts of bids for your items. However, layout can be important if you want to emphasize images or text, or vice versa.

You can also use the Listing Designer to give all of your listings a consistent appearance.

Increase Your Item's Visibility

Next on the Add Pictures & Item Details page is a group of options under the heading Increase Your Item's Visibility, as shown in Figure 9-15. This provides tools with which you can use your photos and text effects to make your listing's title stand out and promote your listing on eBay.

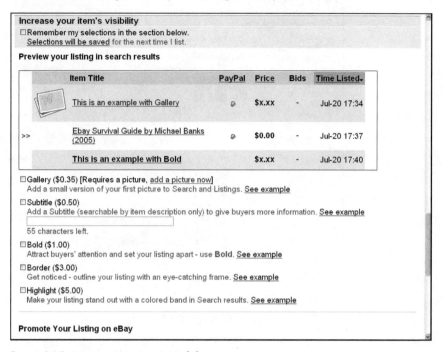

Figure 9-15: Increase Your Item's Visibility options

Choosing Gallery Options

eBay offers several options to use a photo of your item *with your title* to get extra attention. eBay's Gallery option displays a small photo next to an item's title in Search and Browse lists—certainly an eye-catching device. The photo used is the first photo you post with your listing. As of this writing, a gallery photo costs 25 cents.

The photos to the left of the listing titles in the image in Figure 9-16 are gallery images. The listings without gallery photos have camera icons, which indicate that photos accompany the listings.

eBay maintains that statistics prove items with gallery photos not only get more viewers than those without gallery photos, but also more bids. You will notice that more of the listings with gallery photos have bids than those without gallery photos. This would seem to support eBay's contention. Certainly, the eye is more attracted by images than text, and the brain processes images faster.

Buyers can view search or browse results lists in a special Picture Gallery view, as shown in Figure 9-17. This view, which is toggled by links on the line above the first items in a list, shows Gallery Promoted items only, and displays larger photos.

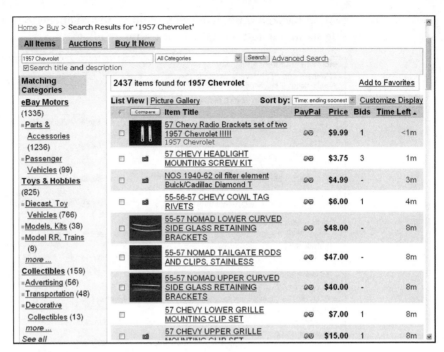

Figure 9-16: Gallery images with auction titles

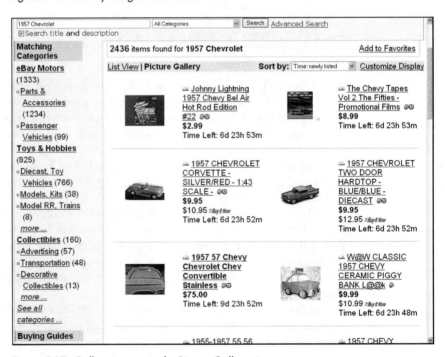

Figure 9-17: Gallery images in the Picture Gallery view

NOTE *If you list a motorcycle, automobile, or other motor vehicle in eBay Motors, the Gallery Promoted option is provided for free.*

The next level up in Gallery options is Gallery Featured. Gallery Featured items have an even larger photo, displayed at the very top of any Picture Gallery display. As of this writing, the Gallery Featured option costs $19.95 (higher for eBay Motors listings).

NOTE *You can also pay to have a listing featured on eBay's home page or on the eBay Motors home page.*

Choosing Options that Make Your Items Stand Out

Along with Galley options, eBay offers some extra-cost options to make your titles stand out:

Bold
> You can emphasize a listing's title by paying ($1 as of this writing) to have the title displayed in boldface type, like the listing titled "Superb Binocular Microscope" in Figure 9-18.

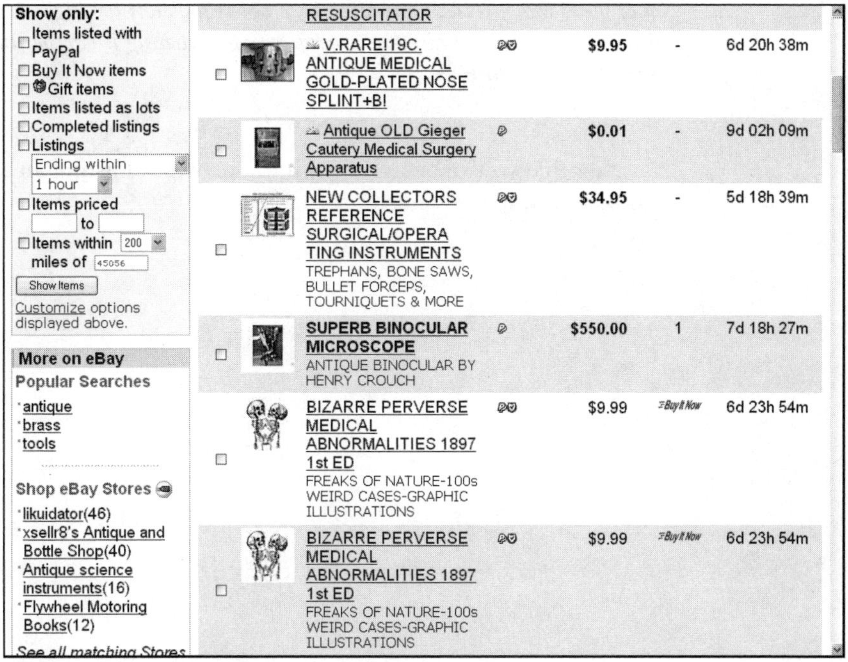

Figure 9-18: Example of a listing in boldface

Border
> Another option for making your title stand out is to put a border around it. This option places a colored border around your listing.

Highlight
> Highlighting your listing puts a colored band behind the listing.

Promote Your Listing on eBay

The Featured Plus! option under the Promote Your Listing on eBay heading will cause your item's listing to be displayed at the top of its category list and search results. The Home Page Featured option places your listing in eBay's Featured Area, and *may* display it on eBay's home page.

Use Gift Services

The Gift Services option places a gift icon next to your listing, and adds notice of gift services you wish to offer to your listing.

Add a Free Counter

At the bottom of the Increase your item's visibility section of the Enter Pictures & Item Details page you will notice a counter. Here you can select or unselect a counter for your page, and change the style of the counter.

NOTE *The number of views an auction gets can say any of several things about it. If the listing isn't getting many views, perhaps you need to change the title, or move it to a different category. Or, it may be that people just aren't interested in the item. If the auction has a lot of views but no bids, your minimum bid is probably too high. A large number of views for an item that also has several people watching it may mean that there will be several last-minute bids.*

Now that you've been through the process of listing an auction, let's take a look at how to create listings that sell.

10

HOW TO CREATE LISTINGS THAT SELL

An effective advertisement grabs attention, generates interest, and gives the prospective buyer all the information she needs to make a purchasing decision. The first thing any ad should do is capture your potential customer's attention. Having secured the customer's attention, the next step is to generate interest in your product. Then you tell your story—the story of what you have to offer and why the customer should buy it.

Write a good pitch, keep the reader's interest, and you have it made. It's almost axiomatic that people who are interested in your product will read everything you have to say about it, provided that what you write is relevant, organized, informative, and not boring. You don't need to be a great writer to create good advertising copy, although paying attention to spelling and the rudiments of grammar helps.

In writing copy for magazine ads, brochures, and even the backs of paperback novels, I developed several methods for reaching those goals. When I began selling on eBay, I decided to test those methods with auction listings. As it turns out, they work as well in auctions as anywhere else. (I sell more than 90 percent of what I list.) This chapter shares those methods.

Advertising, eBay Style

Advertising on eBay is about as simple as it gets. The layout is done for you. All you need to do is fill in the blanks for three major elements:

Title
This is the interest-grabber, but it must also inform.

Description
Here is where you make your pitch. You describe the item and give the customer everything she needs to know to make a decision, all while building interest.

Images
Photos or other relevant images support the description and add interest.

These pieces of information do almost all the work of grabbing and holding the customer's interest.

How to Write Attention-Getting Titles

The first element of your listing a buyer sees is the title. As already stated, a title should do two things: get attention and inform. You want to get the viewer to stop, look at, and think about the auction. At the same time, your title must tell the viewer as much as possible about the item in the limited space available (55 characters).

Before you write your first (or next) auction title, spend some time looking at eBay titles to see what grabs your interest. Look at ads in a variety of magazines, too. You can learn quite a bit by surveying what already works for others. Combine what you learn with the suggestions in this section, and you'll be writing informative and attention-getting titles in no time!

What's Not Permitted in Auction Titles

Here are some things eBay will *not* let you use in auction titles:

- Profane or obscene language
- Website URLs, email addresses, and phone numbers
- Brand names other than that of the item being offered
- Words such as *banned, illegal, prohibited,* or similar terms

Additionally, you cannot use a title that doesn't describe the item you're offering.

Ways to Get Attention

Auction titles are displayed in lists, like the example shown in Figure 10-1. When faced with long, information-rich lists, the eye tends to scan the material, perhaps pausing at a familiar word or symbol, an image, or an unusual phrase now and then, but often skipping words.

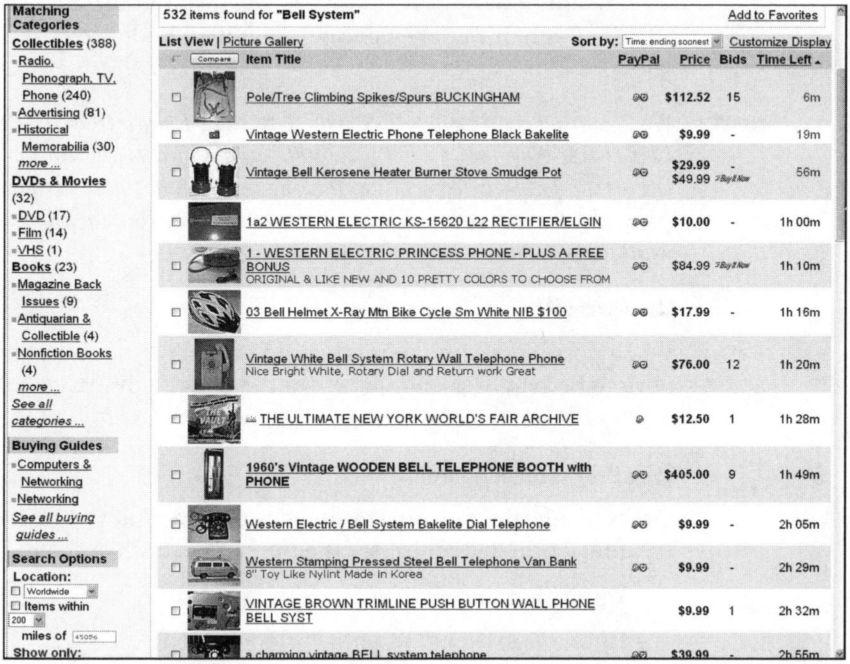

Figure 10-1: List of auction titles

Naturally, you want *your* title to make people pause. The most common way to achieve this is to present something unusual. And what is *unusual*? It's something different, something we don't expect to see, or something we've never seen before. This gives you a starting point for thinking about how your item's title can get attention.

What's Unusual About Your Item?

Ask yourself, "What is unusual or outstanding about this item?" Then use your title to tell the buyer about it.

Here's an example. Thanks to pocket calculators, slide rules were going out of style when I was in high school, but I saw enough of those "slipsticks" to remember that they were either light-colored plastic or wood painted white. So when I came across a transparent slide rule at a yard sale, I immediately recognized it as unusual.

I pointed out this unusual aspect in the auction's title: "Unusual TRANS-PARENT Slide Rule." That grabbed a *lot* of attention; the slide rule ended up with more than two dozen bids and sold for $366! I paid $1 for it.

Another item with an unusual aspect that inspired an attention-getting title was a silent butler from the 1960s. This was a tiny (about 1½-by-1½-by-3/8 inch) brass ashtray that folded up to fit in a pocket or purse. There are quite a few of these around, but this one was different from others I've seen in that the top bore a full-size bas-relief cigarette butt. The fake butt was painted to look like a real, burnt-out, smashed cigarette butt.

The thing was just plain *ugly*, which inspired the auction title, "World's UGLIEST Silent Butler/Ashtray." The silent butler sold for 50 times its yard sale cost.

NOTE   *When writing a title, DON'T SHOUT! By that, I mean DON'T USE ALL CAPITAL LETTERS. When every letter is capitalized, the effect is diluted, and you might just as well use all lowercase letters. Capitalizing is one of the few techniques available to make text stand out in auction titles, and it should be reserved for important words that you want to stand out.*

Use Numerals

When possible, use numerals instead of spelling out numbers. This has the obvious benefit of saving space, but the critical advantage is that the eye slows down when it sees numerals in text.

Take the Personal Approach

Occasionally, the personal approach can be employed to good effect. Try creating a title that addresses the buyer directly, like these:

You NEED this New Niclod 10-Y Camera

Here's Your Next Camera: Niclod 10-Y NR

While this isn't a technique you'll use frequently, titles of this kind will grab attention because they are so different from the other auction titles surrounding them.

Ask a Question

A technique that I don't see used often is asking the reader a question in an auction title. Perhaps the fact that it isn't common is why it is effective, since it catches the eye with the question mark (?) character. It also personalizes the headline.

A seller whose listings I watch uses questions to fill in the empty space left in a title. For example, two of his recent titles read like this:

1938 SOHIO, LET'S EXPLORE OHIO TRAVEL BOOK! Got it?

1939 FORD & WORLD'S FAIR Brochure & Map! Seen one?

Depending on the length of his title, he will sometimes use "Got 1?" or "Seen 1?" as the question. However he phrases it, the legitimate question gets buyers to look twice.

Get Attention with Unusual Words

My auction title examples don't use *Rare, Unique, Awesome, Vintage, Cool,* or any of the many other adjectives that are so ubiquitous on eBay. I avoid them because they are a waste of space; they've been used so much that they hardly register on the reader's consciousness. Saying an item is unique or vintage is almost as ineffectual as saying it's nice or good.

Let's take a look at a few of these adjectives. As used in eBay auctions, *rare* is often redundant, as in saying that an original Mozart manuscript is rare. It's not as if people expect to find these for sale at Wal-Mart or the local convenience store, so you don't need to hit potential buyers over the head with the fact that this is a rare item.

Unique is rarely used properly. If there is more than one of an item, it's not unique. I am unique. You're unique. The *Mona Lisa* is unique. The 40 pairs of hoop earrings you're selling are not unique.

Cool is a subjective term. I think ZZ Top and Boz Skaggs are cool. You think Buck Owens and Loretta Lynn are cool. It is unlikely that I'll accept you as the arbiter of cool and vice versa. Someone who doesn't know you is unlikely to accept your assessment of what's cool, so why even bother offering your opinion? Let the buyer decide what's cool.

As for *awesome*, well, maybe I am missing something, but the diaper bags, maternity shirts, shower curtains, and Gill Tomblin plates I've seen described as awesome on eBay just don't inspire a sense of awe in me. Actually, *awesome* makes me think of the movie *Bill and Ted's Excellent Adventure* or the tornado I lived through. I see few items on eBay that are awesome. Still, sellers routinely describe thousands of unlikely items as having the power to instill awe. All that aside, no one uses these words in searches—unless it's someone curious to see how many fools waste title space with them.

Don't use lame, clichéd adjectives to describe your item. Put your limited title space to positive use with words that have real meaning and that buyers will be using for searches. Use words that really *are* unusual—at least when it comes to eBay auction titles. Describe an unusual item as *odd, strange, eerie,* or *noteworthy.* These are far more effective than *cool, awesome,* or *unique,* and they rarely appear in eBay titles. Image-evoking nouns—such as *relic, objet d'art,* and *artifact*—or antiquated terms like *divan* (in place of *sofa*) can also get attention. Just make sure the words you choose are accurate and not misleading.

NOTE   *A thesaurus or synonym dictionary can be a useful tool when you're writing titles and descriptions. If you use Microsoft Word, you can use its built-in thesaurus feature to suggest attention-getting words (which you may be forced to do after this book has been out for a while and sellers start taking my advice).*

If you can't come up with anything attention-getting, that's okay—just plug in a descriptive word or two. "Clean and neat antique hassock" will get more attention than "Antique hassock."

Print Pyrotechnics and Eyestrain

Forget using textual pyrotechnics, such as "LQQK, KEWEL!!!!!!!! Check it out!!!" in your titles. Many people find this sort of thing childish and annoying. Plus, it makes one wonder how cool an item is if you need to work that hard to sell it.

Loading up empty space with !!!!! doesn't get people excited about your item either. Exclamation points are so common that they're often ignored. At best, an overabundance of exclamation marks tags you as someone who thinks buyers are naive or ignorant enough to believe that !!!!! means something. The same is true of blocks of characters, such as $$$$$$ or 00000000. Ditto mIXeD CapItAl leTtErS and using @, #, %, &, ~, and other symbols in an attempt to force the reader to look at your title. These tricks will arrest the eye, but they do not say anything positive about you or your item. In general, using such tactics repels more buyers than it attracts and wastes space that you could have used to include keywords that buyers use in searches.

Ways to Be Informative

If an item lacks any really unusual traits, focus on its most important elements (which are what you want to communicate anyway). Let the browsing buyer know whether the item is large or small, long or short, and from the 1920s or the 1960s. Use brand names (Wrigley, Crosley, Rolls-Royce, P&G, and so on) as appropriate, because the familiar attracts attention.

"Just the Facts, Ma'am"

Stick with objective facts in describing the item. Don't bother trying to tell the buyer that your item is "great." The presence or absence of greatness is for the buyer to judge. And besides, telling a customer how *great, wonderful, lovely,* or *excellent* something is smacks of high-pressure sales. This makes a person wonder why you need to push the item so aggressively.

So, in instead of writing this:

GREAT watch w/stainless steel band, digital & analog

try a title like this:

Dual-time watch stainless steel band, digital & analog

This puts emphasis on the dual-time feature. If you don't want to be redundant, write this:

Dual-time watch w/stainless steel band waterproof NR

Consider the difference between the first and third examples. The first tells the buyer, "This is a watch *I* think is great. It has a stainless steel band and tells time in digital and analog formats." (The *w/* is an abbreviation for *with.*) It presents three facts and distracts the reader with opinion. And, as the seller, your opinion is pretty much useless; of course, you're going to say it's great—you're trying to sell it! The third example is more informative. It says, "This is a watch that tells time in digital and analog formats. It has a stainless steel band and it is waterproof." NR indicates that there is No Reserve. This title presents four facts and is uncluttered by opinion or the hard sell. Every word conveys information the reader wants or needs to know.

NOTE *You may have noticed that some titles contain spellings or word usages that seem to make no sense. These are a sort of shorthand that enables the seller to pack more into a title. As you've seen, NR means No Reserve, and w/ means with. You can probably work out what many of the abbreviations mean, but to make things easy, I have included a list of abbreviations and shorthand phrases commonly used on eBay in the appendix.*

Make Negative Features Appealing

While it's usually a bad idea to play up an item's negative aspects, you can occasionally use them to your advantage. Imagine that you have a broken antique clock. You could list it with this title:

Seth Thomas octagon wall clock, not working

It identifies the item and provides an important fact. You also get credit for honesty.

Although "not working" gives potential buyers a reason not to bid on the clock, you should keep this fact in the title. But can you find a way to present the fact that the clock isn't working in a positive light? You might break the news with more words (a time-honored technique for blunting sharp truths): "in need of repair."

Then consider, if some buyers won't bid on the clock because it's broken, are there buyers who *will* bid on it because it's broken? As a matter of fact, there are, and you can reach them with this title:

Seth Thomas octagon wall clock, FIX ME!

Or, better yet, try this approach:

Unrestored Seth Thomas octagon wall clock!

Suddenly, the clock's negative characteristic becomes a positive. Mechanically inclined buyers realize that here's an opportunity for a real bargain. It also catches the attention of antique collectors, since *unrestored* is one of their buzzwords. The clock sells, and the crowd cheers!

You can also put a positive spin on negative features in descriptions, where you'll have more room to make your point.

Use Keywords in Titles

Usually, your title is placed in front of potential buyers because of a keyword search. In fact, most searchers search only item titles. A study by Sellathon, creator of the ViewTracker auction data analysis tool, revealed that more than 85 percent of eBay searches are title-only searches, even though a title-only search is less effective. This is largely because it's the default search parameter setting on eBay, although a few searchers choose it deliberately to narrow the number of results.

So, if you want the majority of searchers to find your auctions, put as many keywords in your titles as possible.

NOTE *While titles often draw buyers to look at your auction, they probably landed there first by a keyword search, which makes the presence of appropriate keywords in your title and description vital.*

Occasionally, keywords may be the only words that you can put into a title. Sometimes, it is impossible to come up with a phrase that states everything you want to say about your listing, because your item has too many appealing elements. When this happens, try filling the title with nothing but keywords, as in this example, which appeared on eBay recently:

RUTH NICHOLS 1956 BOOK POWDER PUFF DERBY 99'S AVIATION

The book advertised is an autobiography of a pioneering woman airplane pilot, published in 1956. The title pretty much covers all the basics, in 55 characters. Of course, it might mean little to someone who doesn't recognize the name Ruth Nichols or doesn't know much about early aviation and women pilots. But anyone who is likely to want to buy this book will know immediately what the title is about. And in case you haven't picked them out, the keywords aren't all single words. Two are key phrases: "Ruth Nichols," of course, and "Powder Puff Derby," which was the nickname for a women's air race.

Avoid Misleading Text

Don't mislead people into looking at your listings. Putting an irrelevant title like this:

FREE GASOLINE For Life!!!!

on a listing for designer shoes or a board game may draw some people to view your listing, but they won't be pleased, and they won't be bidding.

On a more subtle level, don't mislead the buyer by juggling words. If, for example, you are trying to sell a new watch with the image of a 1929 Model T Ford on the face, use this title:

New watch with 1929 Ford Model T on face

instead of this misleading title:

Rare 1929 Ford Model A Watch!!!!!!

This implies that you are selling a watch that was made in 1929, perhaps for the use of a Ford automobile owner. (Also, it's probably not rare.)

This isn't technically illegal or false advertising, but it is dishonest.

No Mysteries

Avoid being mysterious in your titles. An auction title like "Car" or "Buick" might draw in two or three people who want to see what kind of item could inspire such an uninformative header, but most browsers will skip to auction titles that give them a better idea of what's being offered.

I have encountered several sellers who used one- or two-word auction titles only because they were sure that buyers would understand what they meant merely by consulting the categories in which the items were listed. A man who was trying to sell a baseball cap with a Ford emblem on it listed it in eBay Motors/Parts & Accessories/Apparel & Merchandise/Car & Truck/Hats, with the title "New Ford Logo." He figured that anyone who saw his title would know it referred to a hat because of the category. What he didn't consider was the fact that the category would not be displayed with the auction title. Another seller made a similar error in trying to sell an antique lamp by placing it in an Antiques category with only the word "Lamp" as the title. Because not everyone pays attention to categories, both of these sellers missed potential bids.

All other considerations aside, it is better to be informative than attention-getting in your titles. When you must choose, go for the words that say something meaningful about your item. More often than not, these are the same words that buyers use in searches.

WHAT DO SPAM, POP-UPS, AND MISLEADING TITLES HAVE IN COMMON?

Being forced to look at ads in which you have no interest is infuriating. When you come down to it, misleading titles on auction listings are no different from spam or pop-up windows, in that they are attempts to force people to look at something they wouldn't choose to view. That's why eBay has a rule against misleading auction titles (sometimes referred to as *subject headers*).

If you think a misleading auction title is a clever idea, stop and consider the tens of millions of spam-hating curmudgeons like me out there, many of whom will go to great lengths to avoid your auction listings once you've proven yourself to be deceptive. And actually, no great effort is involved in filtering a specific seller's listings out of an eBay search; eBay's advanced search offers a tool that does exactly that.

When Items Sell Themselves

Some items sell themselves and don't really need to be described or touted as fabulous, great, or in excellent condition. CDs by well-known contemporary recording artists are like that. Take a look at ads for the latest CDs from companies like CBS, MCA, and RCA, and you'll see what I mean. Most ads for albums by established singers or groups simply show the album cover. The record companies know that all they need to do is advise buyers that the album is available. They don't need to "sell" fans on music from someone they already like.

The same thing is true on eBay. If you're selling a CD by the Beatles, all you need to put in the title is this:

New CD, "Abbey Road," Beatles

People will be interested or not interested based on the title and artist. You can't add anything else that will make more people look at the listing or bid on the CD.

But, harking back to my earlier advice, if there is something unusual about the CD, put it in the title. Maybe it's an import that's not generally available where you live. In that case, you would include that information because it sets your CD apart from others of the same title. So, you might write this:

New CD, "Abbey Road," Beatles, Hong Kong version

How to Write Effective Descriptions

An auction description's primary goals are to inform and interest. It should open with basic, general information about your item, then flesh out the picture with more specific details and any additional information of interest.

NOTE *According to studies by Sellathon, half of all auctions are viewed for 10 seconds or less. This means you have less than 10 seconds to convince the potential buyer to consider bidding on your item.*

In some respects, an effective description is like a newspaper story. The lead paragraph offers the most important facts, and the paragraphs that follow fill in the details. But instead of who, what, when, where and why, an auction description provides facts such as the age, condition, size, and color of the item, as well as any extra information (such as whether the item is damaged, an out-of-production model, and so forth), and payment and shipping instructions.

eBay puts no limit on the size of descriptions but, ideally, your descriptions will be concise and to the point, like the example in Figure 10-2.

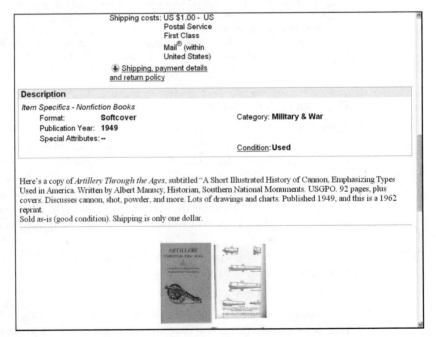

Figure 10-2: Example of a brief auction item description

What to Put in a Description

An important objective in writing an auction item description is to include everything the potential buyer might want to know. This benefits you as well as the buyer by eliminating questions. Some buyers aren't patient enough to ask questions, so if your listing is missing some vital information, you could lose bids and never know it.

Start by asking yourself what you would want to know about the item if you were a buyer. Then write a first draft that describes the item as if you weren't going to post photos of it. Describing something in this way ensures that you will consider all its aspects—size, shape, color, and so on. You can delete extraneous material before you post the listing.

Be honest in your descriptions. If you exaggerate or lie, and someone comes along who knows you're not telling the whole truth, you may end up losing potential bidders in your current and future auctions. Being truthful is the best way to ensure Positive Feedback and repeat business.

When it's relevant, include anything interesting about where and how you came by the item. Antiques dealers and appraisers call this *provenance*. Good provenance can increase an item's value. Something along the lines of, "I bought this at an auction of Howard Hughes' Long Beach storage locker contents," or "I worked on the demolition of Union Terminal and rescued these wall sconces just minutes before the wrecking ball would have taken them out," can add to the item's appeal.

Give the buyer some extra facts or entertaining information when you can. I've added information such as how many companies manufactured similar items or the fact that the company that made a certain toy originally manufactured shoes. This personalizes the item and kicks up the interest factor. It can also catch the eye of collectors who might not be a part of the primary market.

Avoid irrelevant and unnecessary comments, because they're a distraction and can make the customer lose interest. Going into a sob story about how much you need the money from the sale or telling the life story of the author of the book you're trying to sell can lose the reader and cost you a sale.

Inane lines like, "This would look great in your collection!" or "The perfect gift for any collector!" are a waste of space. Do you think the buyer is stupid and doesn't realize that someone who collects coins might enjoy receiving the 1804 silver dollar you've listed as a gift? People who are searching for items are usually quite aware of how collectible those items are, and they're bored by your assessments.

NOTE   *If you do a lot of cutting and pasting of descriptions or plugging in text provided by listing software, double-check the text to make sure it's appropriate. I've seen "Makes a GREAT Gift!" mindlessly appended to things like frying pans and batteries, and "Wonderful for the collector!" used to describe diaper bags.*

As I mentioned earlier, some items sell themselves. If you're selling a CD of the Beatles' *Abbey Road*, you don't need to include a biography of the Beatles or a review of the CD in the description. Such things have no influence on buying decisions; the buyers either want that album or they don't. Cram too much into descriptions, and you may send buyers skittering over to another seller who won't force them to wait for 100 KB of text to load before they can bid.

What's Not Permitted in Descriptions

eBay has some rules limiting what can be put into item descriptions. You can't include the following:

- Racist, hateful, sexual, or obscene language
- HTML or JavaScript functions that read or place cookies on computers or otherwise make changes on computers
- Pop-up windows
- Links to sites that offer to sell or trade goods outside eBay
- Links to sites that offer merchandise prohibited on eBay
- Links to chat systems

Why Bother with Good Writing?

Unintelligible writing is not prohibited on eBay, although it should be. Buyers are going to judge your item not only by what you say about it, but also by *how* you say it. And your item description is going to be the basis for their opinion of *you*. So, if your writing comes across as ignorant and careless, buyers will think the same of you. And they may wonder just how accurate your description is, not to mention your approach to doing business.

For these reasons, you should make your eBay listings as eloquent and well written as possible. Yes, it takes a little longer than pounding out the first thing that comes to your mind and not spell-checking it, but, hey—this isn't like a school assignment; you're being *paid* to write this stuff. Or you will be, if you get it right.

Look at this description for an old radio. It is, unfortunately, representative of thousands of descriptions posted every day.

> here for your bids is on an old wooden crosely tube type radio.radio plays good on am.i bought this at the flea market.case appears to have been refinished and looks good.it is solid but has a few places where the veneer has been patched opr reglued and has a stain on top of it and a small crack on the top left side.cloth also has been replaced.still has the original factory sticker on bottom but solme of it appears to have been scratched off.next is it dial.it is BACKWARDS!!!the numbers are backwards on the dial.when on the high numbers with the pointer you're actually on the low frequency.one of our local stations here is am 700 and it comes in on about 4 instead of 7.very unusual.maybe this was made like this on purpose but i have no idea why.if anyone knows anything about this backwards dial please email me and let me know if i haven't described this radio properly..if you need any more information email me and i'll try to answer any questions.sold as is with a low reserve!buyer pays shipping.

This really appeared in an eBay listing. As you can see, the writer just jumped in and started pounding the keys with both feet when it came time to write the description. It was apparently too much trouble for this guy to use the SHIFT key, not to mention spell-checking his prose. Details such as the size and model number seem to have eluded him as well.

I don't need to tell you that reading this description is torturous. I'm certain more than a few shoppers gave up and clicked the Back button before they got to the fifth line.

The accompanying photos were almost as bad. They looked like this guy just threw the radio on the couch and took three pictures from above.

The radio drew a few desultory bids, no doubt because it was a model easily recognized by collectors despite the poor-quality photos (except those collectors who couldn't wade through the description to get to the photos).

If you read through the description, you probably saw, as I did, that this guy is not illiterate. So why didn't he use that part of his brain when he wrote this? I don't know. Maybe he was just lazy and in a hurry. One thing I do know: This sloppy description cost him money!

NOTE *Make sure you proofread each description you write. There are any number of potential goofs you can make that a spell-checker won't catch. For example, you might describe a commemorative wall decoration as a "commemorative plague." Your spell-checker will think that's fine, but everyone who might be interested in your item will be searching for a plaque. If you are not good at catching mistakes, try printing out your descriptions and proofing them in hardcopy.*

A Template for Auction Descriptions

All the information you need to convey to a buyer can be broken down into four sections or paragraphs:

Basics
The basics paragraph states exactly what the item is and describes its primary characteristics and attributes—everything the buyer wants to know right away.

Details
The details paragraph expands on the basics, addressing secondary issues and answering any questions the first paragraph might raise.

Extras
The extras paragraph lets the buyer know if the item has any special features, such as a reference manual, carrying case, and so on. This section is also where you mention any negatives—defects, damage, missing parts, and the like. This earns the buyer's trust and gives her some assurance of your honesty.

Wrap-up
The wrap-up paragraph gives details about payment, shipping, and the like. It should be as brief and clear as possible. This section usually states the seller's Terms of Service, as described later in this chapter.

Let's try a description using this template. Suppose you're selling a new TimeOx watch that has both digital and analog displays (the same one used as an example earlier in this chapter) with this auction title:

Dual-time watch w/stainless steel band waterproof NR

Someone spots your listing's title, either as she is browsing the Jewelry & Watches/Watches/Wristwatches category or because she ran a search for a dual-time watch. She likes your minimum bid and decides to take a closer look. Now, what facts does this person want to know right away? Put yourself in her place, and you'll probably come up with these questions:

- Who made the watch?
- Is it new?
- Is it styled for men, women, or unisex?
- Is it wind-up, battery-powered, or self-winding?
- What kind of fastener does the band have and is it flexible?
- Is there a guarantee?

Given those questions, the basics paragraph of the description almost writes itself:

> This is a new TimeOx dual-time men's watch. It is battery-powered. The stretch band uses a clasp fastener and is designed to stretch up to a half-inch, and will fit most wrists. It has a limited warranty.

Next comes the details paragraph:

> This watch is in the original package with all papers. It is just like new, with no scrapes or scratches.

Followed by the extras paragraph:

> This watch is a discontinued model, which is why I can sell it at such a low price. If the watch does not work, you can return it to us or to TimeOx for replacement within 30 days of when we ship it.

Finally, here's the wrap-up:

> Shipping is via Priority Mail only, with the watch packed carefully in foam. I accept money orders only. Payment must be made within 10 days of the auction's end, unless you make other arrangements.

That covers everything a watch buyer would want to know, including the negatives: that the watch has a limited warranty and is a discontinued model. But the second negative is also a positive, because it explains why the watch is selling for such a low price, which reassures the potential buyer that this is not a copy or a piece of junk.

Beyond this, you might enhance the description by referring to the watch as "modern" or "Grecian-style." Sometimes, a little extra buzz in the description helps, and sometimes it's meaningless. Ideally, a photo or photos of the watch will accompany the description, so the buyer can decide for herself whether the watch is beautiful.

Let's try this exercise again, this time with a collectible: a radio/record player combo made by RCA in 1942. The radio part works, but the record player doesn't. The cherry wood case is in good shape, though it has a small crack, and you have the original owner's manual and a spare needle. You also have some history of the radio, both of this specific set and the model.

What does the potential buyer want to know? He is interested in whether the set works, its age, its model number, and its primary features.

Here is the basics paragraph:

> For your consideration, a 1942 RCA radio receiver with turntable for playing 78-RPM records, in a cherry wood cabinet. The model number is RM-23AC. The radio works but the turntable does not move.

The fact that the turntable is not working is important enough to state at the beginning, rather than saving it for the extras paragraph.

Next, you write the details paragraph:

> The lighted dial has a green overlay, and the tuner is mounted vertically. The original owner's manual is included, plus a spare needle for the record player.

And then the extras paragraph:

> This model is relatively scarce, because RCA switched to war production just as this model year began. The case has a hairline crack along the front, just beneath the speaker, that runs for four inches. This is otherwise in good condition except for several decades of dirt and grease buildup. (For the last 32 years, this unit sat on top of a refrigerator in the kitchen of my Uncle Bob's restaurant.)

Ending with your wrap-up paragraph:

> UPS shipping for this item will be between $8 and $12, depending on where you live in the U.S. (Will not ship outside the U.S.) We accept PayPal and money orders.

Keywords in Descriptions and Keyword Spamming

Knowing that the majority of eBay buyers find their items through searches, you want to be sure that your listing includes any keywords that might be used to search for your item. You can include keywords in your description, but remember that many people search only by title. So, for the radio/record player combo in the preceding example, you might add keywords and phrases at the end of the title like this:

FORTIES OLD BROADCAST SET RECORD PLAYER ANTIQUE

Some sellers operate under the mistaken impression that getting more people to look at a listing will automatically result in more and higher bids. This is not true, but sellers still try to force people to look at their items by adding totally irrelevant keywords.

For example, a seller may be offering a power-steering gear for a Ford automobile. The gear will not fit on any other kind of automobile, but the seller includes the brand names of other cars at the end of the description, anyway:

CHEVROLET JAGUAR PLYMOUTH HONDA TUCKER
CROSLEY DODGE FRANKLIN HUMBER ROLLS ROYCE
HUDSON KAISER ALLSTATE EAGLE ISUZU TRIUMPH
BENTLEY CHRYSLER IMPERIAL CADILLAC FRAZIER

The item offered cannot be used with any of these automobiles, but the seller mindlessly (or stupidly) includes them, hoping to capture dozens or hundreds of searchers, who will then offer bids. But—surprise!—people who own the cars listed are *not* going to bid on an item that is made for a Ford.

If you do this consistently, the odds are good that enough annoyed buyers will complain to eBay. Additionally, searchers will add your seller ID to the list of specific sellers whose items are excluded from their search results lists. This means you'll lose bids you might have gotten, had you not tried to force people to look at irrelevant items.

NOTE *Saying that an item is "not" a certain brand can be considered keyword spamming as well. For example, posting a handbag and including "not Gucci" in the title or description will cause your item to appear among search results for Gucci handbags— putting your listing right in the faces of people who don't want to see it.*

Similarly, someone selling a TimeOx watch might include the names of other watch brands like Seiko, Bulova, Gruen, Omega, and so on, apparently hoping that someone looking for one of those other watch brands will be persuaded to buy his TimeOx watch instead.

Needless to say, this wastes a lot of time and annoys people who aren't looking for what the seller has to offer—which is why people who indulge in keyword spamming are usually reported and made to remove the keywords.

Those considerations aside, statistical analysis of the amount of time buyers spend looking at auctions indicates that they spend *less* time viewing auctions whose descriptions have unrelated keywords than they do auctions with legitimate descriptions. According to AuctionBytes.com, an analysis of data from thousands of auctions revealed that the average time a buyer looks at an eBay item that interests him is 26 seconds. When inaccurate keywords are used in the auction title or description, visitors spend an average of 2.9 seconds on the auction. You do the math.

Rather than drawing more bids, the most you can expect from keyword spamming is for your hit counter to go up.

How to Use HTML in Listings

To enhance your item descriptions, you can use HTML to format text, such as to set apart specific paragraphs or sentences and add emphasis. HTML code can also be used to insert images into descriptions (provided they are stored online) and link to more information about an item.

eBay's standard editor, shown in Figure 10-3, makes it easy to incorporate simple HTML coding for text size and font, effects like italics and bold, and layout elements such as text centering.

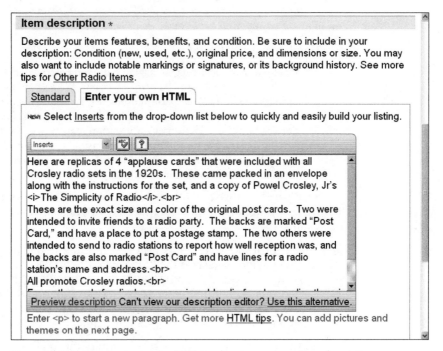

Item description *

Describe your items features, benefits, and condition. Be sure to include in your description: Condition (new, used, etc.), original price, and dimensions or size. You may also want to include notable markings or signatures, or its background history. See more tips for <u>Other Radio Items</u>.

Standard | **Enter your own HTML**

NEW! Select <u>Inserts</u> from the drop-down list below to quickly and easily build your listing.

Inserts ▼

Here are replicas of 4 "applause cards" that were included with all Crosley radio sets in the 1920s. These came packed in an envelope along with the instructions for the set, and a copy of Powel Crosley, Jr's <i>The Simplicity of Radio</i>.
These are the exact size and color of the original post cards. Two were intended to invite friends to a radio party. The backs are marked "Post Card," and have a place to put a postage stamp. The two others were intended to send to radio stations to report how well reception was, and the backs are also marked "Post Card" and have lines for a radio station's name and address.
All promote Crosley radios.

Preview description Can't view our description editor? Use this alternative.

Enter <p> to start a new paragraph. Get more **HTML tips**. You can add pictures and themes on the next page.

Figure 10-3: Using eBay's standard HTML editor to create an item description

With this tool, you can select any of five different fonts, as well as text size and color. You can also mix fonts within the text. Also available are text effects—italics, bold, and underline—and tools that allow you to center, right-justify, or left-justify text; create bulleted or numbered lists; and create a hanging indent for paragraphs. You can also insert prepared HTML, such as a link to your other items or an image with a logo or message. These are the only HTML enhancements most eBay sellers want or need.

This editor will also spell-check your descriptions (an excellent idea).

If you use eBay's standard HTML editor to create a description, do not type or paste in HTML code. It will be ignored and displayed exactly as you enter it.

Seller Terms of Service

Most eBay sellers have a set of rules by which they do business. These are referred to as *Terms of Service,* or, more commonly, *TOS.* A seller's TOS statement is usually placed at the end of a description (in the wrap-up section) and addresses things such as the kinds of payment accepted, how soon after the end of an auction payment must arrive, shipping matters, and so forth. One of the best things you can do to eliminate buyer problems is to make sure your TOS description is as clear and concise as you can make it.

NOTE *If you have had problems with buyers in the past and want to avoid more of the same, eBay offers several features that allow you to block certain buyers and specify criteria for bidders (see Chapter 6). The latter include blocking bids from countries to which you don't want to ship, bidders who have low Feedback scores, bidders who have a recent record of not paying, and bidders who don't have a PayPal account.*

Here's a typical TOS:

> Please write to receive a go-ahead to bid if you have recent Negative Feedback or fewer than 10 Feedback points. We accept PayPal, money orders, checks, or cash (at your risk); payment is expected within 10 days of the auction's end. Shipping is by U.S. Postal Service, only, with Delivery Confirmation mandatory. If you do not buy insurance, we will not be responsible for loss or damage by the Postal Service. Refund of purchase price is offered only if merchandise is returned intact within 15 days.

That's informative and about as lengthy as a TOS should be. Not all TOS descriptions are this polite. Some, like this one, are downright rude and threatening:

> NO BIDDERS WITH LESS THAN 10 FEEDBACK ALLOWED!!!!!
> NO PAYPAL, CASH ONLY!!!!! PAY WITHIN 7 DAYS OR YOU
> **WILL** RECEIVE NPD STRIKE AND *****NEGATIVE
> FEEDBACK!!!!!!!!!!!***** MUST PAY EXTRA FOR INSURANCE!!!!!
> WE ARE NOT RESPONSIBLE FOR LOSS TO POST OFFICE'S!!!!
> NO REFUNDS!!, SO DON'T ASK!!!!!!!!!!!!!

All those capital letters and exclamation points really make you want to do business with this seller, don't they?

This is akin to a shop owner standing inside his door and shrieking, "Nobody allowed who hasn't already bought something here! No shoplifting! No checks! If you go anywhere near the door without paying, I'll call the cops on you! You touch it, you buy it! No refunds!"

Threats don't make friends, and a belligerent TOS can drive away customers. The example shown here reads as if the seller is *expecting* to have problems, and quite often those who expect problems find them, even if they aren't really there. Many buyers know this and will click the Back button as soon as they see this sort of TOS.

In addition to price, your TOS should include an explanation of any handling charges. If you send an invoice to an auction winner saying that her total cost is $6.50 plus shipping of 83 cents, *plus* a $3.00 handling charge, and you didn't mention the charge in your TOS, that's extortion. The buyer will be entirely within her rights to thumb her nose at you and refuse to pay. (Plus, since you were trying to extort money from her, any Non-Paying Bidder report or Negative Feedback from you will be canceled by eBay.)

Would it have still been extortion if you had mentioned the $3 handling fee in your TOS? Technically, no, but it would have been unethical. While it's reasonable for you to have expenses, there is no way that packaging a DVD and driving to the post office will cost you $3. Remember that you're taking another dozen items to the post office with you at the same time. And you're stopping by the grocery store on the way home and running a few other errands. If you're honest with the IRS and prorate the post office part of the trip, that part of your "expense" is a few cents. And you won't even incur that expense if you have the U.S. Postal Service pick up your items at no cost.

Your expenses are part of the cost of doing business, and they should be reflected in your prices. To add a surcharge for expenses is lying to the customer, telling her that she "won" the DVD for $6.50 but she can't actually have it for that price. Instead, she must pay $9.50.

In the end, a "handling charge" is a fiction—a way to dupe the customer into thinking she is paying less for an item. So, rather than mislead your customers, you should build your expenses into your minimum bids or fixed prices.

EBAY IS NOT A MAIL-ORDER COMPANY

Sure, Victoria's Secret pulls the "handling charges" trick on its customers, which is to say that Victoria's Secret is yanking its customers for some extra dollars, too. (And, in some instances, probably exempting the charge from sales tax, not unlike you adding a large handling fee and exempting that part of what you get for your items from the final value fees.)

Does your grocery store shake you down for an extra five bucks "handling fee" on your week's food supply, to pay for those bags and their clerks? No, the cost is built into the prices—the shakedown comes at that end.

If your grocery store reduced the price of coffee, then added a handling charge because it has expenses related to bringing the coffee to customers, you would cry "Foul!" But too many people accept what is effectively the same practice on eBay, simply because they are accustomed to dealing with mail-order companies.

About Audio, Video, and 100+ KB Images

Some of you, after you've been posting items for a while, will be tempted to start dressing up your listings with photos, cartoons, and sounds that have nothing to do with your auction items. This may sound like fun, but I can guarantee you that most auction buyers won't be impressed with photos of your pets, Kermit the Frog, or your grandchildren. Instead, they'll click the Back button, rather than wait for a bunch of cutesy images to load. The only images they want to see are photos of the item for sale.

And *don't add music or video to your listings*! Buyers aren't looking to you to provide some kind of virtual shopping environment. Sharing your musical tastes or a movie of your cat won't entice anyone to buy your item. If anything, it will drive them away.

Worse, music and video slow down the loading of the listing page and may crash some web browsers. Not too many people will be dying to give you money after you crash their browsers!

For similar reasons, you should avoid including photos larger than 100 KB in descriptions. Instead, provide thumbnails with links for viewing the full images. Remember that your goal is to sell your items to buyers, not entertain, overwhelm, or intimidate them.

If you follow the advice in this chapter and have a good item, it should sell. But it sometimes happens that an item doesn't sell the first time around. If this happens, don't despair; read the next chapter!

11

IT DIDN'T SELL!

You sign on to My eBay and scroll down to the Items I'm Selling list, where you find that three of your auctions have ended. From there, you move to the Items I've Sold list, and—whoops!—the number of items sold is the same as it was yesterday, which must mean . . . you didn't sell anything! Why not, and what can you do about it? Although the most frequent reason items don't sell is because the price is too high, that's not the only reason. The problem may be the title, description, or something else. In this chapter, I'll cover how to relist an item and how to improve your chances of selling it.

How to Relist an Item

Relisting an item is simple. Click the Relist link next to an item in your Unsold Items listing or from within the listing itself. You'll see a page similar to the one shown in Figure 11-1.

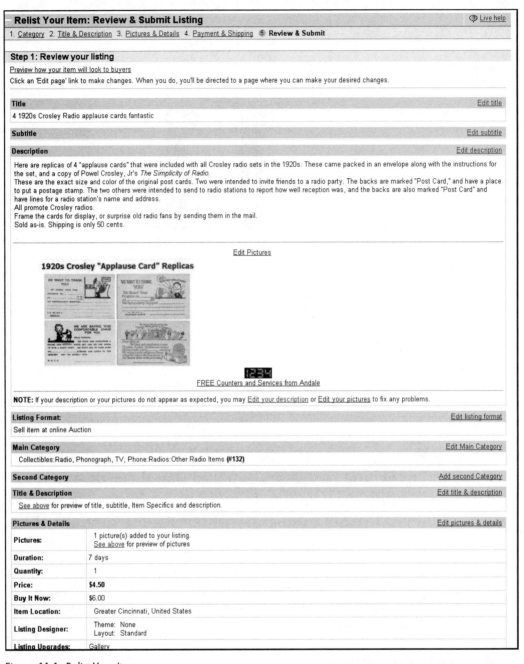

Relist Your Item: Review & Submit Listing   👁 Live help

1. Category 2. Title & Description 3. Pictures & Details 4. Payment & Shipping ⑤ **Review & Submit**

Step 1: Review your listing

Preview how your item will look to buyers

Click an 'Edit page' link to make changes. When you do, you'll be directed to a page where you can make your desired changes.

Title   Edit title

4 1920s Crosley Radio applause cards fantastic

Subtitle   Edit subtitle

Description   Edit description

Here are replicas of 4 "applause cards" that were included with all Crosley radio sets in the 1920s. These came packed in an envelope along with the instructions for the set, and a copy of Powel Crosley, Jr's *The Simplicity of Radio*.
These are the exact size and color of the original post cards. Two were intended to invite friends to a radio party. The backs are marked "Post Card," and have a place to put a postage stamp. The two others were intended to send to radio stations to report how well reception was, and the backs are also marked "Post Card" and have lines for a radio station's name and address.
All promote Crosley radios.
Frame the cards for display, or surprise old radio fans by sending them in the mail.
Sold as-is. Shipping is only 50 cents.

Edit Pictures

1920s Crosley "Applause Card" Replicas

FREE Counters and Services from Andale

NOTE: If your description or your pictures do not appear as expected, you may Edit your description or Edit your pictures to fix any problems.

Listing Format: Edit listing format

Sell item at online Auction

Main Category   Edit Main Category

Collectibles:Radio, Phonograph, TV, Phone:Radios:Other Radio Items **(#132)**

Second Category   Add second Category

Title & Description   Edit title & description

See above for preview of title, subtitle, Item Specifics and description.

Pictures & Details   Edit pictures & details

Pictures:	1 picture(s) added to your listing. See above for preview of pictures
Duration:	7 days
Quantity:	1
Price:	**$4.50**
Buy It Now:	$6.00
Item Location:	Greater Cincinnati, United States
Listing Designer:	Theme: None Layout: Standard
Listing Upgrades:	Gallery

Figure 11-1: Relist Your Item page

As you can see, this page is similar to the Review Listing page you saw when you first posted the item. Click any link at the right to make changes to the item's title or description, price, listing format, photos, and so on.

But Is It Worth Relisting?

Your first consideration for an item that didn't sell is whether it is worth relisting. Sometimes, an item just won't sell on eBay. Your plan for painting smiley faces on old CDs to use as decorations may have seemed like a good idea at the time, but perhaps you should give it another look before reposting. That old die-cast car with the broken axle may not be the collectible you thought it was; a little research might inform you that nobody collects these cars unless they're absolutely perfect. And it just may be that not one of eBay's millions of members is at all interested in an empty oatmeal box from 1997.

On the other hand, if you see other sellers getting a lot of bids for the same or similar items, it's probably worth relisting. The first thing you should consider is cutting the price.

Should You Reduce the Price?

A low minimum bid on a popular or otherwise appealing item can generate quite a bit of activity. At the same time, a minimum bid that is too high can discourage bidders.

Sometimes, people refuse to bid on an item because the minimum bid is too close to what they figure the selling price will be. This removes an element of fun from the auction by eliminating the possibility of getting a real bargain. Placing or watching bargain-level bids is a big attraction for some people, keeping them interested enough in an item to come back and place bids late in the auction, no matter how high the price goes. It's just another human quirk.

But sometimes the price is just too high. Here's a perfect example: an issue of *LIFE Magazine* from the 1930s, now being listed for—no kidding—the eighth time. This is not a particularly outstanding issue; no prominent Hollywood stars or political figures grace its pages, and it doesn't include coverage of any earthshaking events. It's just a typical issue. The seller, however, thinks it's really hot stuff. Perhaps he buys into the theory that, "It's big and it's old, so it must be worth something!" So, he has a minimum bid of $9.99 on it, with a Buy It Now price of $24.99, which is the same price at which he has listed it each and every time.

What's wrong with this picture? First, the seller has thus far spent $3.20 on listing fees. Second, if the seller had spent 15 seconds searching for this magazine on eBay, he would discover that issues of *LIFE* from the 1930s are selling every week for $5.99, which is less than his net profit will be if anyone happens to buy this magazine at his minimum bid.

The moral of the story: Research prices before you list, and if an item isn't selling, lower the price.

Minimize Competition

Before you relist the item, check for competing items and, if appropriate, delay your posting. Depending on how the sales of competing items are going, you may also wish to adjust your minimum bid.

Give some consideration to timing. Maybe your auction didn't end at the best time. Changing it to end earlier or later in the day may make it more attractive to some bidders. See Chapter 9 for more information about auction timing.

How to Improve the Listing

If you feel that an unsold item has potential and that price wasn't the primary reason it didn't sell, it's time to critique your listing.

First, return to Chapter 10 and review the information therein. See if you missed anything, and consider whether the advice in that chapter applies to your item.

Look at other listings for the same or similar items. Another seller may have thought of an angle that you missed.

Now, go back and consider the listing's category, title, description, and photos.

Check Your Category

Some items require unconventional presentation. For example, that 1935 magazine with a feature about the new Chevrolet model didn't sell in the Collectibles category. Maybe it will draw more interest and bids if you post it in the Chevrolet category of eBay Automotive.

Similarly, the old, beat-up trumpet that didn't sell when it was posted in the Musical Instruments category just might attract some buyers if you post it in Antiques.

Or maybe you have the right category, and just need to move to the right subcategory, to catch those buyers who browse categories. For example, I tried to sell a 1955 book on the history of aviation research and development that was published by the U.S. Air Force in the Collectibles/Militaria/1954-60 subcategory. It didn't get any bids. When I relisted it in the Collectibles/Historical Memorabilia/Space Programs subcategory, it sold with a Buy It Now bid within two hours of its posting.

Title Problems

Keep in mind that most eBay browsers and searchers are going to be attracted by your listing's title, so be critical of it. Try to view it as if it had been written by someone else, and ask yourself whether it is as informative and attention-getting as it can be.

If you can't think of any way to improve your title, have someone else read it. Often, all it takes is a different viewpoint to come up with exactly the right phrase.

Check Your Spelling

Imagine what would happen if you posted an Elvis Costello item and spelled the name with only one *l*. Probably nothing—which is the point. If people are looking for "Costello" and you offer "Costelo," they won't find your auction. Misspellings also detract from your credibility, so this advice applies to your description as well as your title. If given a choice to buy the same items from two different sellers, buyers are more likely to choose the one whose listing is free of careless errors. They don't want you misspelling their address so that the item gets lost in the mail.

Too Little Information?

Have you told the buyer everything there is to know about your item? If not, add the missing information. Sometimes, all you need is a couple of well-chosen words. For example, this title really isn't very informative:

> Old tube-type radio

but this one tells the reader exactly what she wants to know:

> 1930s RCA tube-type radio

and this one adds precision:

> 1937 RCA tube-type radio

Too Much Information?

Maybe the problem is that you're trying to tell the buyer too much in the listing title. Perhaps you're packing in information that belongs in the description. For example, this title offers too many details:

> 1930s tube radio with speaker needs repaired but works

And the truncated sentence may leave the reader wondering if you know what you're talking about. The reader probably won't be inclined to take a closer look.

This might be a better title:

> 1930s RCA radio with speaker, fixer-upper

It gives the reader enough information. Now, the browsing buyer knows the brand *and* the age of the radio *and* the fact that it needs repair. This description also accomplishes its task in fewer words, which can often draw attention, especially when everyone else is using lengthy titles.

Also, notice that *tube* is eliminated from the second description. Aside from toy crystal sets, tube-type radios were the only type available in the 1930s, so it's redundant to include both the vintage of the radio and the word *tube*.

The Right Keywords?

Do you have the proper keywords in the title to make it turn up in a search? Consider what you would be searching for if you were looking for the radio advertised by the title in the previous example. You would want to know the age, brand, unusual features, and condition. If, however, you don't collect old radios, you might not know that the age is important or that one brand is more valuable than another.

To find out just what's important to buyers of a given item, do a search for completed auctions and look at the keywords in the titles of the items that brought the highest prices. (Remember that you can sort the search results listing by price.)

Description Problems

You should have few problems with your description if you follow the template in Chapter 10. Still, you may find room for improvement.

Too Little Information?

Take a close look at the descriptions of completed items. Pay attention to the *kinds* of information provided by successful sellers. Maybe you're selling a piece of pottery from a recognized brand name—Rookwood or Roseville, for example. After reading several descriptions of this kind of pottery, you may find that the maker's mark can differ from one year to another. Or you may see that some pieces of this pottery have an extra letter or number on them that makes them particularly rare. These variations are exactly what savvy buyers will look for, but if you aren't a collector yourself, you wouldn't know to include this crucial information.

Too Much Information?

On the other hand, your problem may be that you've told the buyer too much, or at least more than someone needs to know to make a buying decision. This is a common mistake when you know quite a bit about an item and are enthusiastic about it. Keep in mind that too much information—relevant or not—can obscure the facts that the reader needs. Cut everything that doesn't directly drive the reader to consider buying the item you are offering.

Many buyers are turned off by lengthy listings, especially when they drone on about information that's irrelevant to the specific item for sale. For example, a popular fantasy writer has produced most of her work under the pen name Andre Norton. At one point, she wrote some romance novels using her real name, Mary Alice Norton. Her romance novels are highly collectible. That information, along with the title, publisher, and date of the book in question would be enough information for a listing. But I saw a listing for one of these novels that included an entire biography of the author (beginning with her birth) and listing her entire oeuvre. Ms. Norton was a very prolific author, and the description went on for pages. To top it off, the seller had copied the information verbatim from a website.

Questions about plagiarism aside, anyone who was looking for a book by Mary Alice Norton would already know her history. Someone unaware of her real name who was searching for books by Andre Norton might be more likely to buy the novel if he knew about the connection between Andre and Mary Alice Norton. But it's equally likely he would never wade through the description to learn about the connection. So, this seller was doing herself a disservice by dumping all the extraneous information in the description.

Some buyers are turned off by lengthy personal or "cute" stories in descriptions. Someone looking for a pink Princess phone won't necessarily want to slog through your memories of talking to your boyfriend on one of these back in 1962. Instead, she will go bid on someone else's pink Princess phone—one whose description includes the important facts and doesn't go off on a pointless tangent.

Image Problems

Keep in mind that your photos are the only view buyers have of your item. Are your photos out of focus, or are they too dark or too light? Consider reshooting them.

Be certain to capture the visual traits that your buying audience will respond to most strongly and that will make your item stand out distinctly from the competition. Rather than a photo of a computer motherboard just sitting there, a close-up of the main processor chip might be what grabs your buyer. If you're selling an automobile, you might make the main photo a close-up of the grille or the dashboard, instead of a picture of the car sitting in your driveway. Make sure the item is as close to the center of the photo as possible and that the focus is sharp.

Perhaps the issue isn't the quality but your choice of photo. Make sure you choose the most eye-catching visual as the item's gallery photo.

You may need to offer several views of the item you're selling to move your readers from window shoppers to active bidders. Particularly with expensive items, buyers will want to see it clearly from all angles before committing themselves to a purchase.

Revise a Listing Before the Auction Ends

Your auction has been running for three days, and not only are there no bidders, but the number of people viewing the listing is also low. What can you do?

Fortunately, eBay allows you to make changes to your auction listing while it is active, but with some restrictions. You cannot change from an auction format to a fixed-price format; this requires terminating the auction and relisting the item. If an auction has open bids or will end in 12 hours or less, you can only add to the item description or add seller features, such as a bold title or a gallery photo.

To revise an item, click the Revise link at the top of the auction listing. You will be presented with a page that indicates which areas you may change, as shown in Figure 11-2. Follow the same advice as for relisting a completed auction when revising an item that's still open to bids: look at the price, description, keywords, and so on.

Figure 11-2: Revise Your Item page

What Can You Do with Unsalable Items?

Not everything is salable. Some items, like 10-year-old oatmeal boxes, just don't have a market. An item that was sold successfully in the past may not sell when you post it, because only two people in the world want it, and they already bought it from other sellers.

What do you do with such an item? You might just put it out with the trash or donate it to a charity thrift store.

Another idea is to combine it with other items in an auction. Sometimes, the inclusion of a "bonus" item with a group or single item will make the difference between receiving bids and being ignored. Put **FREE BONUS** in the auction title and note that you are throwing in an item as a bonus. Given that the item hasn't sold before, it makes sense to label it as the bonus, rather than as the main item.

If an item doesn't sell after you've listed it several times, or even combined it with other items, you might need to forget about auctioning it. In that case, you can throw it out, donate it, or keep it until you have a yard sale. Or you can do as I have done with several items: wait a few months and try it again. It sometimes happens that the person who was looking for what you have to sell just didn't log on when you were offering it.

PART III

EBAY FOR BUYERS

12

BUYER DO'S AND DON'TS

The ideal eBay buyer bids high, acknowledges her win, and pays via PayPal within minutes of an auction closing. After this, the ideal buyer exhibits great patience while waiting for the item to arrive in the mail, is happy with her purchase, and leaves Positive Feedback and lavish praise for the seller the same day the merchandise arrives. This sort of buyer is also very rare, so eBay has created guidelines and rules for buyers. As you will learn in this chapter, there are more recommendations than hard-and-fast rules, but those rules will usually be enforced by sellers.

This chapter presents an overview of things you should know before you bid and buy on eBay, focusing on dealing with sellers. For actual hands-on bidding instructions and bidding strategies, see Chapters 13 and 14. For details on payment and shipping methods, see Chapter 15.

eBay Buyer Rules

eBay collects no money from buyers; most of its revenue comes from sellers. That being the case, the rules often seem to favor sellers, especially in giving sellers leverage against buyers. For example, while a system has been in effect for sellers to file official complaints against nonpaying buyers for most of eBay's life, it took nearly ten years before a similar system was inaugurated for buyers to file complaints against sellers who failed to ship items.

But eBay doesn't expect as much from buyers as from sellers either (see Chapter 6 for an idea of what eBay expects from sellers). The prime directive for eBay buyers is "Pay your seller quickly." As long as you do that, eBay is satisfied. Oh, you might draw eBay's attention if you post inappropriate material on a discussion board or in Feedback comments, but in the eyes of eBay, the only real crime you can commit is not paying a seller.

Complete information about eBay's rules and guidelines for buyers is available through eBay's Help system. From the Help page, click the eBay Policies link. From the Policies page, click the Rules for Buyers link, and you'll see a page like the one shown in Figure 12-1.

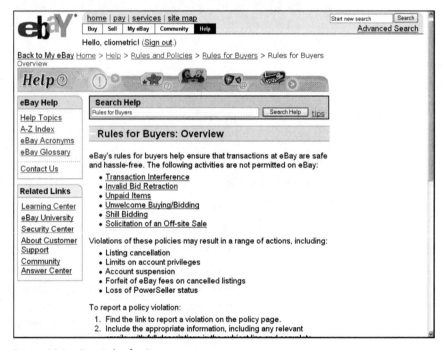

Figure 12-1: eBay Rules for Buyers page

Disciplinary Actions

To keep buyers in line, eBay early on established this commandment: "Each bid you place enters you in a binding contract" (or similar wording). It's often quoted by sellers in their item descriptions, as a sort of threat to bidders. The threat may be real (though it's never been tested in court), but if a bidder doesn't pay a seller, the bidder is not going to go to jail, get a black mark on her credit report, or have her wages or property garnished. The worst that can happen is that the errant bidder's account will be suspended, and her name smeared in email and on eBay bulletin boards.

However, if a buyer does not pay for her purchase in a timely manner, the seller can file a Payment Reminder. This gives eBay notice of a potential problem, and a staff member sends an email to the buyer (copying it the seller), reminding the seller that she still owes money for an item. It also causes a pop-up reminder window to appear when the recalcitrant bidder signs on to eBay. If the buyer persists in not paying, the seller can then file a Non-Paying Bidder Dispute. If that doesn't lead to resolution, the bidder may receive an Unpaid Item Strike, which is eBay's official black mark against a problem bidder. Accumulate three of these, and your eBay account *may* be terminated. For more details about Non-Paying Bidder Disputes, Unpaid Item Strikes, and what else a seller might do if you don't pay, see Chapter 15.

Communication and Payment Deadlines

A certain mythology has grown up around how quickly a buyer must pay a seller. eBay *recommends* that sellers and buyers contact each other within three business days after the end of an auction, but there is no official rule about this. Another misapprehension shared by many eBayers is the idea that payment must reach a seller within a certain number of days of the end of an auction. Here again, eBay offers only a *recommendation*: "As a professional courtesy, please pay the seller within three business days after the listing ends."

Many sellers stipulate a ten-day payment deadline for their own convenience, but eBay itself doesn't set any finite time periods. And it's worth noting that eBay does not allow sellers to file a Non-Paying Bidder Dispute until seven days from the end of the auction, so nothing "official" happens until then. A seller may "require" payment sooner, but his only leverage is the threat of Negative Feedback.

If all this seems a bit of a runaround, it is because eBay has cleverly set up its "rules" so that there is really no situation in which the company is obligated to enforce rules.

Time Limits for Refunds

Several time limits may affect your options involving a late or undelivered item. Unscrupulous sellers have been known to drag out a delivery problem beyond these limits with promises and excuses, so as to eliminate the buyer's ability to take action.

If you use PayPal, you have 45 days to file a claim for a refund on an item that was not received or that differs significantly from the seller's description. (Not all transactions are covered by the plan; if the PayPal Buyer Protection icon is not displayed in the Seller Information box in an eBay listing, it is not a covered listing.) PayPal limits members to three refund claims per year and refunds a buyer's money only after a detailed investigation of a claim. See Chapter 15 for more details about using PayPal.

If you paid a seller directly by credit card or through an online service payment funded by a credit card, there's probably a time limit for filing a "chargeback," which is another name for a refund. Review the rules for your card to find out what the deadline or other restrictions are for your particular account.

There are also limits on filing an Item Not Received report and on making a claim under eBay's Buyer Protection Plan, as described later in this chapter.

Contacting the Seller

Usually, sellers send email to buyers the same day an auction ends. For most auctions, one or more automated email messages are sent to the buyer to let him know he has won the auction—from eBay, PayPal, and/or an auction service. But this doesn't always happen, and for this reason and others, I recommend that you contact a seller directly as soon as you learn you've won an auction. The contact can be via email or through the Request Invoice or Pay Now buttons that accompany an auction's listing, as discussed in Chapter 15.

Some sellers consider the message from eBay about your win to be adequate contact with you. A very few demand that *you* contact *them* within, say, ten hours of the auction's end or forfeit the auction win. You'll find that sort of stipulation in the item description, usually in the Terms of Service (TOS), so be sure to read everything the seller posts with a listing. You may wish to avoid sellers who make such unusual demands of buyers, because they could have other unpleasant tendencies.

eBay isn't going to terminate your account because you waited four days before contacting a seller, but that seller may get nervous if she doesn't hear from you and might assume you aren't going to pay. This is especially true for sellers who have been burned by nonpaying bidders in the past. I know of two sellers who have a "policy" of canceling a sale if the seller is even one minute late acknowledging a win. (Yes, it is a little extreme, but some people *must* control everything.) Others will send a winning bidder several email messages a day until they hear from the bidder. And many, when not satisfied with how a buyer communicates, will give a buyer a Neutral or Negative Feedback rating for "poor communications," even if the buyer pays for the item.

NOTE *If you're going to be away when an auction you're bidding on ends, advise the seller in advance. Let him know that he may not hear from you for a certain number of days after the auction ends, so he won't start wondering whether you intend to pay.*

If you contact the seller and don't hear from him for a couple of days, don't panic. There could be some sort of legitimate problem or a vacation behind the delay. Go back and read the item description carefully; it may include information such as the fact that the seller planned on being away from home when the auction ended. Conscientious sellers usually email all the bidders on their auctions when they are going to be out of touch, but not all do.

Dealing with Problems

Ideally, after an auction closes, the buyer pays the seller, the seller sends the goods, and each leaves Feedback for the other on the eBay website. Sounds fairly straightforward, right? But people *will* find ways to complicate something even this simple. Sometimes, a buyer and a seller will waste days waiting to hear from each other.

All sorts of things can happen on the seller's end to mess up an eBay deal. Sellers get sick, forget to send items, go insane, have computer crashes, and accidentally delete email. Shippers lose or delay items. The list of what can go wrong is endless. There are also sellers who are inept or just don't care if they delay shipping an item that has been paid for.

Sometimes a curious psychology causes seller delays. More than a few people involved in online trade seem to regard their customers as a little less "real" than those they deal with in person. This often diminishes the urgency of fulfilling an online order.

While eBay offers a complaint form and a couple of other remedies for problems with a seller, the system is set up so that eBay members almost *have* to solve problems with other members by themselves. eBay recommends that you exhaust every possible means of contacting your seller before getting eBay involved. This will also usually bring a faster resolution than you'll get if you go through eBay's complaint process. And, as many buyers who have been ripped off will tell you, a complaint about a nonperforming seller typically brings absolutely no action from eBay.

What Are the Warning Signs?

You can usually tell if a seller is the nervous type and likely to be pushy from certain things he puts in his item descriptions. Threats are a big red flag, especially those with lots of capital letters and exclamation marks, like "DEAD-BEAT Buyers WILL BE GIVEN *BAD* FEEDBACK and harassed and MADE FUN OF!!!!!!!" These are usually sellers who have had a bad experience with one or two buyers who backed out on paying for an auction and haven't gotten over their anger.

Also, sellers who spend a lot of time reading and posting on eBay Seller Central's bulletin boards are probably more likely than others to react aggressively to slow-paying buyers. That particular seller culture holds that nonpaying bidders are the Great Satan and are somehow stealing money from sellers. That mentality breeds a lot of hypersensitive sellers who assume the worst of any buyer who doesn't pay instantly. Spend some time reading posts about nonpaying bidders to see just how extreme many sellers are on this subject.

An incredibly long and involved set of rules for dealing with the seller may also warn you that he is going to be a handful (especially, if the rules contain a lot of misspellings and repeat certain points two or three times). In the end, this kind of seller is looking for trouble and *will* find it in the slightest digression from his rules. Think twice before you deal with someone who is an obvious firebrand—unless you like to argue with strangers.

What If a Seller Threatens You?

There are certain kinds of people who, if you don't complete an auction deal with them or if you leave Negative Feedback, may go beyond saying bad things about you. If a seller makes threats or harasses you, whether because you didn't pay or some other reason, your first move should be to collect as much information about the seller as possible (see Chapter 18 for details on finding information about other eBay members). You may need to share this information with eBay, the seller's ISP, or law enforcement.

Next, contact the seller only *once* with a request that he stop harassing you, and send a copy of that message to eBay.

NOTE *When you forward an email message to someone else, make sure you include the entire message—headers and all. The headers contain time and date information, along with additional data that can be used to authenticate the message.*

If the problem continues, send copies of the seller's mail to his ISP. A quick visit to the ISP's website can tell you whom to contact about a customer's abusive behavior. Depending on the severity of the problem, you may wish to report it to local law enforcement—in your jurisdiction or where the offending person lives—even if it's just email harassment. Depending on state laws and the level of Internet sophistication of the law-enforcement officials, your complaint may result in action. In several cases with which I'm familiar (thanks to the fact that I helped identify the perpetrators), local law enforcement officers have put a permanent end to online harassment by simply calling on the perpetrator.

In other cases, sometimes all it takes is a phone call from you to put an end to a problem. Many people who indulge in online harassment stop immediately when they realize their victim knows how to get in touch with them in the real world. On the other hand, there's always the possibility that it can escalate the situation. Use common sense and good judgment before you act.

If the problem moves into the real world (phone harassment, a personal confrontation, and so on), definitely contact law enforcement. Though I don't know of any specific instances where a problem involving an eBay transaction moved into the real world, there are enough cases of online disputes moving to the next level to indicate that it is possible that someone unhappy with you over an eBay deal might want to confront you by phone or in person.

What If the Item Doesn't Arrive?

As an online auction buyer, you are taking a risk. You are expected to send money to a stranger, against whom you may or may not have recourse if you don't get your item. In some cases, all you have is an address; if you use an online payment service like PayPal, you may not even have that. The overall risk is small. Of the many thousands of auctions won every day, only a fraction of a percent involves fraud.

NOTE *eBay's CEO, Meg Whitman, claims that the rate of fraudulent sales is "less than one-tenth of one percent." This is based on eBay's internal fraud tracking system, called the Fraud Automated Detection Engine (FADE).*

Still, most of us have a tendency to get nervous when we're waiting for something important to arrive by mail or delivery service. People have a limit to how long they will wait, and when they reach that limit, the natural reflex is to blame the seller and think, "They're not sending it!"

At the same time, there are many plausible, as well as bizarre, explanations that have nothing to do with fraud. So don't automatically assume the seller is trying to cheat you just because an item doesn't arrive on the day you think it should.

The first thing to consider when you think an item is late is the season. The postal service and other delivery services have extra-heavy loads at certain times of the year—the winter holiday season being the most obvious. A regional or local emergency at or near your seller's location can also slow things down. Remember the anthrax scares of 2001?

Next, review the auction listing; you may have overlooked important information. Perhaps your seller ships only once every week, but you missed it when you first read the auction listing or the seller's email. Or the seller may have found it necessary to be away from her computer when the auction ended but you haven't yet seen the email she sent alerting all bidders on her auctions.

NOTE *Whenever you don't receive a message you've been expecting, check your email program's spam filters. There's always the possibility that an important message from your seller has been filtered out.*

If an item is coming to you by Media Mail or Parcel Post, remember that those services can take two to three weeks. Just visualize your envelope or package in a big cart full of mail, sitting in a processing center for several days while the Priority and First Class mail zip by it.

Then again, some sellers are just incredibly inefficient. They misplace an item and can't find it for a week, or they don't realize they forgot to send an item because they don't keep good records. As a seller, I've been guilty of misplacing an item once or twice. Or it's possible that the seller became ill or preoccupied with a family emergency and has not had a chance to contact you. We're all human!

NOTE *There's a standard joke among eBay buyers about the high mortality rate among relatives of eBay sellers and how frequently eBay sellers have heart attacks or other health crises. This alludes to the fact that quite a few slow-shipping sellers use a death in the family or illness as an excuse for late shipping. Whatever explanation the seller provides, don't question it, as long as you get your item.*

WHAT'S THE HOLDUP?

The reason your item hasn't arrived can range from simple addressing errors to personal problems. For example, I know of two eBay sellers who suffer from profound clinical depression and can let a week or two go by before they mail an item that has been paid for, even though it is sitting right next to their computers where they see it every day. Of course, some folks are simply procrastinators who need some prodding before they can rally themselves to send the item.

There are also sellers who are bad with their finances and spend *all* the money that comes in from buyers, including what was allocated for postage. One seller who was more than a month late in sending an item to me admitted that this was his problem. I was completely exasperated after I had emailed and gotten promises that the item would be sent, so I tried calling the phone number that I got from eBay. It was "temporarily out of service." That gave me an idea. I sent him a self-addressed, stamped, padded envelope, so he could just drop the item in and mail it. He sent it right away and included a note of apology explaining why he hadn't sent the item sooner.

As a seller, I have lost items and never found them. In those instances, I refunded the buyers' money, after making absolutely sure that the item in question wasn't tucked away somewhere around my house. I have also sent items to the wrong buyers several times. Most of them helped me out by forwarding them to the proper recipients (I sent them money for postage, of course). I can think of only one instance in which someone kept an item sent to him erroneously. I know he did because I have receipts for two packages to his address and another buyer who didn't receive his item.

I once broke an item—a rare plastic model kit—after I sold it. It was on the floor and I stepped on it. Here again, I refunded the buyer's money. In this case, I was actually able to sell the kit to another collector who didn't mind that it was broken.

The point of all this is that stuff happens, and sometimes people do stupid things. With luck, if your seller misplaces or breaks an item, or has any other issues that impact your transaction, she will just tell you what happened and refund your money. If it's a matter of the item being mislaid, you might give her a few days to try to find it.

How to Communicate with the Seller

Except in cases where a seller plans to cheat the buyer or the buyer doesn't intend to pay, most of the problems associated with auctions can be solved, if not prevented, with good communication. Whatever your problem, the first step is to email the seller, inquiring as to the status of your item or, if it's something you've already received, informing him of the problem you have with the item.

If you don't get an answer within a day or so, try sending the same note using the "Ask seller a question" link on the item's auction page or the **Contact Member** button on the member's Profile page. It may be that the seller has recently changed his address and isn't checking the address you used first, while mail forwarded through eBay's Contact Member system is going to the new address.

Although you may be a bit upset with the seller, try to avoid hostility and threats. At first, give the seller the benefit of the doubt. Writing something like, "I still haven't received the 1920s coloring book I paid for 17 days and 12 hours ago! I'm going to make your life online a living hell!!!" is unlikely to motivate the seller to address your problem. "Screaming" at the seller in all caps, making threats, and using vulgar language may "motivate" the seller to delay even longer. If you offend or frighten him, he may just keep your money and the item, or refund your money and sell the item to someone else (which, depending on the item, may be the worst possible outcome).

How to Get Seller Contact Information

If you cannot get the contact information you need through eBay (as described in the preceding section), you can try asking others who have bought from this seller for the information you need. Go to the main Search page, click the By Seller tab, and enter the seller's user ID. Click the radio button to include all completed items, and then click **Search**. Select your contacts from winning bidders of completed auctions.

NOTE *If you do a lot of buying on eBay, you may find it useful to keep a list of all the buyers you've dealt with, and information you collect in the course of dealing with them, including their names, addresses, and phone numbers, along with any additional email addresses. (Just don't spam them or send them chain letters!)*

Even if the buyers who've dealt with this seller can't give you any additional contact information, they can at least give you some idea of how likely it is that you won't get your item. A reply like "Oh, yeah—I've bought from this guy several times. He takes five or six weeks to send your items, but they always arrive," or "I'm still waiting on something I bought in 1999!" can tell you a lot.

When you email your fellow eBay members asking about another member, don't be surprised if you don't get any replies, and don't take a lack of information as a negative. Some people don't care to email strangers, and others are too busy to bother or don't remember the person you're asking about. Interestingly, you are more likely to hear from those who had a bad experience with the seller.

You may also find the information about investigating other eBay members in Chapter 18 useful if you are having trouble contacting a seller.

How to Motivate a Slow Seller to Ship

eBay recommends that a seller communicate with her buyer within three days of an auction's end. There is, however, no stated shipping time.

Some sellers note in their item descriptions that they will ship "within 10 days" of receiving payment, or that they ship only once a week, or every other week during the month of a gibbous moon—or whatever. (Ironically, many of these same sellers demand payment within three days.) By and large, sellers can ship whenever they wish, within reason. As a buyer, you can complain about excessive shipping time (as described in the next section), but it is usually better and faster to work things out with the seller yourself.

NOTE *For a seller to be protected by PayPal's Seller Protection Policy, PayPal requires that a seller ship an item within seven days of receiving payment.*

Before you take any action regarding a slow-shipping seller, it is important to take into account that this person has your money *and* something you want, and thus has the upper hand in the transaction. Sometimes, how quickly you get action (or whether you get it at all) depends on how you approach the problem.

If an item is a really long time coming and the seller doesn't communicate with you, it's time to get active. If it has been 15 days since the seller supposedly sent your item Parcel Post or First Class, it's time to send an email inquiring about it. If three days pass and you don't hear back, write again. Ask if the seller has a receipt showing that he sent the item, but don't get confrontational right off the bat.

NOTE *If you think the seller is ignoring your email, and you really want to know whether your messages are being read, consider a service called ReadNotify (www.readnotify.com). This service notifies you when a message you've sent is read, and tells you how long the recipient spent reading it and other information. ReadNotify charges for its service.*

If, after sending two email messages, you don't have a reply and your item still has not arrived, what can you do? One effective tool for speeding up a slow seller is a phone call. This will put you in the forefront of the seller's thoughts like nothing else (unless you go knock on his front door). There is also a strong psychological effect involved in contacting someone in the real world, as opposed to email. A polite request should suffice; identify yourself and tell the seller what you bought and that you've paid for it. Then ask whether the seller has shipped the item, perhaps adding, "The mail has been slow, so I figured I would check to see if I should be expecting the item . . . ."

If your polite requests don't work, and you're up for it, you might try one of several "psychological warfare" techniques described next to get a seller moving. Most likely, you'll never reach the point where you need to consider these methods, but you never know.

Get Their Attention

If you suspect the seller is simply deleting your email messages without reading them, try putting his address or phone number (if you haven't phoned him yet) in the subject line. This can elicit a fast response, especially if the seller knows he didn't give you this information. You don't need to refer to the subject header in your message; just make it a friendly query about your item.

Bring in Reinforcements

Quite often, you can get attention by enlisting a third party, or at least making the seller think a third party is involved. When you write to the seller, address your message to eBay as well as the seller. Try fraud@ebay.com or make up an eBay addressee. (In the latter instance, the mail message will bounce, but the seller won't know that.) In fact, you can write a real complaint letter to eBay and copy your message to the seller. I used this with a problem seller, and he put the item in the mail to me the same day.

A similar tactic is advising the seller that you are contacting the postmaster in her town to report her for mail fraud. If you contact the seller by email to deliver the news, make sure the message's subject line conveys your intentions. Something like "Reporting to your postmaster at *<her town>*" should do. You can also send a postcard or letter advising her of the same thing or do it by phone. Your message might include the phone number and address of the post office in question, so the seller knows you mean business. You can find the phone number and address of any U.S. post office at www.usps.gov (and don't throw away the post office contact information; you may want to use it later if the seller continues to blow you off).

At least one eBay buyer who got stiffed resolved the problem by telling the seller she planned on reporting him to the IRS—a very legitimate threat, since the IRS offers rewards for information about taxpayers who don't report income. This resulted in the seller issuing a quick refund. The seller wasn't necessarily hiding income; it may have been that he just didn't like the prospect of an IRS investigation. Either way, just mentioning the IRS is sometimes enough to light a fire under a shady seller.

Another eBay buyer I know lived in the same county as her troublesome seller. She phoned him and told him she would be filing a claim in small claims court, easy to do as a resident of the same county. Her item arrived two days later.

Tell Everybody

A trick that several eBay buyers report having used to good effect involves the threat of public humiliation. In a case that involved several hundreds dollars, a buyer paid $35 to an online detective service to get a background report on the seller. The report included several of the seller's family members' names, with addresses and phone numbers, as well as contact information for other people in her life. (It is possible to get much of the same information without paying, using the online investigative techniques discussed in Chapter 18.)

The burned buyer then emailed the seller an excerpt from the report with a note that the buyer intended to contact every person in the report and tell them all about the seller's scam. The buyer had her refund within a week.

NOTE *Tactics that involve threats may open you to the possibility of legal reprisals. And with some people, threats could trigger retaliatory harassment or worse. This being the case, you may not want to follow the examples of sellers described here.*

If you still fail to receive your item, or you get it and something is wrong with it, your next steps are to seek help, within or outside eBay.

Recourse for the Burned Buyer

For the first decade of its existence, eBay offered little help for buyers who were ripped off by sellers. The only real option was to convince eBay to investigate the seller, which didn't necessarily result in action. Due to the volume of complaints, quite a few sellers got away with scamming buyers again and again.

Fortunately, eBay now has a counterpart to the Non-Paying Bidder complaint system to protect buyers who don't receive an item or receive an item that is significantly different from an auction's description. eBay also offers a Buyer Protection Program and a mediation service. If these avenues fail, you may be able to take legal action.

Item Not Received or Significantly Not as Described Report

After an auction you've won ends, you will find a link on the item's page labeled "Report the item as not received." Click this link, and you will see the page shown in Figure 12-2.

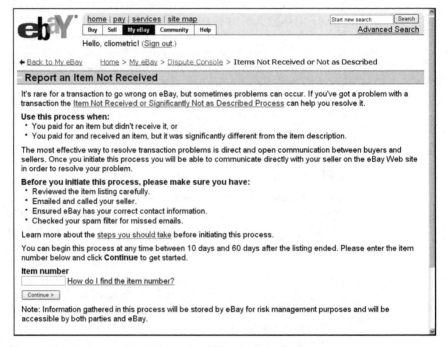

Figure 12-2: Report an Item Not Received/Not As Described page

If, for example, you buy a 24-karat ring and you receive one that is marked "10K," you'll want to fill out this form. Of course, if you didn't receive anything, this is also the form to use.

All you need to provide is the item number, which is already filled in if you click the "Report an item not received" link on the item's page. A report can be sent any time between 10 and 60 days after an auction ends.

Filing the report opens an Item Not Received or Significantly Not as Described Dispute. The seller will receive an automated email from eBay, informing her that you have opened a dispute and encouraging her to communicate with you and settle the problem. The seller must also reply to eBay to report what action, if any, she takes. Opening the dispute creates a special page that you can use to close or escalate the dispute.

If you and the seller resolve the matter, you close the dispute, and that's the end of it. If not, you have the option of escalating the dispute. When you do this, eBay staff members investigate your claim, and, as explained on the eBay Help page that describes this process, "If warranted, the seller's account may be restricted or suspended."

Bear in mind that opening and escalating a dispute won't automatically result in the seller being restricted or suspended. Also, the seller will have an opportunity to defend herself and may convince eBay that your claim has no merit. What happens is entirely up to the eBay staff who investigate the claim. The staff will not inform you as to what (if any) action is taken against the seller; eBay says this is "for privacy reasons."

If you do not escalate a dispute and do not close it, it will be closed automatically after 90 days, after which you're no longer eligible to file a claim under eBay's Buyer Protection Program (described later).

Actually, a live human is not directly involved until you escalate a dispute. The point of filing a dispute in the first place, which is an automated process, is to get the attention of the seller. And most sellers do respond to a dispute filing. For the most part, only seriously motivated buyers will escalate a complaint, as doing so involves more communication and waiting, with no ironclad guarantee of resolution. However, escalating the dispute to a claim entitles the buyer to file a claim under eBay's Standard Purchase Protection Program.

Of course, as eBay advises, you should do everything you can to resolve a problem on your own before filing a dispute. If you go for the dispute before exhausting other options, you may anger the seller and risk not getting your item or a refund. And keep in mind that it's not worthwhile for eBay staff to deal with disagreements over $2 items or someone receiving a blue hat because the seller ran out of green ones. Saving eBay staff from dealing with member problems is the primary purpose of this system.

Other Complaints to eBay

If you're really intent on running down the problem with a seller, you can try filing a dispute, as described in the preceding section, and then lodging a complaint against a seller via the Contact Us link available on eBay's Help pages and elsewhere. eBay will either ignore your complaint or investigate it. Unfortunately, you can't demand an investigation. Just file your complaint and wait. If eBay does investigate and the findings back up your claim, eBay will contact the seller and advise her to stop doing whatever caused the complaint, and/or suspend the seller's account, temporarily or permanently.

To ensure that your problem gets the attention it deserves, when you complain through the Contact Us link, make sure you have included all relevant information. Avoid emotional appeals ("This is driving me crazy!") and extraneous information ("Someone did this last year and they were suspended").

eBay staff will not tell you whether they decide to act on your complaint, but you might be able to figure it out for yourself. If the seller is no longer active, she may have been suspended. (Or she may have changed accounts because she has had too many complaints and Negative Feedback ratings.) If the seller's offending practices have changed, eBay probably warned her. If nothing has changed, the seller is either ignoring warnings or eBay is not acting on your complaint.

What If eBay Does Nothing?

On any given day, eBay members probably submit more disputes and complaints than eBay's staff can possibly handle. So, some legitimate email complaints may get passed over, because staff members are overloaded with more serious complaints, you didn't supply enough information with your complaint, or the complaint is obviously spurious. In addition, complaints are sometimes ignored because an investigation is already ongoing, and eBay is giving the malefactor "enough rope to hang himself."

If your complaint seems to have been ignored but it's really important to you, wait a week and complain again. Better still, look for a new instance of the problem, and complain about that. Do not, however, deluge eBay with complaints; that can result in all of your complaints being ignored.

While you are waiting to see if action is taken, contact other eBay members who have dealt with the seller in question and ask whether they have had similar problems. Urge them to complain, as well.

Also, be aware that while a crime may be obvious to you, it may not be provable in court.

eBay's Buyer Protection Program

eBay offers a Buyer Protection Program under which you can receive up to $175 in partial reimbursement if you do not receive an item. To take advantage of this service, the item's final value (price without shipping and handling) must be over $25, because there is a $25 processing fee. eBay does not cover items paid for with cash or through an instant money transfer service like Western Union or MoneyGram.

Before you can file a claim under eBay's Buyer Protection program, you must contact the seller and attempt to resolve the problem. If you cannot contact the seller to settle the issue, you are next required to file an Item Not Received or Significantly Not as Described Dispute, as explained in the previous section.

NOTE *If you used PayPal or a credit card, eBay requires that you contact PayPal or your credit card company first to take advantage of the purchase protection those entities offer. See Chapter 15 for more information about using PayPal and its protection policy.*

You will, of course, be asked to provide as much information as possible about your claim, and the seller may be contacted as well. The claims-investigation process can take several months. Seeking reimbursement may not be worth your time for lower-cost items. While you may receive $175 for a $500 loss or $75 for a $100 loss, you get only $1 for a $26 loss.

eBay Mediation Through SquareTrade

You can use eBay's SquareTrade mediation service only if the seller has signed up for it, indicated by a SquareTrade logo in his listings. Participation in the SquareTrade program requires the seller to meet certain standards specified by eBay and pay a monthly fee. Membership in the SquareTrade program is like the old Good Housekeeping seal of approval. The seller is less likely to be a bad egg and, if something does go wrong, you know he is willing to seek a reasonable solution through mediation.

SquareTrade (www.squaretrade.com) is an online dispute mediation service. You can file a case for mediation and use a direct negotiation tool that SquareTrade provides at no charge. If a mediator becomes involved, you'll need to pay a fee. A mediator must be involved in any case that involves changing eBay Feedback. Visit the SquareTrade website for more detailed information.

Legal Recourse

If you feel that you have been defrauded by a seller, you may consider contacting law enforcement. Do not count on getting help, though. Local, state, and federal agencies have far more serious crimes to deal with than the small-time fraud that constitutes most lawbreaking on eBay.

The involvement of a large amount of money or stolen property can get the attention of law-enforcement agencies and prosecutors, but sorting out under whose jurisdiction the crime took place may delay an investigation. Also, if a pattern of fraud exists (a number of sellers have been stiffed, sold fake items, or otherwise defrauded people), it may be possible to interest a federal agency such as the FBI or Federal Trade Commission (FTC).

If someone accepts money from you in exchange for merchandise but doesn't give you the merchandise, they have committed a crime. As a victim of this kind of crime, your legal recourse depends on several factors:

- The amount of money involved; $1,000 is going to get more attention than $75
- The level of knowledge and awareness of Internet crime at the law-enforcement agency you contact
- Whether there have been prior complaints against the seller from other buyers

You probably should begin by filing a complete report with your local law-enforcement agency. You may also wish to contact the law-enforcement agency where the seller lives. Quite a few eBay members report that doing this has resulted in some satisfaction (either a refund or seeing the seller investigated), especially in cases where the seller had other complaints filed against him.

NOTE *If you plan to contact the law-enforcement agency that has jurisdiction where the seller lives, be sure to get in touch with other eBay members who have done business with the seller and left Negative Feedback, to see whether they have reason to complain, as well.*

Civil action is also a possibility. You can file a complaint in small claims court or hire an attorney to pursue the action; either route will cost you time and money. And in the end, while you may obtain a judgment against the seller, collecting on that judgment is an entirely different, and often difficult, undertaking.

eBay recommends two online resources for dealing with fraud complaints. The Internet Crime Complaint Center (www.ifccfbi.gov/index.asp) accepts fraud complaints. This is a joint antifraud effort between the FBI and the National White Collar Crime Center. Also of interest is the FTC's site at www.consumer.gov. In addition to displaying pertinent news, this page has links to consumer complaint forms, identity theft resources, and the FTC's Consumer Sentinel pages, which have the latest information on Internet cons and a complaint form.

Feedback for Buyers

If you don't know it already, you'll soon find out that Feedback is a big deal to most eBay users. But can Feedback affect whether sellers are willing to sell to you? The truth is, except where a large number of negatives are involved, Feedback is not as important as some would have you think—not when you stop to think about how few times you have looked at the Feedback of someone you're considering doing business with, and not when you consider the fact that it is possible for bad buyers to extort Positive Feedback from dissatisfied or downright angry sellers (and vice versa). Rare indeed is the seller who will look at a winning bidder's Feedback and cancel a sale because the bidder has too many Negative Feedback ratings.

What About Negative Feedback?

The truth is, a few Negative Feedback ratings for slow payment won't have much of an effect on what sellers think of you. This is because most buyers pay promptly, and the majority of sellers have little reason (and less time) to look at the Feedback ratings of each and every bidder on their auctions. In fact, the only time some sellers look at an eBayer's Feedback profile is when a winning bidder is late paying.

So if you get a Negative Feedback rating, it's not the end of the world. One or two Negative Feedback ratings constitute but a small percentage of your total Feedback and will not brand you as a thief or deadbeat. However, if you collect a streak of Negative Feedback ratings, you will be viewed with understandable suspicion.

If you receive a Negative Feedback rating that you feel is undeserved, you can post a response to it from your Feedback page. Click the **Reply to Feedback** button next to the comment and tell your side of the story, in 80 characters or less.

Feedback Extortion

In addition to communicating with the buyer and shipping the item, the seller should provide appropriate Feedback to the buyer immediately on receiving payment. This is a sensitive issue, as some sellers withhold Feedback in order to extort Positive Feedback from buyers. The stated (and usually bogus) reason for doing this is to give the seller "a chance to make things right."

Obviously, a seller who does this expects problems and does *not* intend to give Positive Feedback unless he receives Positive Feedback. This is wrong; a buyer's Feedback rating is not supposed to be determined by the kind of Feedback she leaves, or by how satisfied she is with the item when she receives it. Buyer Feedback is a rating of how quickly and completely the buyer pays, period.

NOTE *We can only hope that eBay will eliminate Feedback extortion soon. The simplest solution would be for eBay to make it impossible for a buyer to leave Feedback until after the seller has left Feedback. This way, most sellers will leave honest ratings, based on how quickly their buyers paid. And buyers will be able to leave Feedback based on the seller's performance, without fear of reprisal.*

To get an idea as to whether a seller practices this kind of extortion, bring up his Feedback profile, and compare the dates and times of Feedback the seller has left against the dates and times of Feedback he has received. If there is a consistent pattern of the buyers leaving Positive Feedback *before* the seller leaves Positive Feedback, he may be practicing Feedback extortion.

If you want to leave justifiable Neutral or Negative Feedback for a seller but fear retaliation, wait until late on the ninetieth day after the auction ends. In nearly all instances, no one can leave Feedback on an auction that is more than 90 days old. Thus, if you leave Feedback for a seller at 11:57 PM on the ninetieth day after the auction in question ends, it will be too late for the seller to leave vengeful Feedback for you. (AuctionHawk.com offers a tool called 90th Day Feedback that does this for you automatically, so you don't need to watch your calendar.)

Now that you know something about dealing with your eBay sellers, let's take a look at how you can successfully bid on what they're selling.

13

BID TO WIN!

You've found an item you want, researched it and its seller, and you're ready to bid. Should you bid right away? How much do you bid? Is there any way to know how much another bidder is willing to offer? Should you give up if there's a lot of competition? What if the auction ends while you're at work?

You'll find the answers to those and other questions about bidding and tracking auctions here, along with information about techniques and tools you can use to win consistently.

When and How Much to Bid

Ideally, you have determined what the item is worth to you, as discussed in Chapter 5. With that in mind, you now must decide how much you will bid and when you will bid.

As you know, bidding on eBay is incremental. There is always a minimum amount you must bid, and you can place a higher proxy bid so that eBay will increase your bid to (hopefully) exceed any other bids that may be placed. This being the situation, you might feel it best just to bid the highest amount you are willing to pay and hope no one outbids you. But this is not always the smartest approach.

Bid High

You can sometimes win an auction by storming in and placing what seems like an outrageously high bid. You will probably win, but don't count on it. You could end up in a bidding war that has nothing to do with the item being sold and everything to do with being the winner, literally at any cost.

Also, if you are competing with someone who *really* wants to win the auction, bidding high will do nothing more than alert him to return and bid more. I experienced this when I tried to obtain an original, historic airplane photograph and negative. I researched the other bidder and learned that he was the high bidder on more than two dozen similar photos, but hadn't gone over $25 on any of them. "Ha!" I said to myself, "I'll just put a really big bid on this one to be sure I win. Surely, he has already spread his resources too thin to go really high on any of these."

So, I placed a bid of $130, which really was the most I could spend on the photo. The competing bidder came back and outbid me. And he won the other auctions, too—all at less than $25. I know this because I conducted a test and bid a dollar over him on several of those auctions. He hadn't placed a proxy bid on any of them; in each case, he came back later and bid the minimum amount required to outbid me. But with a different strategy, I probably would have won the item, and for far less than my maximum bid.

I should have realized, when I saw that my competitor had not bid more than $25 for any of the photos, that I could have waited until a minute or so before the auction ended, and then slipped in with a $40 bid and taken the photo. My rival bidder would have probably been too busy trying to watch all the other auctions—each of which ended within a minute of each other—to outbid me. That would have given me my opportunity to sneak in with a last-minute bid. I knew from research that this bidder had never bid in more than $5 increments, so bidding an additional $15 within seconds of the auction's close was how I should have played it. He might have bid $30, and then $35 to my proxy bid of $40, but he would still have been outbid, with no time left to place another bid.

This sort of strategy is called *sniping*, a subject I'll discuss in the "Snipers and Sniping Strategies" section later in this chapter. In essence, sniping is waiting until minutes or seconds before an auction ends to place your bid.

Take two important lessons from this story: Timing can be everything, and don't show your hand until you must.

Bid Low

If you want to place a bid immediately, make it well below your maximum. This way, you won't encourage another bidder to bid an amount she may not have otherwise bid without the inspiration of your bid. A sense of competition forces many of us to put forth more effort (or money) than we would otherwise expend.

NOTE *If you are watching the maximum number of auctions permitted by eBay, you can mark an important auction for later attention by placing a small bid on it. If you're outbid, you can make up for it later. An alternative way to mark an auction is to place it on your Favorites list.*

Consider this example: Bidder A places a bid of $55 on a rare book and promises herself she will bid no more than $60. Bidder B comes along and bids $60. Bidder A sees her bid as topped by "only $5" and promptly bids $65, which is $5 over her professed limit. Bidder B returns and bids $70, which bidder A again perceives as "only $5" more, and bids $75—a $10 jump over her preceding bid. At this point, bidder A is $15 over her limit.

Stated intentions are often outweighed by the emotional urge to win. Practicality may tell the bidder that she is $15 over her limit, but it doesn't "feel" like $15. Some reflex or emotion is focused on the $5 increments, making it easy to bid and bid again. The same thing happens at real-world auctions.

At the same time, bidder B might not have pushed his proxy bid up to $70 if bidder A had not responded immediately to the challenge of the $60 bid. If bidder A had waited until just before the end of the auction, she may have gotten the item for $65 instead of $75.

Bid Odd

Some bidders rely on guessing your maximum, rather than trying to knock out your bid of, say $5, with a bid of $8. Maybe the bidder's heart isn't really in it, or he wants to get the item by outbidding you by a few cents. So, he tries to sneak up on your maximum bid with a small increment and places a bid of $5.50. If your maximum bid is $5.50, the bidder will be notified and probably will guess that he can bid $5.51 and win. If, however, you have bid $5.57, the bidder will be notified that he has been outbid. He will probably give up, thinking your maximum bid is several dollars higher, when it's only a penny more.

Bid Late

It is often best to not bid at all until the final day, if not the final hour or minute, of an auction. This way, you avoid alerting your competition, *and* you enter the fray armed with the knowledge of how high at least one bidder is willing to go, although you cannot see who bid how much at each stage until after the auction is completed. You've essentially eliminated some of the competition without giving others a chance to find out anything about you. Indeed, they don't know you exist yet.

In general, the more people who are bidding, the later you should place your bid. If several bidders are active, adding your voice to the auction may discourage one or two, but it's more likely that your new bid will motivate others to bid higher. You never know when one more bid will trigger a bidding war. Some bidders, when prodded one time too many, start taking things personally and decide to go for the win, no matter what the cost.

Bidding late also gives you the opportunity to observe any shilling, or artificial bid inflation, that might be taking place. (Shilling and other scams are explained in Chapter 16.)

Timing of Your Bid

Along with the bid early or bid late timing, you might consider the day, time zones, and time of year before you place your bid.

Day of Week

Is it better to bid on Sunday night or Thursday afternoon? You may hear all sorts of reasons as to why one day is better than another, but the truth is that one day is pretty much the same as the next. The only day that is important in terms of successful bidding is the final day of the auction. Again, you have a better chance of winning an auction by bidding on its final day (or final hour). By that time, a good number of other bidders will have placed their maximum bids, and others may have forgotten to bid on the auction.

Time Zones

Always take note of the time an auction ends and what that translates to in other time zones. Depending on your personal schedule and where other bidders are located, the time an auction ends may affect your strategy.

Auctions that end after midnight or during weekday business hours are likely to have fewer bidders than those that end in the early evening. If you're a night owl or work at home, you may want to focus on auctions that end after 2:00 AM, Eastern Standard Time (EST). This places the end of the auction late at night in all North American time zones. Or you might focus on auctions that end mid to late afternoon, when most of the people in United States and Canada (not to mention Central and South America) are working.

If you're a regular daytime person, you have three options: you can lose some sleep by staying up later or getting up really early, skip work, or use a sniping service (as discussed in the "Sniping Tools" section later in this chapter). Of course, the same approach holds true for night owls or night workers bidding on auctions that end early in the day.

Season

You can get just about anything for less when it's out of season. Winter holiday ornaments (even collectible ornaments) can be bought in July for a fraction of what you would pay in November. Summer sportswear is cheap in the fall, and you can often buy a four-wheel drive vehicle for less in the summer than in the winter.

It's all about demand. The more demand an item generates, the higher the price—just like buying tomatoes in winter. When there's little or no interest in an article, sellers reduce the price to stimulate and increase the demand, after which they will raise prices.

You can find some really good deals on just about anything on eBay from the end of December through early February and sometimes later. Just like retail businesses, eBay goes into a slump during the post-holiday season.

Fewer people bid on auctions, and sellers drop their minimum bids or flat prices to stimulate sales.

How to Research the Competition

Although it may seem like extra work, you can learn quite a bit and maybe gain an edge by researching competing bidders. If you're observant, you can identify behaviors such as when a member is likely to be online, whether she is willing to spend a lot of money, how determined she is to win, and more.

Number of Items Bid On

The number of items on which a member bids may indicate his limitations. Does he have bids in on 33 auctions? Assuming the bidder is not particularly wealthy (and most of us aren't), he may not bid very high on some of his auctions. Someone bidding on multiple auctions can't focus his efforts as closely, which increases the odds that he will miss it when he is outbid at the last minute.

Be sure to check closed auctions in which the bidder has participated, too. If the bidder has won fewer than half of the auctions he has bid on, this may be an indication that he is not a tenacious bidder, and getting outbid once or twice will knock him out of the race.

To see all the auctions a bidder has bid on, including closed auctions, use eBay's Search by Bidder feature. Go to eBay's Search page and click Items by Bidder in the box on the left side of the page. This displays the Search: Items by Bidder page, as shown in Figure 13-1.

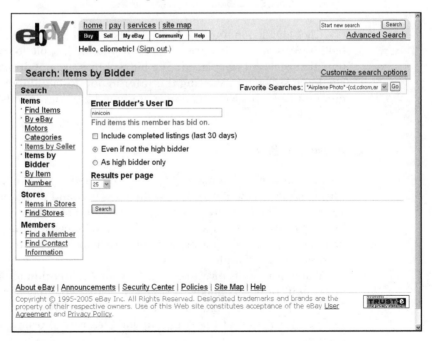

Figure 13-1: Search: Items by Bidder page

Enter the bidder's user ID and check the "Include completed listings" box. Leave the "Even if not the high bidder" choice selected. Click **Search**, and you'll see a search results list like the one shown in Figure 13-2.

Item	Start	End	Price	Title	High Bidder	Seller
6186078377	Jun-10-05	Jun-17-05 18:22:32	US $18.58	ROB REIDER WLW T-5 STATION CINCINNATI, OHIO	cincydp ✉ (*)	htldave
7523254426	Jun-12-05	Jun-19-05 09:09:46	US $9.99	FRED ALLEN at the radio microphone circa 1939!	mamartini (*)	junkhero1
7523270189	Jun-12-05	Jun-19-05 10:13:35	US $1.99	The Rivalry Play by Norman Corwin Souvenir Program	mamartini (*)	steviesbooks
6186816883	Jun-13-05	Jun-20-05 15:06:42	US $26.00	CINCINNATI 1939 TELEVISION PAMPHLET	mamartini (*)	rivercityretro
6539804042	Jun-14-05	Jun-21-05 13:37:29	US $32.50	WLW Radio Cincinnati Oh Letterhead & Original Env. 1940	s7536 (*)	lesterjay
6965098883	Jun-15-05	Jun-22-05 19:36:07	US $61.00	Broadcasting Magazine December 1935 Mutual WOR	radiodavid (*)	nutsk42
7523531831	Jun-13-05	Jun-23-05 08:50:10	US $39.99	Early Original Photo of Eddie Albert & Grace Brandt	mamartini (*)	opal22
7331111598	Jun-17-05	Jun-24-05 17:33:06	US $2.99	1952 Marion Spellman ROSARY LANE Sheet Music NM	mamartini (*)	dbear100
4744937374	Jul-04-05	Jul-09-05 09:36:30	US $5.99	THE COON CREEK GIRLS "EARLY RADIO FAVORITES" LP - OOP	mamartini (*)	fourfinickyfelines
4744390209	Jul-02-05	Jul-09-05 12:40:01	US $44.90	Vintage "PAUL BABY" DIXON Apron - NO RESERVE	wfascott (*)	mjfox7isp
7166706350	Jun-29-05	Jul-09-05 18:50:35	US $12.06	1950s CROSLEY BROCHURE radios,ranges,tv's,refrigerators	ac-fan ✉ (*)	screenheads
7529779600	Jul-08-05	Jul-11-05 17:07:57	US $54.56	Davis Sisters Skeeter Davis Amateur Hour Audition 1949	finjans (*)	moodyjohnson
5218715699	Jul-11-05	Jul-12-05 13:40:00	US $9.99	1960s Cincinnati Reds Hudepohl-Sohio-Colgate Song!	mamartini (*)	shamrockdaddy

1 - 17 of 17 total. Click on the column headers to sort

Figure 13-2: Search by bidder results

Click an auction number to display that auction, and then view the item's bid history. Unless it is a private auction, you will be able to see the date and time that each bid was placed. The bid amounts are not displayed while an auction is still active. Viewing this information for a number of auctions on different days will give you an idea of when the bidder spends most of his time online.

Amounts of Bids

If your competition has made large bids on everything, you may be in trouble. This suggests a fat wallet and the willingness to spend whatever it takes to win an auction. The best way to win against this kind of bidder is to bid late and high. The last thing you want to do when a well-heeled bidder is involved is tip her off that she has competition. Be sure to look at closed as well as current auctions for the complete history.

Watch for habits or quirks. Maybe your competition always bids in $5 increments or always makes her bid a specific percentage or number of dollars higher than someone who has outbid her. You can compile this sort of information by reviewing the bidder's record over a number of auctions.

Number of Bids

How tenacious is your competition? One way to tell is to look at the number of times she bids on an auction. The existence of several bids on an item certainly shows determination, but it may also imply a lack of experience or confidence.

Bid Timing

How closely together in time bids occur can be informative. If most of a person's bids are placed around the same time of day, this tells you when he is most likely to be online and monitoring bids. If several bids on one auction are minutes or seconds apart, the bidder has probably upped his bids in small increments in an effort to outbid someone else's proxy or in response to being outbid, either of which may mean he is a new or, at least, an unimaginative bidder. These things also imply a cautious bidder and one who is not likely to bid much higher than he already has.

Bids every day or so indicate that the bidder checks his auctions regularly and will be right on top of things if you outbid him.

Have a look at the ending times for the auctions on which your competitor bids. If he bids on auctions that end within a few hours or minutes of one another, he may be bidding on only those auctions that end when he can be online, so as to be on hand to battle snipers.

Kinds of Items Bid On

If the bidder is vying for a dozen similar items, he is going to be a very aggressive bidder. If the items are a set scattered across several listings, you can count on even heavier competition. On the other hand, keeping track of a dozen auctions may be distracting and make it easier for you to slip in and win with a last-minute bid.

So, when you are dealing with someone likely to be aggressive in going after items, don't let him know you're there until the last minute. Bid just before the auction ends, when your competitor will have his hands full, instead of bidding hours or days before the auction ends and giving him time to react.

About Me Page

Don't neglect a bidder's About Me page. It may contain useful information about her interests and hobbies that will flesh out her profile. If, for example, the bidder's About Me page mentions that she has the world's largest collection of Cincinnati Reds memorabilia, you are probably in trouble if you intend to bid against her on items that have to do with that baseball club.

Bonus: Let the Other Bidder Work for You!

As you research a competing bidder's auction habits, keep in mind the possibility that you and the bidder share an interest in one or more areas. Following the trail of her bids may lead you to appealing items you might otherwise have missed. For example, maybe you collect beverage memorabilia and you see that she is bidding on a vintage Coca-Cola advertisement you hadn't noticed before. You want in on that action. Continue to check her activity; she might uncover other similar items that you would like to bid on, too.

Cooperative Bidding

My auctioneer friend Doug Ross has a favorite saying that he shares at least once during every auction he conducts: "There are no friends at an auction!" This is mostly true, although I've attended auctions where two or three folks who are interested in the same kinds of merchandise agree in advance to bid or not bid on certain items, so that each gets something he wants. An additional benefit to this approach is that the parties involved spend less than if they had been bidding against one another.

Should eBay bidders cooperate like this? eBay says, "No!" After all, it is a tactic that may reduce the amount a seller realizes on an item. But, depending on your outlook and the circumstances, it could be a good idea. If the item in question is really important to you but you can't spend very much, cooperative bidding might be worth a try.

Say you are bidding against the same bidder on six items, but you want two of them more than the others. You might offer not to bid on the other four if the competing bidder lays off the two you want. As the saying goes, half a loaf is better than none.

Or, in a more likely scenario, you may be interested in one item in an auction that offers a group of diverse objects. If the bidder isn't after the same piece as you and you lose, he may make a deal with you. If you feel this is the case, you can contact the other bidder, ask whether he is interested in the items you really want, and if not, suggest that one of you drop the bidding and split up the lot after the auction is over.

NOTE *The cooperative approach might also be used to "psyche out" another bidder. Say you collect chalkware salt and pepper shakers and are bidding against someone on set A. Then, you see set B come up for auction. Even if it's a set you don't want, you might write your competitor and tell her you won't bid on set B if she lets you win on set A. Of course, you probably wouldn't be this shady, but it's good to keep this in mind if someone contacts you with a similar proposition.*

The danger of proposing one of these plans—beyond the possibility of another person getting snippy and reporting you to eBay for interfering with an auction—is that you have no way of knowing whether you can trust the bidder, unless it's someone you know. It's easy to break a promise to someone you don't know and will never meet.

Place Your Bids

Compared to figuring out when and how much to bid, placing a bid is simple. With the auction you wish to bid on displayed, either click the **Place Bid** button or scroll down to the "Ready to bid or buy?" section. Enter the amount you wish to bid in the "Your maximum bid" box, as shown in Figure 13-3.

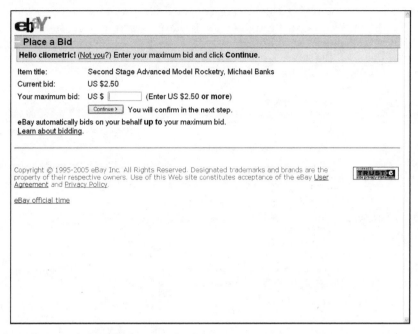

Figure 13-3: Placing a bid

Next, click the **Continue** button. If Buy It Now is available, and you wish to pay the Buy It Now price, click the button labeled **Buy It Now**. Clicking either button will display the Review and Confirm Bid page, as shown in Figure 13-4.

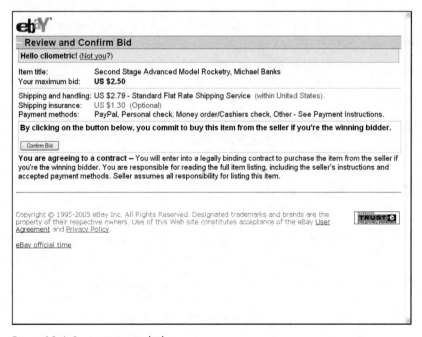

Figure 13-4: Reviewing your bid

If everything is correct (including your user ID), click the **Confirm Bid** button, and you'll see the Bid Confirmation page, shown in Figure 13-5.

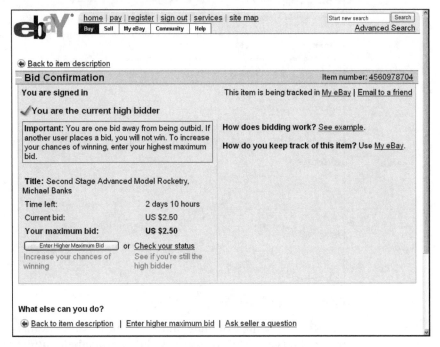

Figure 13-5: Bid Confirmation page

A line at the top of the Bid Confirmation page will advise you as to your bid status. Unless the auction has suddenly been closed by eBay or the seller, you'll see one of three messages. The text will be green for good news or red for bad news:

You are the current high bidder.
  This means just what it says. The notice will remain in place unless someone places a higher bid.

You have been outbid!
  If someone has placed a higher maximum than your bid, this notice will appear at the top of the page. It will remain there until you place a bid higher than the high bidder's maximum.

Reserve not met.
  This means that none of the bids has met the reserve price set by the seller. If the reserve is not met, the item is not sold, and the seller has the option of relisting it or offering it to another bidder through an eBay mechanism called a Second-Chance Offer (explained in the next chapter).

NOTE *On rare occasions, eBay crashes or is otherwise unavailable. When this happens, all auctions are "frozen" as of the time of the crash. So, if eBay crashes two hours before an auction is scheduled to end, you will still have two hours left to bid when eBay comes back online.*

Retract a Bid

Sellers (and eBay) frown on bid retraction. It can be a tool for harassment, and it generally disrupts the orderly process of an auction sale. Placing and then retracting bids—especially high bids—discourages other bidders. But buyers sometimes must retract bids for legitimate reasons.

According to eBay, only three reasons for retracting a bid are acceptable:

- You accidentally entered the wrong bid.
- The seller changed the item's description substantially.
- You cannot contact the seller by email or telephone.

Despite eBay's narrow view, all sorts of personal emergencies can make it necessary or prudent to retract a bid. A sudden catastrophic expense, for instance, may make it impossible for the bidder to go through with a deal. Bidders sometimes misunderstand item descriptions and retract their bids for this reason. Or a bidder could simply have second thoughts. Whatever your reasons, you cannot retract a bid if the auction ends in less than 12 hours.

To retract a bid, go to the Bid Retraction page. Click the Services link at the top of any page, and then click the Retract Your Bid link, and follow the instructions on the next page. You will need to enter the item number and select a reason on a rollup menu. After you cancel the bid, you and the seller will receive an email notification that the bid has been retracted.

Don't worry if you must retract a bid. It's not as if you're stealing from the seller, and it may turn out that you wouldn't have won the auction anyway. Just be sure to tell the seller why you are doing it. Most sellers understand about bid retractions, and some don't even notice retractions.

The consequences of retracting a bid, if there are any, will be minor. The number of bids you retract is recorded on your Member Profile page, which future sellers with whom you deal may or may not take into account (or even see). Beyond this, the buyer may complain, send a nasty email, or decide to put you on his Blocked Bidder/Buyer list to prevent you from bidding on any of his auctions.

Snipers and Sniping Strategies

A *sniper* is someone who waits until the last few minutes or seconds of an auction to place a bid with the intent of being the last person to get in a bid, hoping it will be higher than anyone else's bid.

This is one aspect in which eBay differs significantly from real-world auctions. Instead of sniping, bidders at a real-world auction can, in theory, continue bidding forever, or until the auctioneer says, "Sold!" Conversely, eBay auctions have a time limit. Anyone who wants to bid knows when an auction closes and can choose to be a sniper. This often results in bidders placing one bid after another during the final minutes of an auction, which can be quite dramatic.

Most sellers like this sort of thing. When bidders are competing in real time, they are very likely to go far over what they would bid otherwise. The last-minute competition raises the excitement level and stokes the fire. However, some sellers complain that snipers cause them to get lower prices for their items. Say bidder A has a high bid of $42 on a baseball card, and bidder B places a bid of $43 just 30 seconds before the auction ends. Some sellers maintain that bidder A might have bid $44 or more, if only he had known about bidder B's bid in time. In a real-world auction, yes, bidder A may have come back with a higher bid, if he hadn't already maxed out at $42, just as he may have outbid bidder B online. But there's no way to know, and an auction has to end sometime.

Many buyers don't like sniping, but judging from the number of eBay members who gripe about it, sniping works more often than not. There is nothing intrinsically or ethically wrong with sniping, nor is it prohibited by eBay. It is a simple fact of eBay auctions. Besides, some people snipe unintentionally. They happen to discover an auction a couple of minutes before it ends, so that's when they place their bids. And many, scoring a win with this tactic, become full-time snipers.

Most of the complaints about sniping come from people who have lost auctions to snipers. Some are sore losers, and some are just taken by surprise. They maintain that snipers are somehow "cheating," yet, they are free to do the same thing themselves.

Personally, I'm in favor of this practice, because it's one of the things that keeps online auctions interesting.

How to Beat Snipers

Some auction sites, notably Yahoo! Auctions, have provisions against snipers. At Yahoo! Auctions, a seller can turn on a feature that extends the auction by five minutes if a bid is placed within a few minutes of the auction's scheduled termination. eBay doesn't offer this feature, but you don't need it to beat a sniper.

NOTE *Automatic extensions encourage abuse, in particular shilling (see Chapter 16). With an auction automatically extended every time a bid is placed, shills have leverage against legitimate bidders who are more likely to bid higher as the end of an auction approaches, the excitement rises, and the competitive feeling kicks in. Automatic extensions also provide opportunities for pranksters, who might keep an auction going indefinitely, manually or through sniping services, with no intention of bidding.*

You can beat snipers in two ways:

Become a sniper yourself
If your schedule permits and you can handle the excitement, wait until one or two minutes before the auction ends, and place your maximum bid. Be aware, though, that another equally determined bidder may be doing the same thing, and your last-minute bid may drive him to up his bid further. By the same token, you may find yourself bidding far more than you intended when he outbids you.

Outbid snipers in advance

If you have a bid of $275 on an auction but your proxy bid is $350, the only way a sniper can beat you is by bidding $355. The sniper can squeeze in a final bid in 1/1000 of a second before the auction's end, but if the most he bids is $325 or $349, you will still be the winner.

Of course, the longer your bid sits there, the more likely it is that someone will come along and bid higher than your maximum (as was my experience with the airplane photo). If the auction ends at 3:00 PM, be online and have your bid ready at 2:55 PM. If you need to leave for work at 2:30, place your highest bid before you go. Alternatively, you could get a real proxy bidder to snipe for you: Ask a friend or relative who is familiar with eBay to place your bid a few minutes (or seconds) before the auction ends.

Sniping Strategy

Successful snipers recommend that you open two browser windows, each displaying the auction you're intending to win. Use one to track bids, refreshing it every 10 or 15 seconds so you can see what the latest bid amount is and whether you need to bid again. Use the second window to enter bids.

NOTE *To speed up reloading, turn off your browser's display of graphics and animation. Also turn off sound.*

Enter your highest bid less than 10 seconds before the auction ends. This reduces the possibility that someone else will see the bid in time to respond. Don't despair if you have a conventional dial-up connection rather than cable, DSL, or satellite. You can still win a sniping battle. (I've won against other snipers in several auctions while using a dial-up Internet connection.)

Sniping Tools

Sniping is so popular that there are services and software to do your sniping for you. I recommend using a web-based sniping service to reduce complexity and eliminate the possibility of error, but you may want to see what you can do with sniping software.

Web Sniping Services

Web sniping services are websites that charge for placing bids for you seconds before an auction ends. Sniping services offer several advantages, not the least of which is the elimination of the emotional factor that can compel you to bid beyond your limit. Sniping services let you bid on auctions when you can't be at your computer, and they are sometimes more accurate than manual sniping.

The disadvantages of relying on a sniping service are that you could lose your chance to bid if the sniping site computer malfunctions or if a malfunction in eBay's system prevents the sniping service from communicating with it. Plus, you must give the sniping site your eBay user ID and password, which may be a concern to some bidders.

Figure 13-6 illustrates setting up a bid with a sniping service called eSnipe.

Figure 13-6: eSnipe home page

NOTE   *Bid sniping has become such a hotly contested issue that some auction sites—including eBay in Germany—have at times banned the use of sniping services by blocking bids from the ISPs that provide sniping services. Manual sniping is still permitted on eBay in Germany and other sites, along with the use of sniping software run locally off your computer (which is nearly impossible for an auction site to detect).*

Sniping services offer a variety of features, including the ability to set up a snipe bid as you view an item on eBay. Most have an auction "scouting" service, which conducts searches for you and reports when it finds items of possible interest. A few sniping services require you to download software that interfaces with their websites; most handle everything on their server.

Some services charge a few cents per bid placed, plus a set percentage of the sale price of each item won; others charge a monthly fee.

Whether you use a sniping service or not depends on how important winning is to you. Maybe manually bidding that same amount yourself right before the end of the auction would be equally effective. (I don't use sniping services because I don't feel I bid on enough auctions to make it worthwhile; instead, I almost always bid at the last second, manually.) If you cannot be online and ready to bid just before an auction closes, and winning the item is very important to you, then a sniping service is the way to go. Also, if you bid on a lot of items, a sniping service could be worth its cost. These services are usually more precise than manual sniping in getting a bid in at the last possible second. The more you use the sniping service, the lower the cost on a per-auction basis.

Among the more popular sniping services are AuctionSnipe.com, eSnipe.com, PowerSnipe.com, and BidSlammer.com. It is difficult to recommend one service over another, because improvements are constantly being made. Visit the websites of the various sniping services to learn what they have to offer. Check the boards at eBay, too, to see which services other bidders find the most effective and reliable.

Bulk Bidding

Several sniping services offer what I call "bulk bidding." This allows you to set up last-minute bids on more than one auction for the same item—a digital camera, for example—and cancels all bids if you win one of the auctions. Thus, if you want a particular model Niklod SLR digital camera, and there are 28 auctions for this same camera (a situation that is not uncommon), you can set up bulk bidding to place a bid on each auction during its final seconds. If you don't win the first auction, the service bids on the second auction, and so on, until you win one of the auctions or lose them all.

To work properly, the auctions must end a certain number of minutes apart from each other to ensure that the service can cancel all bids after a win.

Sniping Software

Sniping software is installed on your computer and works through a web browser to place last-second bids. Most sniping programs are actually full-service auction support packages, offering features such as searching, tracking bids, and even posting items for sellers, in addition to placing bids.

Unlike Web-based sniping services, sniping programs, which run on your system, require that your computer be turned on. Most can launch, connect to the Internet, place bids, and log off automatically, although a few require that you set up a connection to the Internet first.

Among the sniping programs you may wish to look into are AuctionSleuth, Auction Station Sniper, and AuctionTamer.

Given the knowledge and tools discussed in this chapter, you may not win every time, but you should win most of the time. And even if you do lose, you may still be able to buy the item in question or otherwise salvage something from the deal. Strategies that enable you to win after losing are the subject of the next chapter.

14

HOW TO TURN A LOSS INTO A WIN

Not being the high bidder or forgetting to bid on an eBay auction doesn't necessarily mean you've lost. Although eBay may not approve of all of these tactics, I'll present some approaches to getting those auction items you've lost.

Find a Similar Item

A first step to obtaining an item after being outbid is to search for the same item over several days after the auction you lost ends. You may get lucky, for several possible reasons:

- Seller A, whose auction you just lost, has more of the same item but is selling them several days apart, hoping to get the best prices.
- Seller B has one of the same items to sell, but was just waiting for seller A's auction to end, to avoid diluting the pool of potential buyers.

- Another seller who has an item like the one you want hadn't planned to auction it, but has now decided there's enough demand to part with it after all.

In any of these cases, the item may not appear for sale on eBay for up to a week after the first auction's end.

It may prove fruitful to search completed auctions, too. It is not unusual to miss an auction entirely for one reason or another, which is why it behooves you to search completed auctions regularly for items you're serious about buying. You may find an auction that has expired without finding a buyer. As I've pointed out several times already, the most frequent cause for an item not selling is overpricing. Some sellers are just too optimistic. Fortunately, when an item doesn't sell, most sellers reduce their expectations and asking price. That being the case, you can just wait for an unsold item to be reposted, or you can be proactive and ask the seller to repost it or try to make a deal with him.

NOTE *Completed item searches look only at titles and not item descriptions.*

Take a Second-Chance Offer

Sometimes, a winning bidder fails to complete a transaction. He may have changed his mind about the item, experienced problems that prevent him from paying for it, or been suspended from eBay for one reason or another.

When a bidder doesn't pay, the seller may elect to repost the item or make what is called a Second-Chance Offer to the second-highest bidder. If you were the runner-up and the seller decides to make a Second-Chance Offer to you, you'll receive an email message from eBay informing you of the offer. At this point, you can ignore the offer or sign in and buy the item. It's all done through eBay, and eBay still receives its cut, so it's not against the rules.

The seller may not be aware of the Second-Chance Offer system, however, or you might have been third or fourth in the bidding rank. Therefore, it is a good idea to email the seller as soon as you can after losing an auction to let her know that you stand ready to buy the item, should the winning bidder not come through with payment.

Second-Chance Offers also can be for duplicate items. As noted, sellers sometimes have several of the same item but sell only one at a time. This happens often enough that eBay has made a provision for a seller to offer the same item to a backup bidder via a Second-Chance Offer. If you lose an item, consider writing to the seller to ask whether she has more of the item. The seller can make a Second-Chance Offer with a duplicate item up to 60 days after the auction ends. (Or the seller can just sell the item to you directly, which is against eBay's rules.)

Finally, Second-Chance Offers may come as a result of a reserve auction where the reserve price was unmet, so the item is not sold. The seller can try relisting the item or, if the auction had multiple bidders, the seller can offer the item to any of one of them—at the bidder's last bid, even though it did not meet the reserve. This is done through the Second-Chance Offer system and proceeds just like a regular auction sale. The offer cannot be made to anyone other than a bidder.

SHILLING AND SECOND-CHANCE OFFERS

If you receive a Second-Chance Offer for an item that someone else won, it may be prudent to look into the winning bidder's recent history, as described in Chapter 13. It is possible to disguise shilling by using the Second-Chance Offer system, rather than having the shill openly cancel a bid. In this case, the seller simply pretends that the shill bidder didn't pay, and sends the Second-Chance Offer to the second-highest bidder.

If you get a Second-Chance Offer, check to see whether the winner made several bids to force your proxy or manual bid higher. If this is the case, check the winner's feedback. If he bids primarily on items from the seller who made you the Second-Chance Offer, it could be a setup. You can ignore the Second-Chance Offer, and wait to see whether the item is relisted. Then if the suspected shill places bids on this auction again, don't participate.

Make a Deal with the Winner

If an auction consists of a group of items and you want only one of them, you might try emailing the winner to see if you can buy the one piece you wanted out of the lot. Possibly, the winning bidder didn't want that particular item and will be glad to sell it.

Occasionally, you will lose an auction because you forgot to bid or didn't bid enough. In this situation, the winning bidder might have purchased the item for far less than you would have bid. If this happens, you can ask the winner if he wants to sell the item at a profit. Or you can spend a little time researching his bidding habits to see what other sorts of things he buys. You may have something to offer as a trade or partial trade with additional cash.

Having said that, it's important to remember that there are some members who will report you for proposing to make a deal outside the purview of eBay. These individuals are either very scrupulous or just tattletales. Others may fear that they're being "tested" by eBay, to see if they'll jump at this unauthorized proposal.

You can cover yourself by suggesting that the eBay member sell the item to you through eBay, if he would be more comfortable doing that, rather than brokering a deal off the books. Most of the time, that show of good faith will be enough to dispel any fears he has, and he'll just make the deal with you directly.

When making deals of this type, where you buy directly from the seller, be aware that you are no longer shielded by the protections that buying through eBay affords.

On the other hand, if the winner (or anyone else you want to make a deal with) puts the item up for sale on eBay at your request, you're not circumventing eBay's rules. If someone agrees to post an item on eBay for you to buy, urge her to categorize it as a fixed-price item and to notify you immediately when she posts it. This reduces the risk of someone else coming along and snatching the item before you can buy it.

Make a Deal with a Seller

Strictly speaking, you cannot go to a seller and ask him to sell something to you that someone else has already won. It is against eBay rules, and you will probably encounter quite a bit of hostility from the seller. A seller who would agree to this opens himself up to Negative Feedback and a possible report back to eBay.

Of course, if the item is truly one-of-a-kind and important to you (such as the long-lost lamp your great uncle made in high school shop class in 1938), and you *really, really* want it, you might try offering the seller a $25,000 bonus. He can always say he lost or damaged the item and refund the buyer's money.

But that's an extreme example. The fact is that very few sellers will back out of a closed deal. Despite my cavalier treatment of the subject earlier, people are, as eBay's Community Values statement says, basically good. You're better off trying to make a deal with an auction's winner than attempting to corrupt the seller.

By the terms of the eBay User Agreement and by most ethical standards, eBay has a right to demand that a buyer and seller not make a side deal involving an item that has been posted for auction or sale on eBay, even if it did not sell. eBay urges members who are solicited via email (especially using eBay's Member Contact system) to report the person doing the soliciting, so you are at risk if you try this. The best way to avoid problems in this context is to contact the seller and request that she repost the article. Again, ask the seller to repost the item with a Buy It Now option at an agreed-upon time, so you don't have to wait through another auction period and don't risk losing it to someone else.

That said, from my viewpoint, eBay's entitlement should not prohibit one eBayer from contacting another to say, "I see you're interested in old radios. I have two for sale," or, "I see that you sell old radios; do you happen to have any made by Crosley?"

NOTE *Unless it's through the Second-Chance Offer system, it's a monumentally bad idea for a seller to make a deal with another eBay member for an unsold item. The idea is that eBay deserves a piece of the deal, having brought together seller and buyer in the first place. Of course, plenty of dealing goes on in email, no matter what eBay thinks of it.*

So, if you do want to make some sort of deal with a seller, you might be able to get some leverage by finding out what the seller likes. Not all sellers are also buyers, and the ones who are buyers don't always use their same seller ID. But it may be worth running a seller's ID through the Search: Items by Bidder page. Be sure to click the Yes radio button next to "Include completed items" and "Yes, even if not high bidder," as described in the previous chapter. This may uncover the fact that the seller collects or is otherwise interested in something you have, giving you a bargaining chip.

If you contact the seller and she agrees to do a trade or partial trade, follow the same procedure as you would in making a deal with the winner of an auction you've lost.

Ideally, you won't have to concern yourself with finding a replacement item or trying to make a deal with a seller or an auction winner, because you'll win every auction you bid on (well, most of them, anyway).

After the initial exhilaration, it's time to get down to the business of paying for the auction and getting the seller to send the item to you, which is what the next chapter is about.

15

PAYING FOR AND GETTING YOUR ITEMS

When you win an auction it's certainly a time to rejoice, but this is only the first step in getting your item. It remains for you to pay for your win, and for the seller to send it to you. This chapter covers the steps and options involved in paying for and getting your items. You'll also get some insight into what may happen if you don't pay for the item you've won.

Invoices

When you win an auction, eBay sends an email message advising you of that fact. It will look something like the message shown in Figure 15-1.

If the seller doesn't use PayPal, you won't see the PayPal logo and Pay Now button in the message. If the button is there and you want to pay by credit card, check, or your PayPal balance, click it. (See the "Payment Methods" section later in this chapter for more information about PayPal.)

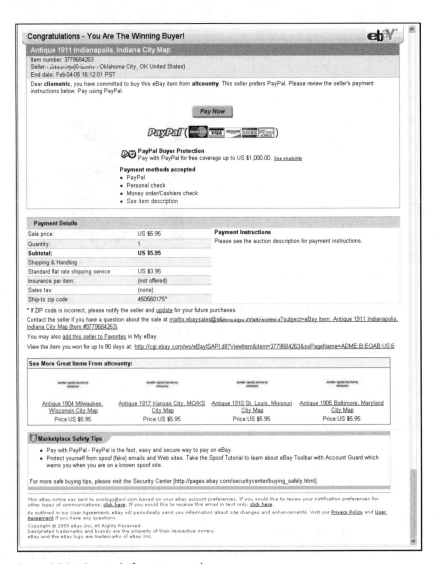

Figure 15-1: eBay end of auction email message

The seller may also have set up things so that PayPal or another service sends an email with an invoice to you. And some sellers send the same thing to winners manually. This can get annoying, but some sellers don't seem to realize that all those other emails are flying around out there. I suggest that you just ignore the extraneous messages. As long as the seller acknowledges that she has heard from you and knows payment is on the way, you can relax. See Chapter 12 for details on communicating with the seller.

Shipping Charges

If the seller did not put in shipping charges when she created the auction listing, the system will not have that information and, hence, the invoice you receive will be incomplete. You'll need to look in the item description or email the seller to learn the final cost.

If the seller has opted to have the cost calculated based on the winner's location, there will be a form on the item page where you can enter your ZIP Code to find out how much shipping will cost. (This form is available in item listings before the auction ends, for bidder convenience.) This is common for heavy items, because the shipping cost will vary depending on the buyer's distance from the seller. The cost calculated here will include handling fees (if any) along with the shipping charge, so you may want to use the U.S. Postal Service's (USPS's) website and/or United Parcel Service's (UPS's) website to see the true shipping cost.

NOTE *Some sellers don't provide the shipping cost form in their listings but do tell you the weight of the item and their ZIP Code. Given these elements, you can calculate shipping costs yourself at the USPS website (www.usps.gov), the UPS website (www.ups.com), or the sites of other delivery services.*

What if the seller doesn't include shipping charges in her email and there's no information about shipping in the listing? In such a case, I typically calculate the postage myself and include that amount with my payment. I'll also include a note that says, "Payment is included for First Class [or Media Mail or Priority Mail] shipping." I have never had a seller object to this arrangement.

Request an Invoice

If you need to, you can file a request for an invoice for the item you won. This is particularly handy for communicating with the seller (see Chapter 12). It's simpler than email and puts your contact on record with eBay. It can serve as a polite reminder if you don't get an email reply from the seller after a day or two. This also will furnish you with the shipping amount, if it is not included in the auction's description.

If you look at the Items I've Won list on your My eBay page, as shown in Figure 15-2, you'll see a button labeled Request Invoice to the right of each auction's sale date. Clicking this button will lead to a page that sends an email request to the seller to contact you with complete information regarding your total payment. This button is also available within an auction listing.

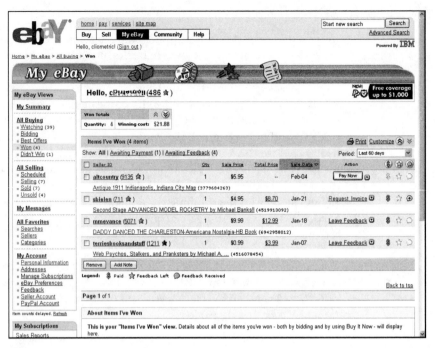

Figure 15-2: Items I've Won list

Pay Now

In addition to emailing your seller as soon as possible, you might also want to use the Pay Now button you'll find next to the item you've won on your My eBay page. (The button will also be displayed on the item's page, and in the confirmation email you receive from eBay.) This button appears only if the seller included the shipping cost when she listed the item. This is, in effect, an automated means of generating an invoice.

NOTE   *Clicking the **Pay Now** button on your My eBay page will take you to a different page. If you don't want to leave your My eBay page, you can right-click the **Pay Now** button displayed in your Items I've Won list (not the Pay Now button displayed at the end of an item's listing page) and open the link in a new browser window. This speeds things up because you can return to the My eBay page without needing to reload it.*

Click **Pay Now**, and you will see a page titled Review Your Purchase, where you can check the terms and select a payment method, as shown in Figure 15-3. (Payment methods will vary, depending on what the seller accepts.) The next page displays a prewritten note notifying the seller how you plan to pay. You can add your own comments to the note if you wish, but be aware that they will be pasted in near the end of eBay's canned note, which means the seller may not see your comments. If you have something important to tell the seller, do it in a separate email message.

If you select PayPal as a payment method, a new browser window will open at the PayPal website. After you sign on to PayPal, you'll see a page with all your purchase information filled in, ready for you to approve payment, as shown in Figure 15-3.

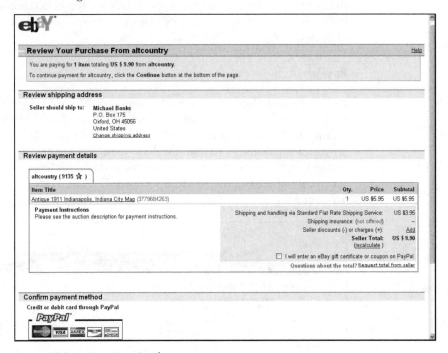

Figure 15-3: Review Your Purchase page

Third-Party Checkout Systems

A number of sellers use third-party checkout systems. These are websites that collect information about the auction you've won, how you're going to pay, and your shipping address. Most such services also handle credit card payments, but this does not mean that you must pay by credit card. As a rule, these systems are far more complex than eBay's checkout.

NOTE *Several of the website checkout systems I've used (as a buyer) have proven to be infinitely annoying and inefficient. One site, for example, refused to work with Microsoft Internet Explorer. When I contacted the email address provided by the site, I was told that the site worked only with a "real" browser, meaning Netscape. Another site, which several sellers I've bought from have used, froze at a certain point every time I tried to use it. In each case, I advised the seller by email that payment was in transit, and the deal was completed without any problems.*

The first time you use one of these services, you will need to provide quite a bit of information about yourself (name, address, phone number, and so on), which it will save for next time you use it. That's convenient, but it's up to you whether you want to give your personal information to yet another website that you may never visit again.

Payment Methods

The usual payment plans offered by eBay sellers are online payment systems, money orders, and personal checks. Some accept cash as well, but it's risky to trust that to the postal system, especially for big-ticket items. Because the PayPal online system is owned by eBay, it's the quickest way to complete an eBay deal.

PayPal

PayPal membership offers several advantages. Members have the option of getting a PayPal ATM card, which can be used just like a regular MasterCard, online or off. Both buyers and sellers find PayPal particularly useful in international transactions, as PayPal handles currency conversions. PayPal pays interest on money in member accounts, and certain levels of membership receive small rebates on purchases. Figure 15-4 shows an example of a PayPal account page.

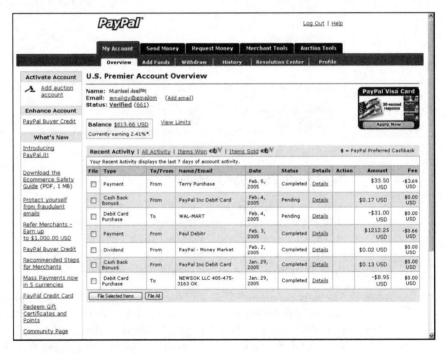

Figure 15-4: PayPal account page

To sign up for PayPal, you will need either a credit card or a checking account, as well as a physical mailing address (not a post office box), which PayPal will use to send postal mail to verify your existence. (The mailing address must match the address used by your credit-card provider or bank.)

You do not need to deposit money to open a PayPal account, although you can easily transfer money from a credit card, debit card, or checking account to your PayPal account. Most buyers transfer money from credit cards, as this is faster than transferring money from a checking account, which takes more than a week.

To spend or withdraw money from their accounts, most PayPal members use their PayPal ATM cards. Others transfer money directly from PayPal to bank accounts. A few have PayPal send checks when they want money from their PayPal account (there is a small service charge for this).

NOTE *If you want to reduce the chances of losing money—even temporarily—use PayPal's ATM card instead of a credit card when you make online purchases, and keep a relatively small balance in the account. That way, if someone gets his hands on your card number and expiration date, or the card itself, you'll have minimized the amount that can be stolen.*

WHAT IF YOU DON'T WANT TO USE PAYPAL?

Some sellers list PayPal as the *only* payment method accepted. (Of course, PayPal entices sellers to use its service exclusively, such as by offering a feature called Require Immediate Payment with PayPal.) To use PayPal, you must have a credit card, checking account, or a bank debit card (connected with a checking account). Not everyone meets these requirements. Until such a time when universal cash cards are more readily available, some people will prefer (or need) to pay with a money order, cash, or check.

If you encounter this in a listing, write to the seller and ask whether you can pay by other means.

If you end up winning an item whose seller accepts only PayPal (and you didn't notice this before bidding), you can make an end run by paying the seller your way before she has a chance to protest. Get the seller's snail mail address (use the Contact Information form on the Find Members page if necessary, but be aware that the address that eBay has may be wrong). Then send your payment to her as soon as possible. I have done this, and the deal worked out fine.

PayPal offers a buyer protection plan, a money back guarantee, and a buyer complaint service. In order to qualify for any of these forms of protection, there must be a physical item involved (services, e-books, and downloaded or emailed products are not covered).

PayPal Buyer Protection

This plan can reimburse buyers up to $1,000 for items not received. If you used PayPal Buyer Credit to purchase the item, the amount may be higher. You must file your claim within 45 days of an auction's close. You cannot use the PayPal Buyer Protection Plan if you file a claim through eBay's Buyer Protection Plan (discussed in Chapter 12) or if you file for a chargeback through your credit card company.

PayPal Money Back Guarantee

When you pay for an item with PayPal, you can buy a PayPal Money Back Guarantee to protect your purchase, up to $1,000, on selected items from eligible sellers. The purchase must involve physical goods, and the reimbursement request must be filed within 45 days of payment. If a buyer's money is to be refunded, the buyer must return the item in question before receiving a refund.

PayPal Buyer Complaint Process

This process provides a means of filing a formal grievance against a seller. The program offers the possibility of reimbursement for a percentage of the amount lost in a transaction. As with other buyer protection plans, the disputed purchase must involve a physical item.

A number of restrictions apply to each program. Details of other limitations are available at PayPal's website.

NOTE *A few sellers demand that buyers who pay with PayPal add a certain percentage of the total sale "to cover PayPal fees." This is an unreasonable demand. The PayPal fee is part of the seller's overhead, and making the buyer pay for this is like a clothing store adding a surcharge to your total "to cover our bank fees." Any such costs should be built into the price. If such an extra charge is enough to dissuade you from bidding on an item, write to the seller and let him know. The response may well be, "You'd give up a great deal over a few cents?" Which is, of course, precisely what the seller is doing. Maybe you can get him to come around to your way of thinking.*

Other Online Payment Systems

Online payment systems require that you register (usually at no charge) and provide credit card and/or checking account data, as well as full contact information. If you are not comfortable doing this, you can't use the online systems. They are convenient, however, particularly the larger services, like PayPal, which can be used with other online merchants, not just eBay.

Realize that not all payment systems operate like PayPal, transferring money to the seller's account at no charge to the buyer. A very few, like Western Union Auction Payments service (formerly BidPay), deliver the money by snail mail in the form of a check.

Western Union charges the buyer for this service. Next to PayPal, Western Union Auction Payments service is probably the best way for someone outside the United States to pay for an auction. To use this service, you go to the Western Union website (www.auctionpayments.com) and use a credit card to pay the amount you owe the seller, plus the service charge. Western Union cuts a check in the United States and mails it to the seller.

NOTE *Western Union and eBay specifically recommend that you do not use Western Union or MoneyGram money-transfer services to pay for auctions, as they can easily be turned to fraudulent uses. You should use money-transfer services only if you know the person to whom you are sending money. If a seller says he will accept* only *money transfer, forget the deal and report the seller to eBay.*

Money Orders

As a rule, sending a money order is safe and results in a faster turnaround by the seller than a personal check. With a money order—especially a postal money order—the seller has a 100 percent guarantee of payment.

The only drawback for the seller is that, with the exception of postal money orders, a money order must be handled like a check; that is, most money orders must be deposited or cashed at a bank. This can come as a surprise to some recipients who discover, for example, that Wal-Mart will not cash a Wal-Mart money order. For this reason, it's usually best to use USPS money orders for eBay purchases. They can be cashed at any post office (and just about every seller goes to the post office), and banks welcome them, too.

For international payments, most sellers should be willing to accept an international money order from the USPS. If the auction is in another currency, you will need to work out the dollar amount with the seller. (If you pay with PayPal, the exchange rate and amount in your currency will be calculated for you, for most countries.)

NOTE   *eBay auctions posted by sellers outside the United States have a price listing in the seller's local currency, plus an approximation in U.S. dollars, based on the most recent exchange rate eBay has obtained.*

Checks

Many sellers are suspicious of personal checks. There is no guarantee that a personal check will be good, and if it bounces, the seller loses $30 or more. As a result, some sellers will not accept personal checks under any circumstances. Those who do usually hold the merchandise until the check clears. So, if you're in a hurry to receive an item, don't pay with a personal check.

A cashier's or bank check is another thing entirely. Sellers usually treat a cashier's check like a money order and will ship your merchandise as soon as they receive it.

You will find few foreign sellers willing to accept checks of any kind. This is because banks charge a stiff fee for handling checks from other countries. The payee will have to wait—sometimes weeks—to get the money.

Escrow Services

An escrow service is a third party that, for a fee, holds payment for an auction item and does not release the money until the buyer has reported satisfactory delivery. This is useful for particularly valuable items and represents the only condition under which a seller should send merchandise to a buyer before receiving payment. The only issue to resolve is who will pay the escrow fee, which is normally a percentage of the payment amount.

There have been scams reported involving illegitimate "escrow services." In some, the seller instructs the buyer to send payment to an escrow service. When the buyer doesn't receive the item and investigates what happened, he learns that there was no escrow service at the address to which he sent his money (and maybe there was never really an item up for auction). More sophisticated scams have involved websites that purport to be escrow services, and then disappear after scamming several people.

So, be wary if a seller insists that you use an escrow service. Indeed, this should be the buyer's choice, since its purpose is to protect him. eBay also advises, "If you are a buyer or a seller and choose to pay or be paid through an escrow service, you should use only Escrow.com (www.escrow.com), eBay's approved escrow service."

Shipping Methods

The method used to ship items is usually up to the seller. I've noticed that the majority of sellers either ship by the cheapest method possible or offer a choice of shipping methods. For example, if you buy a book, a seller may offer you a choice of Media Mail or First Class. eBay recently added a feature whereby sellers can offer buyers a choice of shipping method, and then eBay automatically calculates the postage.

Some sellers use Priority Mail exclusively because, for a small charge, a Priority Mail envelope or package can be assigned a tracking number that both the buyer and the seller can enter at the USPS website for a status update. Other sellers force you to pay for Priority Mail shipping simply because this service entitles them to free boxes and free pickup from the post office. This is unfair and exploitative, not to mention extortionist. Whenever you see Priority Mail offered and you feel it is too expensive for what is being shipped, ask if the seller will ship by another method.

NOTE *If your purchase is small, perhaps a postcard or antique brochure, consider sending a self-addressed, stamped envelope to the seller. I usually do this when I win a small item, on the theory that the seller is likely to send my item right away—and remember me next time.*

When bidding on multiple items from the same seller, ask about combining shipments and getting a break on the shipping cost. It seems only logical, right?

If you have concerns about shipping, consider having your item shipped with a tracking number. This is standard with UPS and Federal Express, and is available for a small extra charge from the USPS. Where an expensive or one-of-a-kind item is involved, insurance may be advisable as well.

In-Person Pickup

On occasion, you may win an auction by a seller who lives close enough that you can pick up the item in person. Or, if the item you won is too large to ship, you might choose this arrangement. In either case, you may find that the seller prefers to bring the item to you or to meet in public to exchange money and merchandise; some people do not like the idea of strangers coming to their homes.

Excessive Shipping and Handling Charges

Sometimes, a seller will grossly inflate his shipping or "handling" charges—for example, $20 to mail something like a photograph or a magazine with a final bid of $3. This is obviously far more than it costs the seller to send the item, even though he may claim he has "expenses" such as shipping materials, gasoline for trips to the post office ("Gee, whaddaya do—make a separate trip for each package?"), his time, and other bogus claims. In reality, all of these elements should be built into an item's price or minimum bid. Sellers who add such handling charges are extorting additional profit. In effect, they are letting the buyer believe she is buying an item for the bid amount, when she is really paying the bid *plus* $20.

Before you bid, make sure you know what the shipping charge is and whether there are any "handling" charges. If this information isn't included in the listing, write to the seller and ask. If you consider the shipping/handling charge to be excessive, consider looking for the same or a similar item offered by another seller.

If you feel a handling charge is unwarranted, try negotiating with the seller. Tell him that you know the handling charge is padded and that you're not willing to pay it, but you might pay a lesser amount. You could also offer to send the seller a postage-paid, self-addressed box or envelope to reduce the seller's "packing costs."

NOTE   *I remember one seller who added a handling charge of $8 for each and every item he sold (in addition to postage). He had several items I would have bought, but I didn't like the handling charge. I wrote to him to ask whether he could reduce it, since the items he sold were, with few exceptions, small things like photographs and documents. His reply explained that he was a retired man living on a fixed income, and that he had to pay kids to pack and ship things for him, or else he could not run this business. Needless to say, he didn't last long as a seller.*

eBay calls such extra charges "excessive." eBay discourages excessive handling charges because it recognizes this con not only as an attempt to make a buyer think she is paying less for an item, but also a way to beat eBay out of money. eBay levies a final value charge on every item sold online. Shipping and handling charges are exempt from the final value fee, which means the more a seller folds into "handling," the smaller eBay's cut.

eBay urges members to report such sellers. If you find yourself offended by bogus shipping and handling charges, go to eBay's Main Help page and click the Contact Us link. You'll see a Contact Us form, with selections to help you describe your problem, as shown in Figure 15-5.

In the first box, select "Ask about bidding or buying." In the second box, select "Problems with sellers," and in the third box select "Shipping cost is too high or unfair." Click **Continue**, and you will be taken to a page with links to explanations of eBay's policies on shipping, as well as an email link. Click the email link to send a report to eBay about the seller's excessive shipping charges.

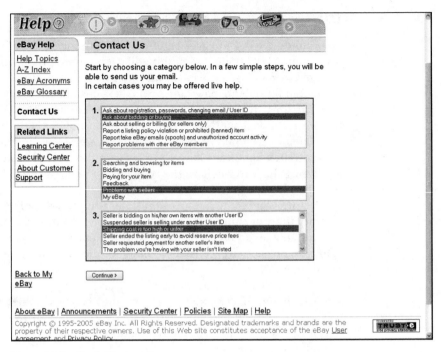

Figure 15-5: eBay's Contact Us page

NOTE *Rather than reporting the violation as excessive shipping/handling charges, you may wish to report it as circumventing fees. eBay gets a little more excited about sellers ripping them off than they do about sellers ripping off buyers.*

If a seller tries to ambush you with handling charges that were not mentioned in the item description, let him know that you will cancel the deal and report him to eBay for excessive shipping and handling charges, extortion, *and* Feedback extortion (since the seller will threaten you with Negative Feedback).

Payment Problems

It's obviously better to pay for an auction than not, but sometimes the vicissitudes of life put obstacles in the way of meeting our obligations. If that happens, it's time to communicate with your seller.

What If You Can't Pay Right Away?

If you are going to be late paying for an auction you've won, you should let the seller know right away. This allays any fears that you may not pay, and reduces the possibility of Neutral or Negative Feedback. If there are extenuating circumstances, most sellers will understand and give you the time you need. The same is true if you forgot to pay for the auction or are otherwise delayed in remitting. Again, the key is to *communicate* right away.

A few curmudgeons will respond to an honest explanation with accusations or threats, but there's nothing you can do with such people. Simply pay them as soon as you can, hold on to your proof of payment, and ignore everything else.

If you continue to delay sending payment, the seller will eventually give up and put the item up for resale. She may or may not leave Negative Feedback for you, too.

What If You Can't Pay at All?

If you spend some time reading the posts in Seller Central or the bulletin boards of eBay sellers' groups, you will probably find that many more people than you thought fail to pay for items. The nonpaying bidder (NPB) is among sellers' most popular topics of discussion. So what can happen to an NPB? Can an NPB really be forced to pay for an auction item? Probably not, but there *are* consequences.

On eBay, not paying for an item can result in any (or all) of three possible penalties:

- The seller can leave Negative Feedback for you.
- The seller can block you from bidding on her auctions again.
- The seller can file an Unpaid Item Dispute against you, which can lead to an Unpaid Item Strike.

There's also the possibility of legal consequences.

Unpaid Item Disputes and Strikes

Filing an Unpaid Item dispute isn't just about slamming an NPB with an Unpaid Item Strike. The seller can get a refund of the final value fee that eBay charged her when the auction ended if she files an Unpaid Item Dispute. But before a seller can file an Unpaid Item Dispute, she must file a Payment Reminder, which is an email message recorded with eBay that reminds the buyer that payment is due. Sellers must wait until ten days after the auction to do this.

If a seller files an Unpaid Item Dispute against you, eBay notifies you by email. For the next 14 days, a pop-up window will appear when you sign on to eBay reminding you of your outstanding payment. At this point, you and the seller have the option of agreeing to abort the transaction. If this happens, the dispute is closed, you do not receive an Unpaid Item Strike, and the seller receives a refund of her final value fee.

If you, the NPB, don't respond to the email or pop-up window within seven days, the seller has the option of closing the dispute and receiving a final value fee credit. But you will not receive a strike. This filters out the vindictive sellers from those who merely want their final value fee refunded.

According to eBay's rules, the seller also has the option of closing the dispute, receiving a credit, and giving the buyer an Unpaid Item Strike, if the buyer has acknowledged the reminders but still hasn't submitted payment or hasn't responded at all after eight days. (This may seem arbitrary, but it's how eBay lays out the rules.)

As the buyer, you can close the Unpaid Item Dispute by paying for the item (the quickest way is by using PayPal) or you can provide proof that you've already paid (a money order receipt, PayPal or credit card statement, and so on). And, of course, you and the seller can resolve the issue between the two of you however you decide.

To check the status of, respond to, and otherwise deal with a Non-Paying Bidder Dispute, go to your My eBay page, scroll down, and click the Dispute Console link at the left side of the page.

An Unpaid Item Strike is separate from your Feedback record and does not affect your Feedback score or member profile, but eBay keeps track of Unpaid Item Strikes. If a buyer accumulates too many Unpaid Item Strikes in too short a time period, she may be suspended from buying or selling on eBay. In typical corporate style, eBay doesn't publicly define the number or time frame.

If you have an Unpaid Item Strike, you can remove it if you provide eBay with proof of payment. It may also be removed if you provide proof that the seller canceled the transaction under dispute, such as an email or other written communication from the seller.

Beyond leaving Negative Feedback, locking you out of her auctions, and filing an Unpaid Item Dispute (with the possibility of an Unpaid Item Strike), there's nothing else the seller can do to you on eBay except say bad things on bulletin boards and in Feedback comments. It is up to you, as a buyer, whether you want to risk these consequences by not paying for an item. If you just don't have the money, these things don't matter. But if you suffer a case of "buyer's remorse" or just change your mind, take a moment to consider how your standing on eBay can be affected.

Legal Consequences of Not Paying

Can an NPB be taken to court? eBay's shtick that "your bid is a binding contract" scares some people, but it is almost guaranteed that no legal action will be taken against you if you don't pay for an item. It's just as unlikely as a real-world auctioneer taking you to court after you bid on an item and then walk away without paying or taking the item. You would be banned from future auctions, though.

There is always the potential that an overzealous seller will actually go to the trouble and expense of making a case against an NPB in his local small claims court. He may or may not win a judgment; if he does, it will be nearly impossible to collect, unless the seller lives in the court's jurisdiction.

I hope that all of your deals on eBay will come to quick and successful conclusions. You can enhance the chances of having positive eBay experiences by avoiding shady deals. And this is where the next chapter comes in. It shows you how to avoid shills, sleazes, and seller scams on eBay.

PART IV

HOW NOT TO GET RIPPED OFF AND WHAT TO DO IF YOU DO

16

SHILLS, SLEAZES, AND SELLER SCAMS

Just about every social or commercial activity that exists in the physical world has been duplicated on the Internet: dating, stalking, theft, entertainment, extortion, prostitution, identity theft, education, impersonation, libraries, and, of course, auctions.

In this chapter, we'll look at some common (and not-so-common) scams and downright illegal activities that take place on eBay. Many scams that sellers direct at other sellers (and would-be sellers) are detailed in Chapter 17, but even more scams are designed to misinform and rip off buyers, which is what this chapter covers.

The Case of the Bidder Who Wasn't There: Shills and Shields

Shill bidding is, as eBay defines it, "the deliberate placing of bids to artificially raise the price of an item."

Say you are bidding on an item—alone or against other bidders—and the price is at $65. If an unscrupulous seller isn't satisfied with the amount, he may get someone else to bid for him. The person who does this is called a *shill*.

eBay doesn't allow sellers to bid on their own items. Otherwise, they would unfairly drive up bids. However, sellers have been known to create phony buying accounts (which don't require a lot of verification) and use these to inflate bids for their items. Or the seller may enlist an acquaintance to place a fake bid. Either way, shill bidding is unequivocally against eBay's rules, and both the seller and the shill can be suspended for engaging in it. Shilling is also illegal in real-world auctions.

Because shill bidding is such a problem, eBay has made it against the rules for a seller's family members, employees, and roommates to bid on items offered by the seller—unless they buy a Fixed Price item, or use Buy It Now to purchase an auction or store item.

NOTE *Shilling is enough of a problem that law-enforcement agencies sometimes get involved in investigating it. Go to www.usdoj.gov/criminal/cybercrime and enter "shill" in the Search box to read about cases of big-time online shilling fraud and what happened to the perpetrators.*

Is a Shill at Work?

Although you may not be able to know for sure that a shill is bidding on an item, there are certain tip-offs. If you notice multiple bids from new bidders or multiple canceled bids, proceed with caution.

Multiple Bids from New Bidders

Shills may be recognizable by the fact that they are new eBay members, with few or no feedback points. Perpetrators often create user IDs for one or two auctions solely for shilling purposes. If the user ID of the person bidding against you was created about the same time as the auction began, he may be a shill.

Since a shill's objective is to drive up the bidding, he may bid several times. These bids will often be in small increments, in order to inflate the current high bid without going over the legitimate high bidder's maximum proxy amount. Clumsy shills will sometimes outbid the high bidder, and then immediately withdraw their bid.

You can view an item's bid history by clicking the link that shows the user ID of each bidder, in the order that the user bid. (You will not be able to see bid amounts until after the auction is over.) As shown in Figure 16-1, a bidder's ID is listed each time that person bids. A bidder who has bid on the item *in small increments* several times in a row may be bidding to drive up the item's price on behalf of the seller.

Canceled Bids

Several withdrawn or canceled bids from the same bidder (or two or three bidders) near the end of the auction may also indicate a shill at work, particularly if the canceled bids were higher than that of a remaining bidder. Since the shill has no intention of buying the item, she will withdraw her bids, or the seller will cancel them for her.

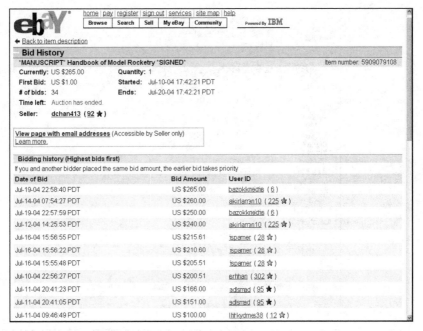

Figure 16-1: eBay bidder list

If you suspect another user of being a shill, spend some time looking at completed auctions in which she has bid. Go to the Search page and click the Items by Bidder link. You'll see the Search: Items by Bidder page, as shown in Figure 16-2. Enter the bidder's user ID, click the "Include completed listings" check box, and then click **Search**.

In the bidding history results list, keep an eye out for multiple bids and canceled or withdrawn bids. A pattern of these may indicate that the bidder is a shill.

Hot Item with Only One (Shill) Bidder

Because items with numerous bids are listed on eBay's home page as "hot" or "top 10," a seller may have a shill bid a dozen or more times in a row to attract more bidders. To see whether a seller is doing this, go to the auction's page and check out the item's bid history. (Click the link that lists the number of bids the item has.) If the bids are all from the same bidder, the bid count is being artificially boosted. The same may be true if the bids are from only two or even three bidders. Investigate the bidders' histories to determine whether this is likely.

Think You've Encountered a Shill Bidder?

After you've checked the item's bidding history to get the user IDs of the bidders involved and you've used the Search: Items by Bidder page to investigate the suspicious bidder, take a look at the profiles of both the bidder and seller. If the two are in the same town or region and/or have similar user IDs, there's a good chance the bidder is a shill.

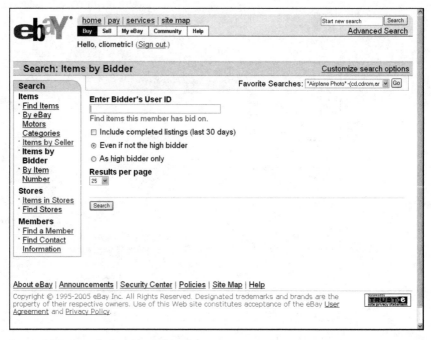

Figure 16-2: Search: Items by Bidder page

Check the bidder's Feedback rating and look for several Positive ratings for the same seller left by the suspect bidder in a brief span of time. You should also look at Feedback the suspect has left. If you see several Feedback items in a row for the seller whose item you're considering purchasing (or if this is the only seller for whom the suspect has left Feedback), you may have a shill on your hands.

Also, check to see if the suspect has had any items for sale. Look for patterns of shill bidding in those auctions, too.

If you think you have enough evidence, report it to eBay. eBay staffers will investigate, weigh the available evidence, and make their own determination on the matter.

Judging from discussions at Seller Central, however, eBay sometimes doesn't recognize a clear-cut case of shill bidding when it sees one, so don't expect much. Oddly, eBay doesn't even remove the Feedback profiles of shills whose accounts are suspended. But this is not necessarily an indication of inaction on eBay's part. The company usually does not report actions it takes on complaints to the public. And sometimes Feedback profiles remain up for a time even after an account is closed. If you report a shill bidder, keep an eye out for any bidding activity from him. If you don't see any, he has probably been suspended or left voluntarily.

It's up to you to cancel your bid and contact any legitimate-appearing bidders with your evidence. Ditto if you want to share the information on a bulletin board. If you cancel a bid because you suspect a shill is at work, it's unlikely that the seller will complain about your public discussion of his auction. If he does complain, point out that there appeared to be shilling connected with the auction, and that you'll be happy to take it up with eBay. Also explain that eBay probably took action against the suspected shill bidder, but as a rule, does not tell members when it does so. That should end the matter.

NOTE *If you choose to expose a shill bidder or other shady character to the eBay community, do it with a user ID other than the one you normally use to sell or buy. Note this in your message and explain that you're posting the note with the new ID to avoid Negative Feedback or other reprisals from the suspect seller. Do be aware that there's a good chance that eBay staff will delete your message, especially if your charges are not well supported or your message is too emotional.*

Bid Shielding

Bid shielding is a means of temporarily inflating an item's price in order to discourage other bidders. An eBay user places a bid and, shortly thereafter, her partner in crime places a really high bid. Just before the auction ends, the second bidder cancels her high bid. Since the second bidder's high bid has discouraged others from bidding, the first bidder wins—with a far lower bid than she might otherwise have placed.

If you suspect someone of bid shielding, take a look at past auctions she has bid on. If there is a pattern of high bids followed by bid cancellations, report the abuse to eBay. As with shilling, you may wish to report your suspicions to the eBay community at large and refrain from bidding on the seller's auctions.

Lies in Listings

Sellers can be deceitful in their listings, by using misleading titles, false images, and deceptive descriptions. It's true that a confusing title or unclear description may be the innocent result of poor writing, rather than an intentional con, but either way, you should take a few minutes to make sure what you're buying is what you think it is.

To check the seller's record on descriptions, view a list of her completed auctions. Have a look at the feedback comments to see if previous buyers were satisfied with similar items that they bought from this seller. You might email a few winners of the seller's auctions and ask how accurate the descriptions were. And you can always email the seller directly with some pointed questions.

Misleading Auction Titles

Misleading titles are usually just an annoyance, but they can sometimes trick buyers into bidding on items they don't really want. Using a title that is misleading is against eBay rules, but that doesn't stop some of the site's more dark-hearted sellers.

Consider this title:

"Rare 1920 Ford Model A Watch!!!!!!"

The item was a brand-new watch with a picture of a 1920 Ford on the face. A legitimate title for this item would read something like, "Watch with a 1920 Ford Model picture," but that wouldn't con anyone into looking at the item. The misleading title might make a few people think the item is an 80+ year-old watch made by Ford, and maybe one of them would actually buy it.

Here's another example:

New 1950s dial telephone!!!!

The item was a reproduction telephone, still in its original box, and "new" as in "manufactured last year." This sort of trick relies on the fact that, as readers, we tend to skip or filter out certain words and phrases that we see too often, such as *new, best, fully loaded,* and *bargain.* In this example, the part of the brain that parses written words may ignore "New" and focus instead on the "1950s dial telephone" part. If the description is sufficiently misleading and doesn't say that the telephone is a reproduction, a buyer might be fooled into thinking that this is a telephone manufactured in the 1950s that is still in its original shipping box. You'll see an example of such a description in the "Sins of Omission" section later in this chapter.

Next, consider the "Not" type of title:

"AM-FM set! Not an RCA radio"

The item was a Watashiwa-Dai radio, a brand you've never heard of and probably never will see again. The phrase "Not *<whatever>*" in an auction title is a trick used to force an item to appear in search results. For example, "Not RCA" might be attached to an item made by General Electric, Sharp, or any other company, just to entice buyers who really are searching for RCA. The seller hopes that, even though the buyer is looking for an RCA product, he will see this item in his search results and be moved to bid on it anyway. This specific trick is against eBay rules.

Some sellers resort to using abbreviations in titles, hoping you'll overlook them or click through to find out what's being described. Instead of writing "replica" they might use "rep," or they might say "styl" instead of "style." If you don't understand a term in a title, ask about it.

Not all clever auction titles are intended to deceive. Sometimes, the seller is trying to pack in as much information as possible, while relying on the item's category to dispel any confusion. For example, I offered a 1968 press photograph of a model of the Cincinnati Reds' Riverfront Stadium, taken when the stadium was still in the proposal stage—an item of obvious interest to baseball historians, Cincinnati Reds fans, and collectors of Cincinnati ephemera. I wrote a title with keywords that appealed to each of those groups:

1968 Riverfront Stadium architect model, Cincinnati Reds

The only problem with the title was that it did not indicate that the item was a photograph and not the architect's model itself. I didn't want to pay extra to add a subtitle, but I thought that the fact that the item was listed in the Collectibles/Photographic Images category would tell careful browsers that they weren't actually looking at a model. I really should have used the word "photo" or "foto" in the title, but no one complained.

A more subtle example is a title I encountered while looking for some classic car parts:

1951 VW Beetle Junker

The current bid was $69.51—what a dream! I clicked the title, expecting to see an auction with the reserve price not met. Instead, I found a creatively rendered diorama, the centerpiece being a die-cast Volkswagen Beetle toy made to look "aged," sitting in front of an old fence. This sort of creative titling may or may not have been intended to deceive the shopper or misrepresent the item. From an ethical standpoint, however, it *is* misleading. To report a deceptive title, go to eBay's Help page, enter "Misleading titles" in the Search box and click **Search Help** for instructions.

Looks Can Fool You

The *photo* in the 1951 Volkswagen Beetle auction was more blatantly deceptive. While the toy car was displayed in an attractive setting, the auction was for the model car *only*. A good many bidders probably looked at the photo and thought they were getting the car *and* its display setting. Wrong! I saw no mention of the diorama in the description, so I looked at other auctions for similar die-cast cars and found that the seller used the same background for those, too. I ended up emailing the seller, and he confirmed that he was offering only the cars. The photo, however, led the bidders to believe otherwise, and the description did nothing to correct this impression. The seller claimed that he was just trying to display the car in a favorable setting. It certainly *looked* deceptive, though.

Similarly deceptive is the "glamour shot" displaying an item in an exotic setting or in the arms of a pretty model. The intent is often to distract the viewer from a negative aspect of the item (or perhaps the seller wants to show off his girlfriend). Photos showing an item among a bunch of junk or out-of-focus shots may also be attempts to deceive.

Then there are "stock photos." These are typically used by the original manufacturer or retailer for promotional purposes, such as product brochures. Using stock images is common in book auctions; in fact, eBay provides a service that posts images of book covers for sellers, as well as other products (see Chapter 9). But a stock photo, which the seller may have copied from a manufacturer's website, may not accurately represent an item that has been used. If the item in the photo looks brand new, or if the seller provides a limited description and refers you to the photo for information, ask questions.

Deceptive Descriptions

Probably the most frequent kind of eBay scam involves deceptive descriptions. Some sellers go to great lengths to make an item seem like something it's not. Or they conveniently neglect to mention the item's flaws. These scams take several forms, including hiding or disguising critical information, cleverly rephrasing important facts, claiming that a fake item is authentic, and offering ambiguous descriptions that lead the potential bidder to believe that an item is more valuable or in better condition than it really is.

The following examples illustrate the techniques used to mislead buyers and the kinds of merchandise to which they're applied.

Clever Ways to Hide the Facts

As in commercial advertising, an unscrupulous eBay seller may obscure essential facts. For example, an important part of a description might appear in small print, as in "THIS 1920 RADIO HAS A WONDERFUL WOODEN CABINET AND WORKS WELL! (it is a repro)." The bidder may not notice the note that the item is a reproduction, but the seller is protected because, "It said so in my description, and all sales are final!"

Look for words such as *retro, repro, reproduction, remake, redesign, reissue, replica,* and *remix.* Also watch for use of the word *style,* as in "ANTIQUE style 1930s WALLET." Antique style is not the same as genuine antique.

As in titles, some sellers will even misspell or truncate words that would otherwise give away the fact that the item in question is not an authentic original. For example, instead of *repro, style,* or *replica,* the seller will type *rep, sty,* or *replc.* You might see "This is a replc in the sty of the VICTORIAN ERA." Note the all-caps emphasis of the last two words. This is clearly an attempt to trick buyers and pacify eBay. The seller uses the abbreviations repl and sty not to tell the browser anything, but so she can say to anyone who complains, "I wrote in the description that this is a replica in the style of the Victorian era; it's your problem if you can't understand abbreviations."

I've seen this sort of dodge used more than once, and, invariably, when I checked the sellers' Feedback, I found buyer complaints that the sellers had been misleading about their items being replicas. Unfortunately, people continue to be fooled by this, especially those who tend to skim through blocks of text, instead of paying close attention to what's really being auctioned.

Since this type of deception is quite common on eBay, the site administrators should require that the description for *any* item that is a reproduction clearly state that's what it is. But until that happens, if you have any doubts about an item's authenticity, write to the seller and ask if it's a reproduction. An honest seller will give you an honest answer. A dishonest seller might reply with a defensive or belligerent note or may not reply at all. A few sellers will lie outright and tell you that the reproduction they are selling is not a reproduction. I have experienced this and ended up buying a book touted as having been published in 1951 but which was, in reality, a 1990 reprint. Fortunately for me, it cost less than $10.

Unscrupulous sellers also hide unflattering descriptive elements at the end of the item's description or place such details in a statement of shipping terms. Or they use slippery wording, such as this description of the 1920 radio reproduction: "When this model was first manufactured in 1920, it used leading-edge technology." This could easily be read as applying to the reproduction radio up for auction. The seller's defense would be that he didn't actually say that, but referred only to the original model on which it was based. The seller is counting on such misinterpretation.

Some sellers use wordplay to fool buyers into bidding on nonworking, fake, or otherwise undesirable items. Table 16-1 shows some examples you'll see frequently on eBay.

Table 16-1: Translating eBay Doublespeak

Doublespeak	Translation
It looks complete, but I don't know enough about this sort of thing to know if any parts are missing.	Some parts are missing.
I don't have any batteries to test it.	I don't want to test this item, because I might discover that it doesn't work and would have to ask less for it. Alternate translation: I'm only saying this because I know it doesn't work.
Fresh from an Estate!	I'm not saying this is old, but I want you to *think* this is old. Alternate translation: This stinks of mold and mildew because the previous owner kept it in a damp basement.
RARE!!!!	I haven't bothered to look or I'd have seen that there are 43 of these up for sale at a tenth of what I'm asking. Alternate translation: Personally, I have never seen one of these before.
Really hard to find	There are only three of these up for auction right now.
Vintage	I'm not sure what this means, but everyone else is using it, and it sounds sexy.
These were my grandfather's when he was a little boy.	I'm lying; these weren't made until 1995. (And if you try to pin me down, I'll plead ignorance.)

Too Much Information

Another technique that dodgy sellers use to mislead buyers is to put so much textual information in the description that potential bidders give up before they've read it all. You've probably seen such listings, loaded with 10 or 20 pages of text. The information the seller doesn't want you to see, but which must be in the description if he wants to be able to claim a legitimate sale, will probably be somewhere in the middle.

Irrelevant, extraneous, or just plain erroneous information is some-times used by subtle criminal minds to encourage buyers to believe that an item is something it is not. For example, a seller may post an "autographed" Stephen King or Bram Stoker novel and clearly state that it is not guaran-teed to be authentic. But along with this, the seller includes an exhaustive biography of the writer, which has the effect of reinforcing the buyer's hopes that it is, indeed, authentic and worth bidding on. (Worse still, this shady seller probably stole the biography text from a copyrighted website or book.) The same technique is used with works of art, designer items, and antiques.

Extra text is also a form of keyword spamming. A biography of the late Ronald Reagan or Winston Churchill can be twisted around to include just about anyone's name to clutter legitimate searches with junk. For example, someone selling a biography of Ronald Reagan might include a summary of cultural events that occurred during his term as president. This description might include "Alice Cooper had few hits during Reagan's term, and 'The Jerry Springer Show' was yet to be aired." So, the person looking for tapes of old Jerry Springer episodes will conduct a search that returns the Ronald Reagan biography auction, too. Sellers actually do this sort of thing, thinking it will get bids!

All this being possible, you should read any overly long descriptions thoroughly. Better still, simply write to the seller and ask exactly what the item is. Or just ignore the listing and keep browsing—perhaps the best choice, as you avoid encouraging deceptive selling practices.

Sins of Omission

Rather than lie outright, some sellers simply omit an important fact, such as that an item is a reproduction. Consider the "New 1950s dial telephone" title I used earlier as an example of a misleading title. Here's the kind of deceptive description that might accompany it:

> Brand New 1950s Rotary DIAL TELEPHONE in the Original Factory Box
>
> Rotary Dial with Buttons, Volume Control, and Black Finish
>
> The original dial telephone of this style was introduced in 1950. It is a reminder of the past. Your grandparents had one.

Nowhere does the description say this is a reproduction, but the seller would maintain that he said the telephone is "new" and, therefore, the buyer should know it was not made in the 1950s. Or the seller may add the name of the manufacturer, which is a company that did not exist in the 1950s.

Often, all a dishonest seller needs to do is leave out one bit of informa-tion. For example, omitting the copyright date of a rare book might lead hopeful buyers to infer that it is a first edition.

Illegal Knockoffs

After not getting anything at all for their money, the second most frequent complaint among eBay buyers seems to be that they were sold a fake item or an item of lesser quality than that described. Plenty of eBay sellers offer cheap reproductions of Rolex watches, rare collectibles, bogus Ralph Lauren clothing, and other sought-after name-brand items. They are usually sellers who offer a wide variety of items, often obtained at auctions or flea markets. They usually don't actually know very much about most of their merchandise, and may or may not know that they are distributing illegal knockoffs.

As a rule, someone who specializes in something like expensive watches probably has legitimate items. The same is true of eBay sellers who operate brick-and-mortar stores, because they depend on building customer loyalty. But even these sellers can turn up with fakes—knowingly or unknowingly.

Fakes Offered by Careless and Uninformed Sellers

Sometimes a knockoff ends up in the hands of a seller who really believes it is authentic, usually because she is not terribly familiar with the item but has heard that it can sell for quite a bit. This happened to me once, when I bought a used car and found an old watch under the back seat. The watch looked expensive and carried the brand name Tag Heuer. I did a search on eBay for Tag Heuer and found that this was indeed a standout brand, right up there with Rolex for some collectors. So, I posted the watch with a price a bit lower than others of the same model and included photos.

I had already accumulated several bids when another seller emailed me to tell me the watch was a fake. I was naturally a bit suspicious, thinking perhaps the seller was just trying to eliminate the competition. I wrote both to him and to an acquaintance of mine who had bought several Tag Heuer watches at auction, and I asked each what identified the watch as a fake. It's always a good idea to consult more than one source. Their answers were consistent, so I agreed that the watch had to be a fake. Rather than risk an unhappy buyer, I emailed the high bidder and gave him the disappointing news. He still wanted it, and I picked up $35. The watch might have gone for as high as $200, but I did not want to deal with charges of fraud. The moral of the story is that sellers can be fooled as easily as buyers, so don't take everything they tell you at face value.

Photocopies

Some sellers offer photocopies or printed scans of documents, articles, magazines, or books. This is illegal if the material is still protected by an active copyright.

Some of these clowns won't bother to mention that the item is a copy. Instead, the description will include a misleading line like, "Sharp as the original," or "Excellent quality photo paper," which the seller hopes is enough to cover his tail if it sells to someone who hadn't recognized it as a copy. If you think you might be looking at a copy of an original, write to the seller for confirmation.

NOTE *You will see many original magazine articles for sale. Be aware that these don't always come as part of the complete, intact magazine. Read listings for articles carefully, so you are aware whether you're being offered an entire magazine or just a cutout page.*

How to Identify Fakes

Whether or not the seller is intentionally peddling a fake, she may claim to know nothing about the item she is selling (nor about the category of the item) and fall back on the old "Sold as-is" line, leaving it up to the buyer to determine its authenticity.

Given how little recourse an eBay buyer has, you should do as much legwork as possible to verify the seller's claims *before* you bid on anything. This is even more important if you are thinking of bidding on a high-priced collectible, an original artwork, or any sort of item that is potentially counterfeit. Items in this category include paintings, pottery, sculptures, autographs of famous persons, and rare books.

You can take several approaches to this problem, and you should use more than one.

Ask the seller.
First, write to the seller and ask whether she can provide any assurance that the item is for real. Is it accompanied by a certificate of authenticity? Will she back up her claim with a refund if the item isn't legitimate?

Go see the item.
If feasible, you can travel to the seller and confirm the item's authenticity yourself. Alternatively, you can hire an expert authenticator to view the item on your behalf and give you a report.

Ask others.
Look for other sellers who offer items in the same category and ask one or two of them how to identify a fake. You can also search the Internet for collectors and buyers of the kind of item you are seeking, or you can consult with local collectors in your town. These sources are most likely to be willing to tell you how to detect a fake.

Refer to publications.
Many books for collectors have information about verifying an item. You may also be able to find magazines dedicated to the item and its category, and these can be good references. These sources may also tell about fakes in circulation.

Use an authentication service.

If the item in question is high-priced and you cannot easily determine its validity just by looking at photos, and if the item is in a category of merchandise that is noted for fakes, you should consider using an authentication or grading service. eBay provides links to companies that provide authentication services for a variety of items. To view the links, do a search for "authentication" from the main Help page. You'll be linked to a list of companies that assess the quality or grade of an item. Like most appraisers, authentication experts usually charge a flat fee plus a percentage of the item's value, plus any expenses incurred.

Look for similar items on eBay and the Internet.

If you don't know whether reproductions are in circulation, you could look for similar items offered on eBay (or among closed auctions) to see if one or more are described as reproductions. If so, you will be fore-warned to look at the item with a more critical eye, and ask questions to help determine whether it is a reproduction. You can search for this information on the Internet, too. Check other auction sites, and use Internet search engines like Google to see if anyone else is selling the item in question on another website.

For example, I was once considering paying $45 for a 1920 booklet about the then-new science of radio—quite a collectible—but the price gave me pause. So I did some Internet searches on Google and AltaVista and discovered that someone had reprinted the book in 1975. The reprint was easily identifiable by a pattern of wrinkles on the cover.

I compared an image from the publisher's site, where the reprint was only $8, with the item I had seen on eBay. Sure enough, the eBay offering was one of the reprints. I suspect the seller had set such a high price because she had never seen the booklet before and figured it must be worth a lot of money.

This kind of inconsistent pricing happens most frequently with paper collectibles: comic books, automobile manuals, advertisements, and postcards. For example, if you do a search on eBay right now, you will probably find something called the "Hollander interchange book." This is a big reference book with cross-listings of parts used in automobile manufacturing. It might list parts used on American Motors cars in the 1960s that were also used in 1970s and 1980s Dodge automobiles but which no one stocks under "American Motors" anymore. It's a valuable guide for mechanics, as well as anyone who owns a classic car. Copies of this book are often offered for $70 or more, but you can buy them from the original publisher for far less.

So, do a little research before you buy. You may be able to verify the authenticity of an item, and you might get lucky and find a less expensive source for it—on eBay or elsewhere. And don't be afraid to alert a seller to the possibility (or fact) that something he is offering is a reproduction or fake. You'll be doing the seller, as well as potential buyers, a favor.

Spam Scams

Spammers *love* getting email addresses for people who use eBay. They can do this easily with eBay's Contact eBay Member or Ask Seller a Question services. They send an insipid message like, "Do you have anything else for sale?" or "Do you want to buy any more of these?" Quite often, the recipient replies in an honest effort to answer the question or to ask for clarification. At that point, the spammer grabs the person's address.

eBay lets you hide your address when you reply to someone who has contacted you through eBay's system. You should use this feature any time you receive email through eBay.

Sellers can be spammers, too. Some sellers maintain lists of people who've bought from them and regularly send email messages announcing new items up for sale. Most sellers who send sale announcements will drop you from their list if you ask. Most will also keep you off their lists, even if you buy from them again. A few, however, ignore "remove" requests or restore you to their lists saying, "It's automatic if you bid on anything from me." When you encounter this situation, keep complaining—with copies to eBay—until the seller removes you from the list. You can also complain to the seller's ISP. If your email system allows, you can block mail from the seller's address, too.

Identity Theft Scams

You may receive email messages that seem to be from eBay but are not. The messages may tell you that someone has stolen your account, your password is compromised, your help is needed in stopping eBay scammers, your eBay account is about to be suspended, or you have been awarded PowerSeller status. These messages are often tricks to get your eBay ID, password, or other personal data. They are called *spoofs*.

What can someone do if he gets his hands on your password? He may change information in your profile so that email from eBay members is directed to a different address. He can misdirect payments or merchandise intended for you to someone else's PayPal account or mailing address. He may use your account to harass sellers (and you) by bidding on items and not paying for them. Some scammers have stolen eBay accounts and used them to sell items that they don't deliver.

You can identify spoofs in several ways, some of which involve examining message headers, but you don't need to know anything technical like that. Here are some simple methods:

- If an email message asks you to reply with your eBay ID, password, or other personal information, it is a spoof. Neither eBay nor PayPal (nor your own ISP, for that matter) will ever ask you to send a password via email. No matter who is asking for your password and no matter what reason is given, any request of this sort is a trick, intended to steal your private data.

- If the message has an attachment, you can be sure it's not from eBay. eBay never sends mail with attachments.

- If a message provides a link and asks you to click it and "sign in" to eBay with your user ID and password, it is a spoof. While legitimate messages from eBay may contain links to auctions or other eBay pages, they *never* contain explicit login instructions referencing your ID and password. If you see this, it should raise a big red flag.

NOTE *eBay advises that you should never enter your eBay password on a page, unless the web address (URL) begins with http://signin.ebay.com/. A link that contains characters after .com (other than the forward slash) may not be a genuine eBay sign-in page. Links in spoof messages may contain the word "eBay" but may not actually direct you to real eBay web pages.*

Even though the message that accompanies a link may be very compelling, do not click it and sign in. One spoof message going around tells the recipient that she has been selected to be an eBay PowerSeller and must click a link in the message to log in and accept the honor. Tempting, huh? Another tells the recipient that his credit card information is about to expire, and he must log into eBay via the "special link" or his account will be terminated. Your first impulse may be to take immediate action, but *don't use the link provided in the email.* Sign on to eBay as you usually do, via the eBay website. There, you can check your eBay profile to confirm whether the email was authentic. Or, you can send email via eBay's Contact Us page to inquire about the message's validity.

When you receive a spoof message or any message purporting to be from eBay about which you have doubts, forward it to spoof@ebay.com. Then delete it.

Now, on to the next chapter, where we'll take a look at product scams, including those tantalizing "moneymaking opportunities" and "secrets" you may have seen offered. If you're considering wasting your money on such offers, read before you act.

17

BOGUS PRODUCTS AND MONEYMAKING SCAMS

eBay is an open market. Just about anything that is not illegal or harmful can be offered for sale. eBay imposes no requirements as to quality or value—a fact highlighted by the statement eBay adds to every auction listing: "Seller assumes all responsibility for this item." This lack of control lets in a category of sellers who try to pass off useless collections of information as "products." These sellers spend a lot of time and effort trying to make the products look like something they're not; in other words, they perpetrate frauds.

The main requirements for these "products" are that they be cheap, fast, and easy to produce. There are few things that are cheaper and require less effort than computer files delivered on CD or by email, which is why you find so many "information products" offered on eBay. (Some may argue that commercial music CDs and downloads are similarly cheap to deliver, but those have a value-added element that the owners of the files went to some effort and expense to create; furthermore, this value-added element cannot be obtained elsewhere.)

This chapter looks at several types of products that aren't what they appear to be. My aim is to provide enough information here to satisfy your curiosity about these items and prevent you from wasting your money on them.

E-Books

Remember back in the mid-1990s, when people started talking about how the Internet would empower writers to publish their own books? At last, they could circumvent the stifling control of publishers and be richly rewarded for their noble efforts. What we got was a flood of really bad electronic books (e-books).

Many e-books are published in that format because they weren't good enough for a real publisher. If you buy one, you are taking a chance on being seriously disappointed. Indeed, some don't even qualify to be called books.

A few years ago, I saw an e-book offered on eBay that was purported to be a guide to finding good locations for vending machines. Because I was once in the vending machine business, I was curious what the author had to say on the subject. I bought the "book" for a dollar or two and found that it consisted of *two pages* of useless "instructions." Basically, the author's advice was to ask anyone who owned a business if you could place a vending machine at his site and pay him ten percent of the machine's gross.

There are a few worthwhile e-books here and there. As with traditional self-published bound books, some e-books just don't have a large enough market to warrant a publisher's interest, though they might sell enough copies to make it worthwhile for the author to publish them. Many hobby and how-to books fit in this category, as do some local tour guides and regional histories.

Is the E-Book What It's Purported to Be?

It is difficult to determine whether an e-book is what it is represented to be without seeing it. Generally speaking, the better e-books tend to be in the special-interest and how-to categories—how to train your dog, build model airplanes, repair your computer, tune up your motorcycle, and the like. Local, regional, corporate, or family histories usually have real content, as well.

If you are buying the book from the author, so much the better. She is less likely to be offering junk products for sale than someone who just makes copies of existing material.

Most e-books of dubious value are those with "glamorous" subjects like how to make money fast or lose weight without diet or exercise. Books that tell you how to change your luck in life, win the lottery, get 100 miles per gallon of gasoline, or control other people are in the same category. And it's safe to say that just about any e-book that claims to reveal "hidden secrets for success" won't tell you anything you don't already know.

But some histories and how-to e-books can also be worthless. For example, you might find an e-book about the assassination of John F. Kennedy to contain nothing but conspiracy rants. Similarly, an e-book that claims to show you how to build your own computer for $100 could also be useless—perhaps just a few pages of instructions telling you the kinds of stores and online vendors who sell computer parts.

Before you buy an e-book, write to the seller. Ask who wrote the e-book and what kind of material it contains. Also ask how large the e-book is (in pages or file size). Finally, ask whether the material in the e-book is original. The overwhelming majority of e-books offered on eBay are *not* original in any sense of the word; they are simply copies of text and graphics files that someone scanned or obtained from elsewhere on the Web.

If the seller isn't the author and hedges on where he got the files, or if he replies with a sales pitch, the e-book is most likely material you can find online yourself or do without. If the seller doesn't reply, that says something about the e-book, too.

Giant E-Book Collection!

You may have seen CDs for sale on eBay offering hundreds (or even thousands) of books in one collection. These range from classics of all sorts to a variety of intriguing and boring titles. They're mostly titles you would be unlikely to buy in hardcopy—obscure or out-of-copyright works by Charles Dickens, Lucien of Somasata's first short story (circa 2500 B.C.), *How to Beat Vegas, The Complete Works of Shakespeare,* and a lot more of the same. You can also find two- or three-page text files that aren't books; rather, they are essays or short stories.

On occasion, these sellers will scan a real book or two, but for the most part, all of the books or other text offered were picked up from the Internet—something you can do yourself. In addition, there have been instances of these CDs containing the text of books still under copyright, though out of print.

Because of the often poor quality of the text files and the potential for illegally distributed copyrighted material, I advise against buying such batch lots of e-books. Instead, check out Project Gutenberg (www.gutenberg.net), where you can download more than 15,000 e-books *for free.* The odds are good that much of what a giant e-book contains is available at this site. Also, try searching the Web for "ebooks." You'll get plenty of links to free e-books.

Image Compilation Products

Whenever you see a CD of video or photographs for sale on eBay, stop and think about how easy it is to copy files to a CD. Then ask yourself whether you would be willing to pay someone $20 plus shipping for time spent sitting in his bedroom copying files that he downloaded from the Internet. The fact that you can get the files yourself, at no cost, rather diminishes the "value-added" element.

You can usually tell whether a photo or photos are available on the Internet with a few quick searches. Start by doing an AltaVista or Google search (use the Images search feature). If the photo subject involves American history, check the National Archives (www.archives.gov) and the Library of Congress (www.loc.gov). Note that other countries have their own versions of national archives on the Web. Also check the American Memory collection online (http://memory.loc.gov/ammem).

NOTE *Here and there, you will find listings for rare, antique, or historic photographs. Some are original, but some are scanned copies printed on high-quality photo paper. Responsible sellers will identify reprints as such, but on occasion, a seller will simply describe the photo with a line like, "Photo of Orville Wright and Charles Kettering." Or the seller may obscure the item's true nature using some of the techniques described in Chapter 16. If the photo's authenticity is important to you, write to the seller to ascertain its status.*

If a state or city is involved, check its historical society's website. Quite a few cities and states have placed extensive collections of photos online. One good example is the Cleveland Memory Project (www.clevelandmemory.org), which offers an exemplary collection of historic photos, including thousands from the files of the *Cleveland Press.*

Hundreds of libraries and universities also offer historic photos. Large, high-resolution photos of historic places and events are just waiting for you to download them for free—exactly the same photos being sold by some unprincipled sellers on eBay. Historic photos and videos in the public domain (the copyright has expired) can be found at other sites on the Internet as well. Do a Google search and see for yourself.

You can also obtain historic and other photos for your own use at no cost from some stock photo agency websites, as well as from government agencies and corporate websites. For example, Corbis, www.corbis.com, is a stock photo agency that allows users to preview high-resolution images, and NASA offers loads of free images to site visitors at www.nasa.gov/multimedia/imagegallery/index.html. Other stock photo agencies and corporate sites, like www.boeing.com, offer historic photos for a small fee.

No matter what the source, the photos are usually offered for personal use only, which means you cannot sell copies or use the photos in publications.

NOTE *Savvy copyright holders foil thieves before they strike by digitally watermarking images so they can't be reproduced illegally. At some point, you would think the Library of Congress or one of the stock photo agencies would clue into what's happening with their property on eBay and come down hard on the copyright violators.*

Photos aren't the only sort of images offered on eBay that you can get for free if you take the time to look around. For example, as I write this, dozens of eBay sellers are offering collections of patent drawings ("suitable for printing out and framing—a great gift for any occasion!"). Patent drawings are the drawings that an inventor is required to submit with a patent application. They typically illustrate the item in question in great detail, and depending on the subject, may be quite appealing. Additionally, many patent drawings show how to build the patented item.

But you don't need to buy these; you can get them from the same place the seller got them. Go to the U.S., Canadian, Japanese, or British patent offices' websites, where you can download TIFF and JPEG images of every patent ever filed. Better still, go to the worldwide patent search hosted by the European patent office, at http://ep.espacenet.com. It's more efficient and offers more than the U.S. Patent Office website.

NOTE   *Among the few CD compilation products sold on eBay that contain images you can't easily find on the Web—not for free, at any rate—are collections of amateur nude photos, many of which are antique. Few photographers and artists sell their work in electronic format because it is so easily copied. You can, however, buy hardcopy prints and originals on eBay, which you won't find included in image compilation CDs (or shouldn't).*

Find Out Anything About Anyone for Free!

Like the schemers who try to scam gullible people with shady email offers, some unscrupulous eBay sellers offer information and tools you can use to look up anyone/find anyone/get dirt and revenge on anyone on the Internet. Don't be fooled. In addition to the fact that you *cannot* literally find out everything about anybody on the Internet, you will have to pay for a lot of the information you can get.

This exciting secret information package usually consists of a bunch of poorly categorized lists of URLs. A good many of the URLs are public databases, such as www.anywho.com, Internet Address Finder (www.iaf.net), and www.four11.com. Others are URLs for government agencies offering information online or by mail for a fee. Still others are the websites of private investigators and businesses that conduct investigations offline and for a fee.

Sometimes, the information product will include a bunch of public domain and shareware programs, too, billed as "spy" or "hacker" software. With or without the software, this is the same garbage that you've been spammed about for the past ten years, and you can download these programs for free. You're better off spending an hour or two on Internet search engines. As for the software, you can download shareware and freeware from sites such as www.software.com, www.download.com, or hacker websites.

NOTE   *You'll do even better buying* Steal This Computer Book 3, *by Wallace Wang (No Starch Press). It provides a plethora of such information and quite a bit more. It is available at www.nostarch.com or in your local bookstore. Tell all your friends!*

Buy This and Make a Fortune!

Con artists have been promising ways of getting rich quick since capitalism was invented. They clog your inbox with spam, run bogus classified ads, and post shady offers on job boards. They also seek out vulnerable prey on eBay.

One reason so many eBay sellers are flogging "moneymaking secrets" (especially those that can be emailed or copied to a CD) is that they got into buying them from someone else, and the only way for them to come out ahead is to sucker other people in turn. Of course, they already know the product's claim has great appeal—they fell for it, after all. So, rather than try to sell it via a website or email spam (or in addition to these methods), they offer it on eBay, usually copying the very same sales pitch that conned them, complete with poor grammar and misspellings. Try searching the Web for some of the sentences in a get-rich-quick item description posted on eBay; the odds are good that you'll find dozens of websites that are selling that item, too, as well as a lot of discussion threads where duped customers offer cautionary tales.

Not everyone is going to bother to ask those questions, which is what the sellers pushing these wonderful opportunities are counting on. This section describes some of the more common scams disguised as valid opportunities on eBay.

If you come across a get-rich-quick or miracle cure that isn't explained here, there's a fast and easy way to find out if it is legitimate: ask someone who bought the item. You can contact anyone who left Feedback for the seller, but you'll get the most revealing responses from a disgruntled buyer. The quickest way to find people who have been duped is to check the Negative Feedback at http://auctiononlinedirectory.com/cgi-bin/negs.

Sell "Information Products"

Information products are files—e-books, software, images, or whatever—on CD or delivered by email. They are distinguished from image compilation or giant e-book products only by the fact that they're called information products. I mention this because eBay has an Information Products category, which it created largely to stop these CD and email products from cluttering categories such as Books and Business. Note the existence of the category doesn't attest to the validity of these offerings.

As with most CD products, you can get the majority of the files offered as information products for free on the Internet. Worse, if you're thinking of reselling this sort of thing, the "product" you buy is already being sold by 3,000 other sellers.

NOTE   *Literally anything you encounter that claims to be a fast and easy way to make money is already being sold by thousands of others, which means you aren't going to make a fortune reselling it.*

Purchase Email Lists

Email address lists, as well as spamming services, often show up for sale on eBay, despite the fact that they're not allowed. eBay prohibits the selling of email address lists or any other personal information, so if you see these things up for sale, report them right away. Although the lists are usually described as composed of people who want to receive spam, they're not. Some bogus business operations will even sell you spam messages that you are then supposed to send out. As a rule of thumb, steer clear of any lists of contact information.

Buy a Website Business (Cheap)

Useless websites and web "tools" are a favorite of those who prey on would-be Internet millionaires. Free or incredibly cheap website hosting, complete with a domain name, is frequently offered. The catch (hidden in a confusing contract) is that the third year or the sixth month of service is free, with the preceding time period billed and payable in advance. And, of course, you must provide your credit card number up front. There are also people running multilevel marketing (MLM) or pyramid plan scams on eBay, requiring you to pay a "registration" fee in advance.

NOTE *No matter what it is called or how it is presented, whether you're supposed to sell products to others or join a club, MLM is a scam. If making money is contingent on you register-ing others, it's MLM and it's illegal. Educate yourself by reading the Federal Trade Commission's list of top cons at www.ftc.gov/bcp/conline/pubs/online/dotcons.htm.*

To sum up, very few CDs or downloadable information products for sale on eBay are worth the cost. Yes, there are some exceptions, such as copies of truly rare books. I've seen a few of these on eBay, although they are often overpriced. Again, it's also a good idea to see if you can find the text of the books on the Web yourself for free.

In case you're wondering, yes, there are eBay members who buy these types of products, and then make copies for resale. Probably none of the people selling these CDs on eBay created the original.

By no means have I covered every moneymaking scam out there, and new ones are popping up all the time. As P.T. Barnum said, "There's a sucker born every minute." Otherwise, scammers would have given up long ago. So, if you encounter something that seems attractive, don't let the hype and promises dazzle you into lining the scammer's pocket. Use common sense and take the time to research any questionable business opportunities or claims. And remember that if it sounds too good to be true, it probably is!

18

HOW TO INVESTIGATE OTHER EBAY MEMBERS

When you have a problem, or think you are going to have a problem, with another eBay member, the first thing you should do is learn as much as you can about that member. A little investigation may prove your concerns are false. If there *is* a problem, a little knowledge can often foster a solution. In this chapter, I'll suggest how you might go about getting information about an eBay member, through eBay and other channels.

Feedback

As you've read in earlier chapters, the place to begin learning about a member is the member's Feedback Profile page. In examining an eBay member's profile, look for Negative and Neutral Feedback. The comments that buyers or sellers leave about the member ("He didn't pay!" "She never sent my item and told me to cram it!") may tell you a lot about the member. Don't forget to use the Negative Feedback tool, at www.toolhaus.org/cgi-bin/negs, to uncover older Negative Feedback.

What buyers and sellers have to say about the member in Positive Feedback comments can speak volumes, too. Positive Feedback accompanied by unenthusiastic comments like "Okay deal" or "Item arrived" may have been left by someone who was a victim of Feedback extortion.

Take a look at some of the Feedback the member you're investigating has left for others, as well. This can tell you a lot about how easy or difficult it is to deal with the member.

Other Buyers and Sellers

Write to those who have posted Feedback (Positive or Negative) in the past month or so to solicit intelligence about the member in question. Let these eBayers know why you are collecting information—because you are in a deal or contemplating a deal with the member—and assure them that you won't mention them as your source.

As long as you're contacting other members, ask them for the email address, physical address, and phone number they used to communicate with the member. It may be that the person you are investigating has moved or given eBay false information.

Action Listings and About Me Pages

Your next step is to see how much information the member includes about herself with her auction listings. In their listings, some sellers provide a phone number and physical address that are different from what you find in their profile.

After this, check out the seller's About Me page. Here, the seller may list the URL for a personal website. You'll want to visit that website to gather contact information and to get an idea of what sort of person you're dealing with.

The lack of contact or general background information in a listing isn't necessarily a bad sign. Some sellers prefer not to clutter up listings. The same is true of About Me pages. But it could indicate that the member is trying to avoid being found and contacted.

eBay Contact and Member Information

eBay will provide a seller's contact information on file only if you are currently involved in a transaction or have been involved in a transaction with that seller in the past 60 days.

NOTE *The email address a seller gives you may not be the same address he used to register with eBay. So, it is a good idea to use the **Contact Member** button on the seller's Member Profile page. It may be that he has missed email sent to his other address.*

To request information about an eBay member, use the Find Contact Information link on any Search page. You will see a form like the one shown in Figure 18-1.

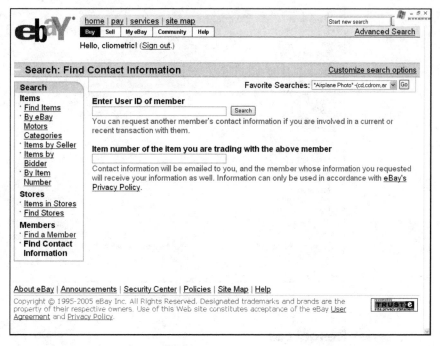

Figure 18-1: Search: Find Contact Information page

To request a member's information, you must provide both the member ID and the number of the item you are trading. After sending the request, you will receive an email from eBay with the address, phone number, and email address that the member has on file with eBay. At the same time, the seller will receive your contact information.

If the address and phone number provided are incorrect or incomplete, contact eBay; eBay requires members to keep their contact information up-to-date. (Interestingly, this is often the only time eBay bothers to check member information.)

Another link on the Search page, labeled Find a Member, takes you to a tool for verifying a member's account by entering an email address, as shown in Figure 18-2. As with the Find Contact Information tool, you can use this tool only if you have been involved in an eBay transaction with the member in question in the past 60 days.

The Find a Member page can be useful if someone contacts you about paying for an item and you want to make sure the person using that email address is indeed the same seller whose auction you bid on. On this page, by entering an email address, you can learn the eBay member ID associated with that address. You can also do a reverse lookup by entering an eBay ID.

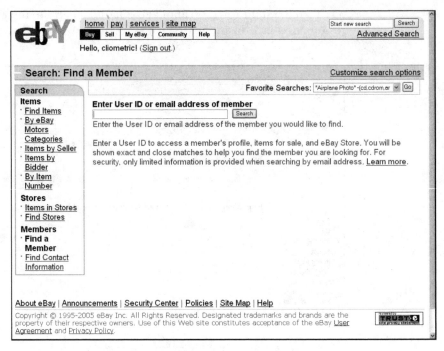

Figure 18-2: Find a Member page

Internet Resources

eBay itself shouldn't be your last resource for finding member information. eBay doesn't confirm the accuracy of information provided during registration, so it is certainly possible that a phone number or address on file is bogus. Or the seller could simply have moved without updating his profile. Therefore, here are a few ideas on Internet resources that might shed additional light on your eBay member's whereabouts:

Reverse phone number lookup
To check out a phone number, you can call it, or you can use the reverse lookup services at www.anywho.com or www.whowhere.com to see if it is connected with the name and address you have for the seller.

NOTE *Libraries in many cities will look up a number in their local telephone directory for you.*

Address lookup
If the address doesn't match the information you have, or if the address checks out but not the name, it may be a mail drop—a business like Mailboxes, Etc. You can use www.anywho.com's business lookup service or directory assistance to see whether there is a mailbox service at that address or in the town in question. You can also find out whether the address you're using is a mail drop by entering the address in a search engine (like Google or AltaVista) as a phrase, like this: **"1213 Kehrn Rd."**

If the address is common, include the city, like this: **"1234 Main" Coving-dale Maine**. Be sure to search newsgroups, as well. If you are dealing with a physical address, not a post office box or mail drop, you'll still want to search www.anywho.com or www.whowhere.com. You may not find the name listed with the phone number at that address, but if the last name is the same, it's almost certain that your seller lives there, too (perhaps she is a spouse or relative of the person listed in the directory).

NOTE   *Running an address through a search engine may turn up useful information in addition to revealing whether the address is a mail drop. Sometimes, a home address is used as a business address, and vice versa. A home or business address may also appear on the Web in connection with something that has nothing to do with eBay— a club membership, another business, and so on.*

Name lookup

In a search engine, do a search on the seller's name (in newsgroups as well as on the Web). If the seller has a fairly common name, include the town or some other identifying search term, like a personal interest. Names turn up on the Web and in newsgroups for a variety of reasons. You can also try searching with just the last name and a town (unless you're dealing with the name "Smith" in "Los Angeles").

Email address and eBay ID lookups

Also search using the seller's email address(es) and eBay member ID. Rip-off artists are often stupid enough to post on a website or in a news-group using an email address or ID that is the same as or similar to what they use on eBay—enough for you to be able to glean useful infor-mation. You can try one or more of the online "directory" services to see whether you can find an alternate email address or other information about your subject. Try http://people.yahoo.com, www.bigfoot.com, www.worldemail.com, and www.four11.com. Also, do a Google or AltaVista search with the seller's email address; you may turn up yet another address.

Online investigative services

Many websites offer, for a fee, a report on an individual's current and past addresses, phone numbers, businesses, assets, and so forth. Links to several such services can be found at www.consumersreview.org/investigate.html. Another place to look is www.records-search.net.

I have found the home addresses and phone numbers for several slow-shipping sellers by searching the Web. In one instance, the seller had provided only a post office box on eBay for payment, and a request for his seller infor-mation turned up only a disconnected phone number. I had noticed, however, that he bannered his listing pages with the name of a bookstore—for the sake of this example, we'll say it was Ogo Eskar's Bookshop. I did a search for "Ogo Eskar's Bookshop" and found the web page for a physical store that had been forced to close due to lack of business. The eBay seller, a.k.a., the bookstore proprietor, posted his home number (and address) on the web page for those interested in buying books. I called him, and my item was delivered within days. I mentioned where I had gotten his phone number.

As much as possible, cross-check the information you get to reinforce its validity before making contact.

Ideally, you won't need to use any of the information in this chapter. If you have a problem with another member, it's a good idea to remind yourself that most problems can be cleared up by communicating with the other party. It is also good to maintain a sense of proportion; when a small amount of money is involved, it's often best to file a complaint and move on. Don't treat a $3 deal like a $500 transaction.

EBAY-SPEAK: ABBREVIATIONS AND ACRONYMS

Many abbreviations and acronyms are used in eBay auction titles and descriptions, as well as in eBay discussion boards. The intent is to save space and time, but these codes can sometimes be cryptic, especially for newcomers. Table 1 defines the most commonly used abbreviations and acronyms.

Table 1: Common eBay Abbreviations and Acronymns

B&W	Black-and-white photo
BC	Back cover
BIN	Buy It Now
EXC	Excellent condition
FAQ	A list of frequently asked questions with answers
FB	Feedback

(continued)

FVF	Final value fee
GC	Good condition
GU	Gently used
HTF	Hard to find
INIT	Initials
JPG	JPEG image format
LTD	Limited edition
MIB	Mint in box
MIJ	Made in Japan
MNB	Mint, no box
MNT	Mint condition
MOC	Mint on card
NARU	Not a registered user
NBW	Never been worn
NC	No cover
NIB	New in box
NM	Near mint
NOS	New old stock
NPB	Nonpaying bidder
NR	No reserve
OEM	Original equipment manufacturer
OOP	Out of print (or out of production)
PM	Priority Mail
Sig	Signature
TM	Trademark
TOS	Terms of service
UPD	Unpaid item dispute
UPS	United Parcel Service
UPI	Unpaid item
USPS	U.S. Postal Service
VHTF	Very hard to find
XC	Excellent condition

INDEX

ABOUT THE AUTHOR

Michael Banks started trading online in 1983, when he sold an old printer for parts. More than 20 years later, he's still at it. He's been an eBay seller and active bidder for several years and considers eBay the most fun, efficient, and varied online auction site. A full-time writer for 22 years, Banks has authored more than 40 books and has published countless articles on topics as varied as technology, model rockets, and writing. He lives in Oxford, Ohio, home of the 1960s Preservation Society.

THE CULT OF MAC

by LEANDER KAHNEY

The Cult of Mac is an in-depth coffee table book that brings us into the world of Mac users and their unique, creative, and often obsessive culture. Like fans of a football team or a rock group, Macintosh fans have their own customs, with clearly defined rites of passage. From people who get Mac tattoos and haircuts, to those who furnish their apartments with empty Mac boxes, this book details Mac fandom in all its weird and wonderful glory.

NOVEMBER 2004, 280 PP., $39.95 ($55.95 CAN)
ISBN 1-886411-83-2

THE EBAY PRICE GUIDE

by JULIA L. WILKINSON

More than 125 million people are registered eBay users, creating a vast community of sellers and buyers all looking for the right price. No one wants to pay too much and everyone wants to get what they think they deserve for whatever they're selling. *The eBay Price Guide* is a one-stop shop for pricing information and tips for successful buying and selling on eBay, accessible both through the book's pages and via the Hammertap software on the included CD-ROM. The author has done extensive research to compile this exhaustive guide, which helps readers determine which items will fetch big bucks and which will go for rock-bottom prices. Sellers learn how to price their items competitively to attract more customers, while buyers learn which categories tend to be overpriced and where they can find the best bargains. Fun stories, statistics, lists, and eBay trivia round out the book. A must-have for the serious eBayer.

NOVEMBER 2005, 304 PP. W/CD, $29.95 ($40.95 CAN)
ISBN 1-59327-055-0

JUST SAY NO TO MICROSOFT

by TONY BOVE

Just Say No to Microsoft begins by tracing Microsoft's rise from tiny software startup to monopolistic juggernaut and explains how the company's practices over the years have discouraged innovation, stunted competition, and helped foster an environment ripe for viruses, bugs, and hackers. Readers learn how they can dump Microsoft products—even the Windows operating system—and continue to be productive. The book also shows how to work successfully and seamlessly with computers and people who are still hooked on Microsoft software. Includes full explanations of alternate operating systems, such as Linux and Mac, and outlines various software applications that can replace the familiar Microsoft products.

SEPTEMBER 2005, 256 PP., $24.95 ($33.95 CAN)
ISBN 1-59327-064-X

STEAL THIS COMPUTER BOOK 3
What They Won't Tell You About the Internet

by WALLACE WANG

An offbeat, non-technical book that explores what hackers do, how they do it, and how readers can protect themselves. Thoroughly updated, this edition adds coverage of rootkits, spyware, web bugs, identity theft, hacktivism, wireless hacking (wardriving), biometrics, and firewalls.

MAY 2003, 384 PP., $24.95 ($37.95 CAN)
ISBN 1-59327-000-3

STEAL THIS FILE SHARING BOOK
What They Won't Tell You About File Sharing

by WALLACE WANG

Steal This File Sharing Book peels back the mystery surrounding file sharing networks such as Kazaa, Morpheus, and Usenet, showing how they work and how to use them wisely, and revealing potential dangers lurking on file sharing networks, including viruses, spyware, and lawsuits, and how to avoid them. Includes coverage of the ongoing battle between software, video, and music pirates and the industries trying to stop them.

NOVEMBER 2004, 296 PP., $19.95 ($27.95 CAN)
ISBN 1-59327-050-X

PHONE:
800.420.7240 OR
415.863.9900
MONDAY THROUGH FRIDAY,
9 A.M. TO 5 P.M. (PST)

FAX:
415.863.9950
24 HOURS A DAY,
7 DAYS A WEEK

EMAIL:
SALES@NOSTARCH.COM

WEB:
HTTP://WWW.NOSTARCH.COM

MAIL:
NO STARCH PRESS
555 DE HARO ST, SUITE 250
SAN FRANCISCO, CA 94107
USA

COLOPHON

The eBay Survival Guide was laid out in Adobe FrameMaker. The font families used are New Baskerville for body text, Futura for headings and tables, and Dogma for titles.

The book was printed and bound at Malloy Incorporated in Ann Arbor, Michigan. The paper is Glatfelter Thor 50# Antique, which is made from 50 percent recycled materials, including 30 percent postconsumer content. The book uses a RepKover binding, which allows it to lay flat when open.

UPDATES

Visit **http://www.nostarch.com/ebaysg.htm** for updates, errata, and other information.